IMAGES of Modern America

USCGC MACKINAW (WLBB-30)

Mike Fornes

ARCADIA PUBLISHING

ISBN 978-1-4671-1367-0

Published by Arcadia Publishing
Charleston, South Carolina

Printed in the United States of America

Library of Congress Control Number: 2014949107

For all general information, please contact Arcadia Publishing:
Telephone 843-853-2070
Fax 843-853-0044
E-mail sales@arcadiapublishing.com
For customer service and orders:
Toll-Free 1-888-313-2665

Visit us on the Internet at www.arcadiapublishing.com

To those who served . . .

Contents

Acknowledgments

Many thanks are due to those who helped make this telling of the *Mackinaw's* story possible. First and foremost, the U.S. Coast Guard's assistance is appreciated in providing many of the photographs used in this book. Lt. David Lieberman was of particular help in answering technical questions, identifying locations, and providing access to the ship and its archives. In addition, I was assisted by Lt. Matthew Kempe, Lt. (jg) Jeannette Killen, Ensign Elizabeth Newton, Ensign James Connors, Lt. (jg) Shane Alexander, Lt. (jg) Katharine Braynard, and Lt. (jg) Rebecca Follmer. They have all no doubt achieved higher ranks since I worked with them while covering the *Mackinaw*!

Thanks as well go to the *Cheboygan Daily Tribune* for access to its archives and the many articles that I wrote and photographs I took of the ship while employed there on the Coast Guard beat. Of special assistance were Shawna McManus, Mary Barker, Jerry Pond, and Renee Glass of the *Tribune's* staff.

Finally, grateful acknowledgement is due to the District 9 Office and those captains and officers of the *Mackinaw* who welcomed me aboard and encouraged me to tell the ship's stories and those of the crew. Deserving of particular respect and admiration is Cmdr. John Little, who taught me so much about icebreaking, leadership, and how to conduct a loyal command.

INTRODUCTION

The U.S. Coast Guard knew as early as 1990 that the original icebreaker *Mackinaw*, built in 1944, was in the twilight of its useful life. It had become an inefficient and expensive resource to operate, due to its World War II–era systems and its single-mission capability. In 2002, a plan was developed to design a Great Lakes icebreaker-class ship that would replace the aging original. In addition to icebreaking, the new vessel would have multi-mission capabilities, including servicing buoys, conducting search-and-rescue missions, law enforcement, and the ability to deploy an oil-skimming system to respond to oil spills. If an oil spill occurs on the Great Lakes, the new *Mac* gets the call.

The new Great Lakes Icebreaker (GLIB) is 50 feet shorter than the original version. It is thinner and more high-tech, requiring fewer crewmembers. It does more types of work with significantly less people needed to operate the ship. Today's Coast Guard requires more comfortable accommodations for mixed-gender crews, and the new ship is designed with that need in mind.

Model tests demonstrated that the GLIB would be significantly more maneuverable than the old ship in ice, thanks to the dual Azipod engine systems, which are able to rotate 360 degrees. The 1944 version had two propellers aft and one bow propeller, as well as a hydraulic system that shifted thousands of gallons of ballast water from side to side, allowing the vessel to "roll" out of ice jams. The new vessel has a simpler engine plant, with appropriate power.

The 2005 *Mackinaw* is designed to meet or exceed all international, federal, state, and local environmental requirements, including consideration of possible future requirements. The new cutter's environmentally friendly systems include a double-bottom hull, to move fuel tanks away from the hull bottom; box-type coolers for machinery cooling water (all cooling water stays internal to the ship, preventing any potential leakage from being improperly discharged, similar to a nuclear plant's design); zero discharge of all gray water and retention of all trash on board; diesel engines that meet the latest regulations for engine emissions; propulsor pods, which incorporate multiple seals between the lubricated parts and the pod exteriors, including a void space to detect water leaking in or oil leaking out; and a system that skims oil from the surface of the water to inflatable oil barges. The cutter can handle two barges holding 28,000 gallons each.

The new *Mackinaw* can handle buoys with the same ease as the 225-foot Juniper-class buoy tenders, and it has a 40,000-pound-capacity crane on the forward deck. It has fully automated systems for control of the ship and the machinery plant. Driving the vessel is much like operating a video game, officers say.

Today's Coast Guard operates within the Department of Homeland Security. The new *Mac* carries a variety of guns, including big ones. The vessel is outfitted with two M-240 machine guns to reinforce its role in marine law enforcement.

This is a story of a continuing legacy. The name *Mackinaw* implied strength, trust, and capability to Great Lakes mariners throughout the original cutter's service life, and that has carried on to a new era, with a new ship. Both have been regarded as "Queen of the Great Lakes" during their respective careers.

One

The *Mackinaw* Legacy

How does one replace a legend, especially when the motto "We move ships when no one else can" is painted on its deck? For many years, it seemed that the original *Mackinaw* (WAGB-83) would last forever—that it would always be on duty in the Great Lakes. A particularly rough era of malfunctions in the early 1990s was followed by a resurgence in funding and repairs, bringing the great ship back to fighting shape.

Even so, the *Mac's* aging 1940s-era systems, built by companies long out of business, would often break down, with no parts available for repair. When it got to the point that engineers visited a Texas train junkyard and brought back parts for refabrication to repair broken engine-room machinery, the end could not be far away. Amazingly, the *Mac* retired in 2006 to a new life as a museum ship and was in perfect working order, doing the same heavyweight job it had done for 62 years.

That career was envied by the crews of even the most decorated Navy vessels. Stories abound of *Mackinaw's* heroic rescues of ships stuck in ice windrows during blinding snowstorms and in subzero temperatures. There are tales of ships towed to safety by the *Mac's* giant towing winch, spectacular centerpiece vistas with the ship among a fleet of racing yachts, and search-and-rescue missions in the darkest nights. When there was trouble on the Great Lakes, the radio calls from ships always asked, "Where's the *Mackinaw*? We need the *Mackinaw* to come and help us!"

The ship's World War II–era lines and proud profile was indeed an impressive sight on the horizon. In port, the ship appeared almost larger than life. They were big shoes to fill, indeed, but the idea was to honor the legacy and keep doing the job. Nobody expected the new ship to be the *same* ship. There were plenty of projections that the technological advancements would improve performance. But some predicted that the original 1944 ship would have to come and rescue the 2005 version during icebreaking.

What version of the new *Mackinaw* would the shipyard produce?

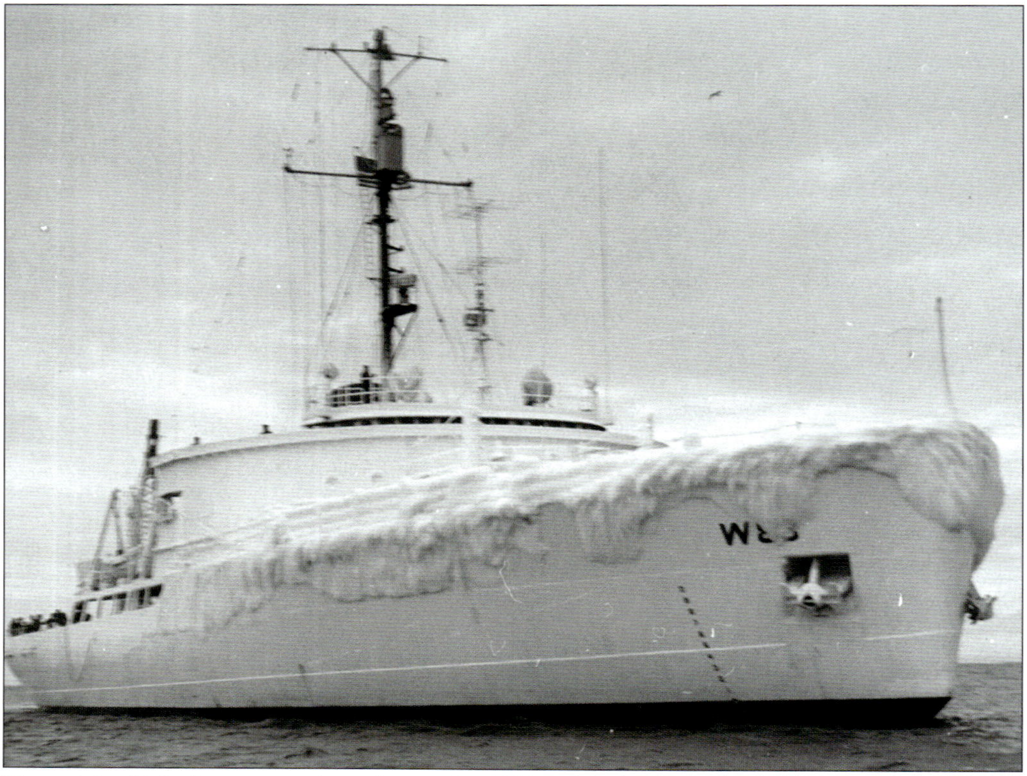

The original *Mackinaw*, seen here during the 1958 icebreaking season, had a simple appearance. Already 12 years into its career, the Wind Class designation (W83) was thus far the only official marking on the ship, other than the draft marks. The all-white paint, intended to camouflage the vessel in ice during World War II, remained as a trademark. (Courtesy of Jack LaLonde.)

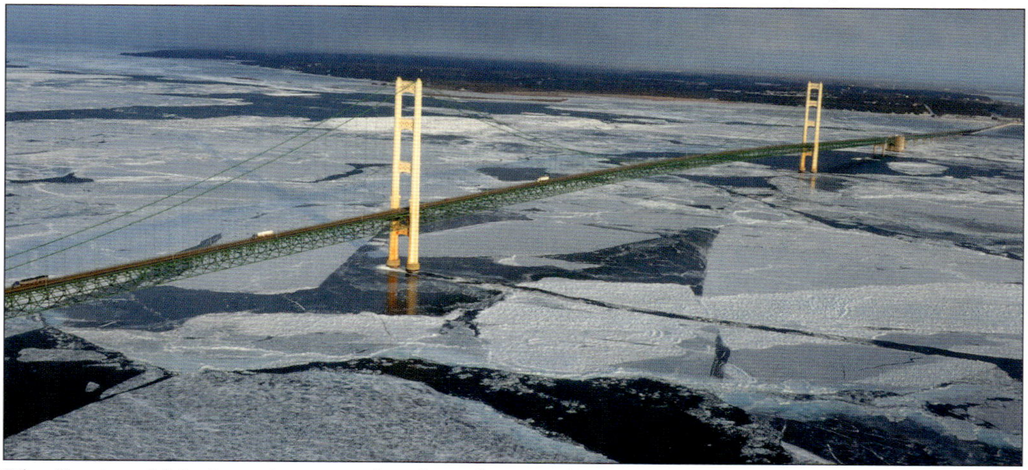

The Straits of Mackinac's narrow bottleneck annually clogs with heavy ice, a key reason why Congress authorized funding for the original *Mackinaw* just 10 days after the bombing of Pearl Harbor in 1941. Shipments of iron ore and steel needed to transit the Straits and reach the steel mills of the lower Great Lakes for the construction of ships, planes, and tanks for the war effort. (Author's collection.)

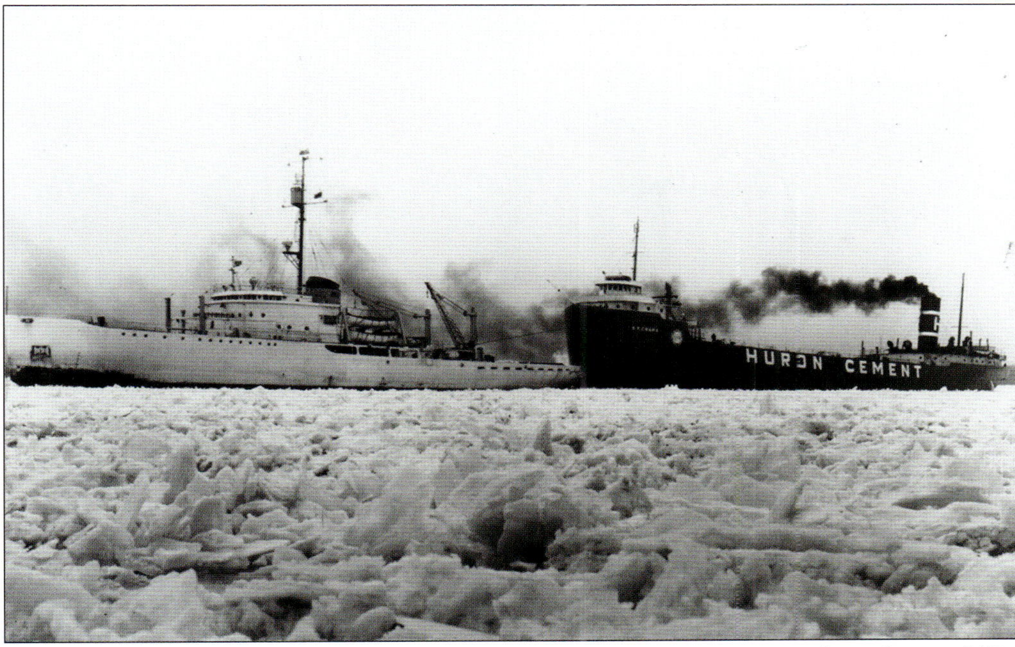

Mackinaw's brute strength included a massive constant-tension towing winch, nicknamed "Big Bertha," which utilized a three-inch diameter cable. This mid-1940s photograph shows a towing job for the Huron Cement carrier *S.T. Crapo*. The icebreaker's stern was notched, so the bow of a following ship could be drawn into a hard rubber boot for towing. (Courtesy of Ed Pyrzynski.)

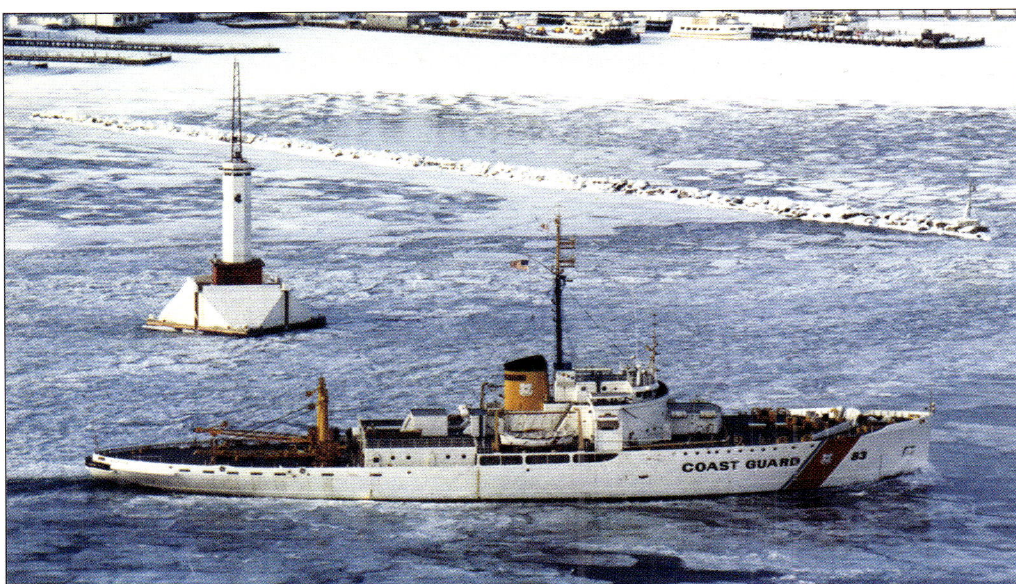

The Round Island Passage, a frequent icebreaking route near Mackinac Island, is the scene of this 1971 aerial photograph of the *Mac* sporting the Coast Guard's racing stripe logo adopted in 1967. Pres. John F. Kennedy approved the design as part of an effort to improve the images of all the armed forces. (Courtesy of Ken Rocheleau.)

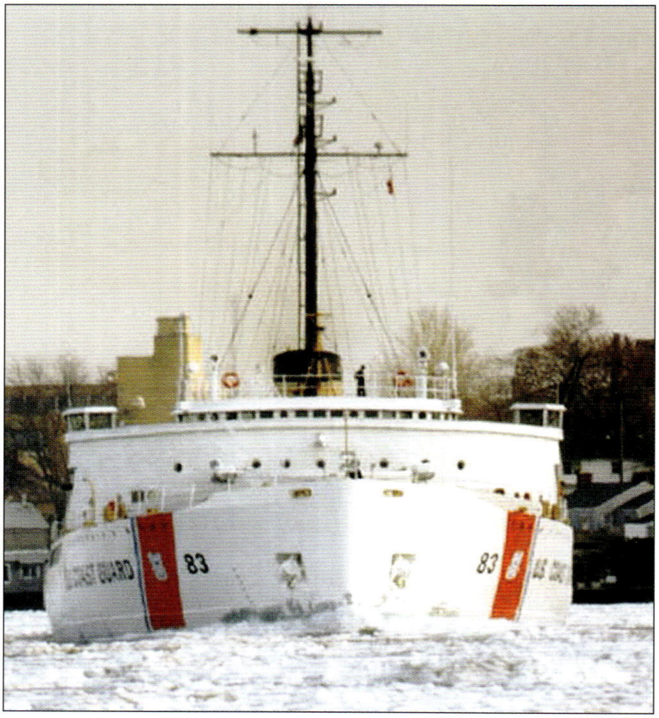

The wide, football-like shape of the *Mackinaw* is evident in this icebreaking view from near Port Huron, Michigan. At 74 feet, 4 inches wide, the ship's 5,200-plus tons of displacement could crush all the ice the Great Lakes could form in the coldest of winters. This ability earned the *Mac* a reputation of being able to "move ships when no one else can." (Courtesy of Neil Schultheiss, www.boatnerd.com.)

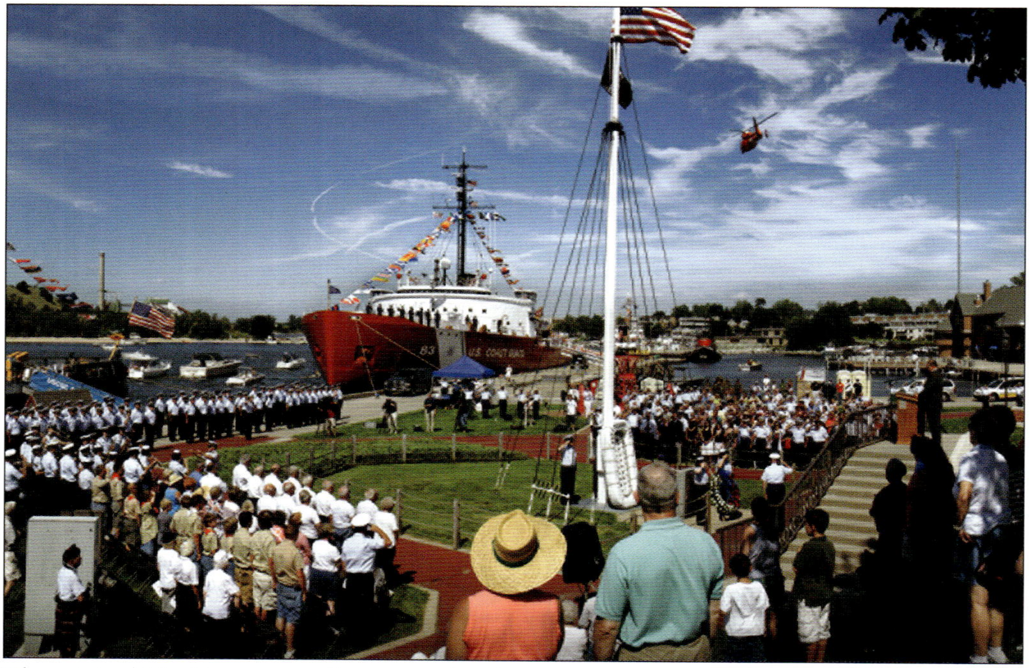

The original *Mackinaw* annually appeared as the centerpiece in Grand Haven, Michigan, at the Coast Guard Festival. Here, the National Coast Guard Memorial Service takes place to honor the memories of those lost in the line of duty, including those of the USS *Escanaba*, lost in the North Atlantic during a World War II German submarine attack. (Courtesy of Chris Winters.)

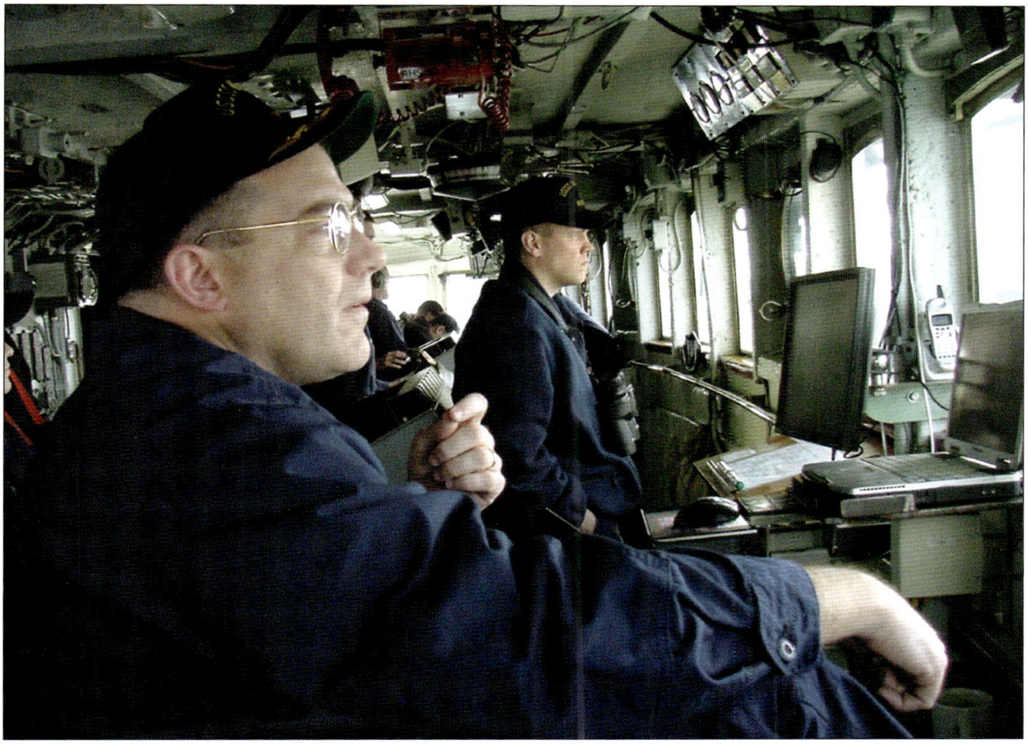

Cmdr. Joseph C. McGuiness (left) is pictured conning the *Mackinaw* during its last season of icebreaking in 2005. He oversaw the decommissioning of the ship and its eventual transfer to a new life as the Icebreaker Mackinaw Maritime Museum. McGuiness worked to ensure that all systems and equipment were ready and able for service and could be accurately displayed for future visitors to see. (Author's collection.)

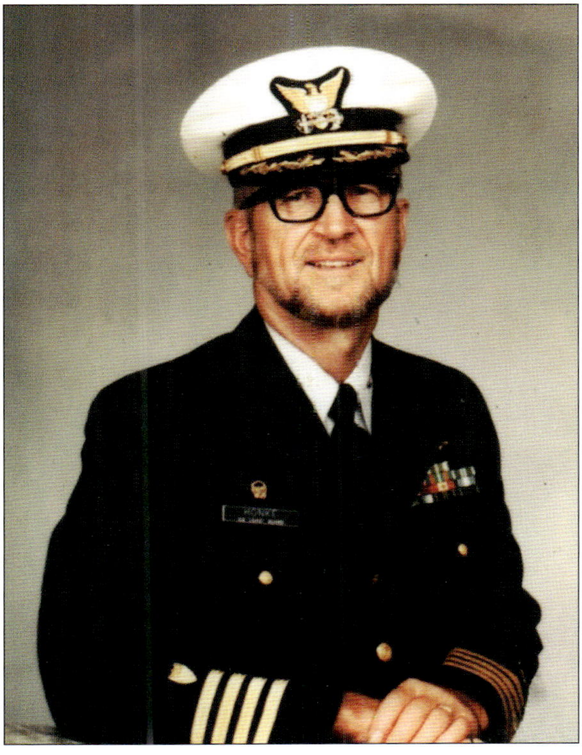

Capt. Jim Honke, widely regarded as perhaps *Mackinaw's* most popular commanding officer, served from 1980 to 1983. Honke, known as a "crew's captain," kept himself and his shipmates very active in the Cheboygan community. Honke and his family lived in town, oversaw the building of the Coast Guard Housing Complex in Cheboygan, and then moved there to prove its acceptance as a great neighborhood in which to raise a family. (Courtesy of Shirley Honke.)

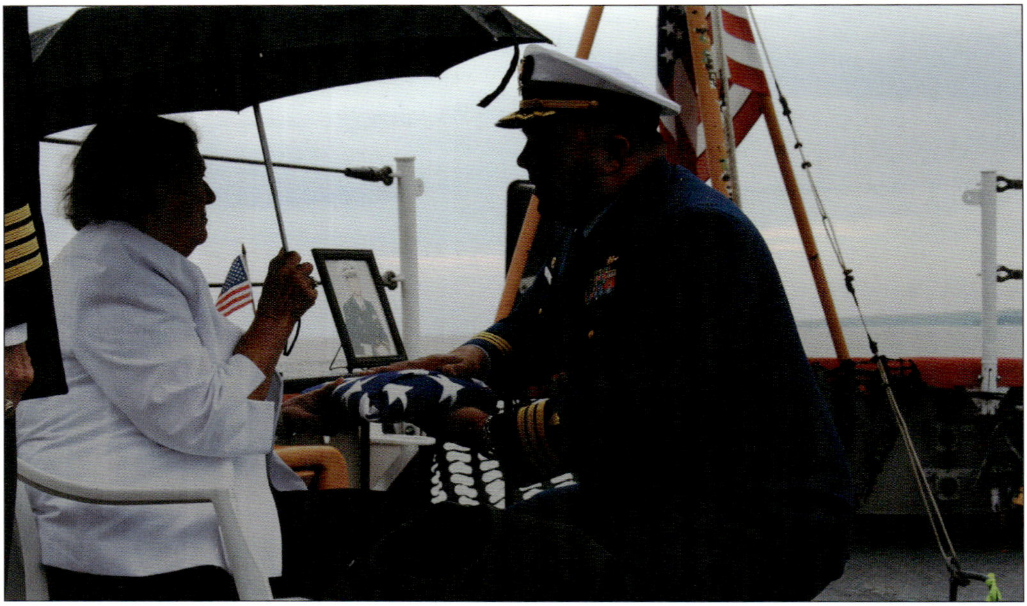

Cmdr. Scott Smith of the new *Mackinaw* presented the American flag to Shirley Honke, widow of Capt. James Honke, at the captain's committal service in July 2011 aboard the original *Mackinaw*. Crewmembers of the new *Mac* stood guard as raindrops began to fall near the ceremony's end. It was easy to imagine that the original *Mackinaw* was shedding tears for the popular captain as his ashes were scattered at sea. (Author's collection.)

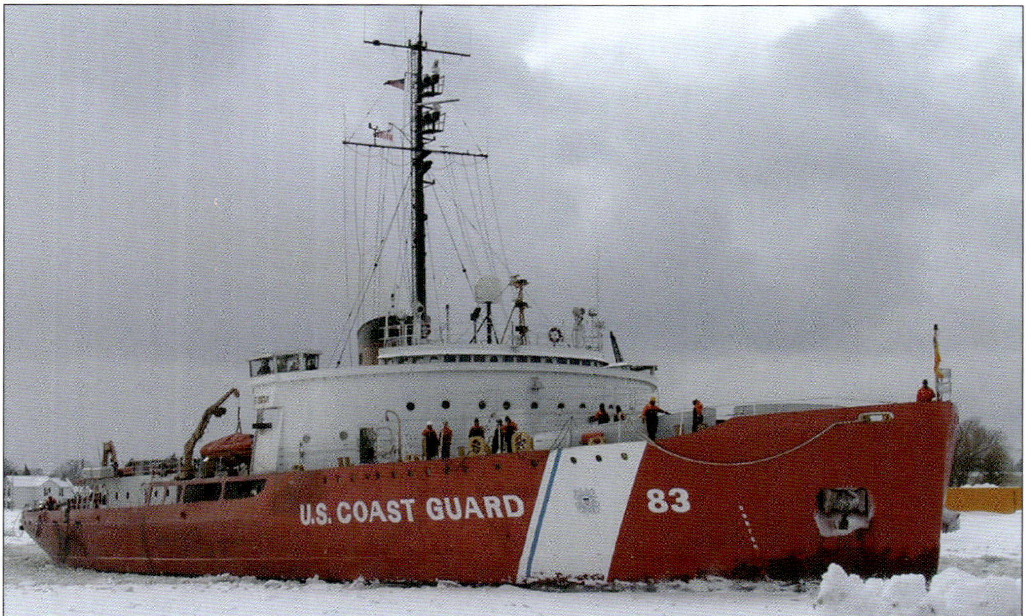

The original *Mackinaw* returned to the Cheboygan River after its final icebreaking mission in March 2006. The ship conducted a farewell tour of sorts, working in Lake Superior and doing the same great job it had done for 62 years, then passing through the Soo Locks and the St. Marys River one final time. (Author's collection.)

Two

Planning, Building, and Launching the New *Mackinaw*

The Coast Guard was directed by Congress to begin planning to replace the original *Mackinaw* (WAGB-83) with funding provided in the 2000 budget. A contract for the design and construction of the new GLIB, or Great Lakes Icebreaker, was awarded to Marinette Marine Corporation in October 2001.

A long process of planning, funding, and construction preceded the launch of the icebreaking buoy-tender. The new ship needed to do the same job with fewer crewmembers, and it needed to add buoy-tending and oil response to its duties due to the decommissioning of the U.S. Coast Guard cutter *Acacia*, which had been stationed nearby in Charlevoix. The design and construction contract provided Marinette Marine Corp. with a performance specification, a compilation of acceptable design and construction standards, and a point design developed by the Coast Guard. The design effort included proven state-of-the-art technology and required the shipbuilder to include logistics, life cycle costs, maintenance requirements, and crewing as part of the process. From the beginning, the GLIB was to be designed for multi-mission capability.

A number of modeling analyses were performed as a part of the design process through 2002. An extensive series of open-water and icebreaking model tests were completed in Sweden and Finland, where ice thickness exists far beyond that experienced in the Great Lakes. Among the items tested were two bow configurations and three stern configurations. Open-water tests focused on ensuring that the sea-keeping requirements for the aids to navigation mission could be met while finalizing powering and maneuvering predictions. The icebreaking model tests focused on documenting the maneuvering capabilities of the ship in ice and refining the hull form for backing in ice.

A thorough propulsion-system dynamic analysis was completed to prove the effectiveness of the chosen machinery, confirm the system level control strategies, and identify areas where additional control strategies needed to be developed. In addition, analysts examined the system's transient loading and power requirements and confirmed that the performance requirements could be met.

During the tests, models broke 32 inches of solid level ice at three-knot speeds and completed 180-degree turns inside an arc 300 feet wide. Marinette Marine Corp. delivered the ship on time and perfectly constructed to specifications.

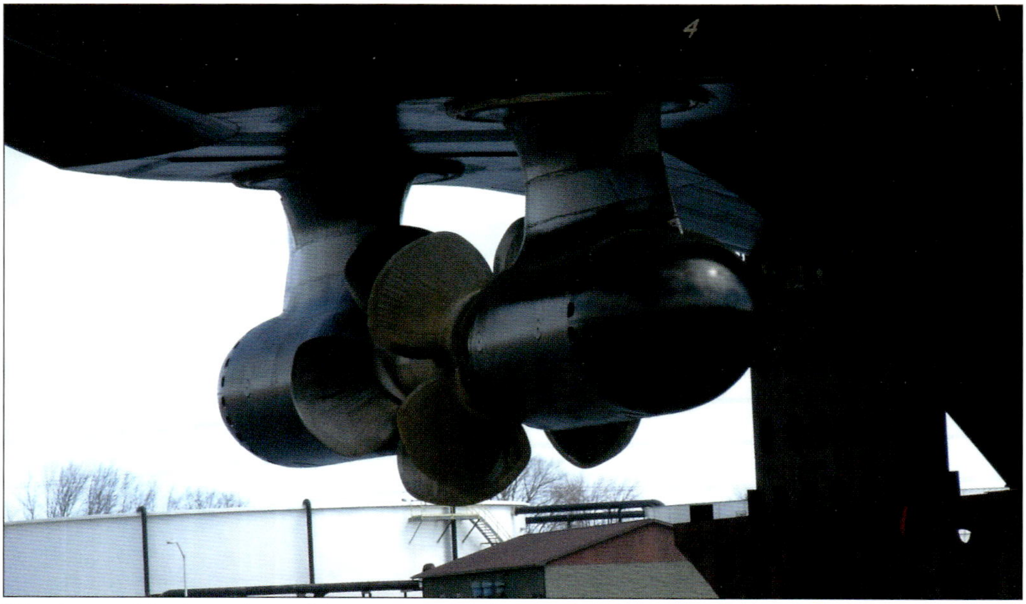

The key to *Mackinaw's* nimble maneuverability is the incorporation of two fully azimuthing podded propulsors, meaning its "podded" (or protected) propellers can rotate 360 degrees and operate without a rudder. The design was the first for the U.S. Coast Guard fleet and the first for any vessel in the American military. The Azipods deliver a combined 9,200 horsepower. (Author's collection.)

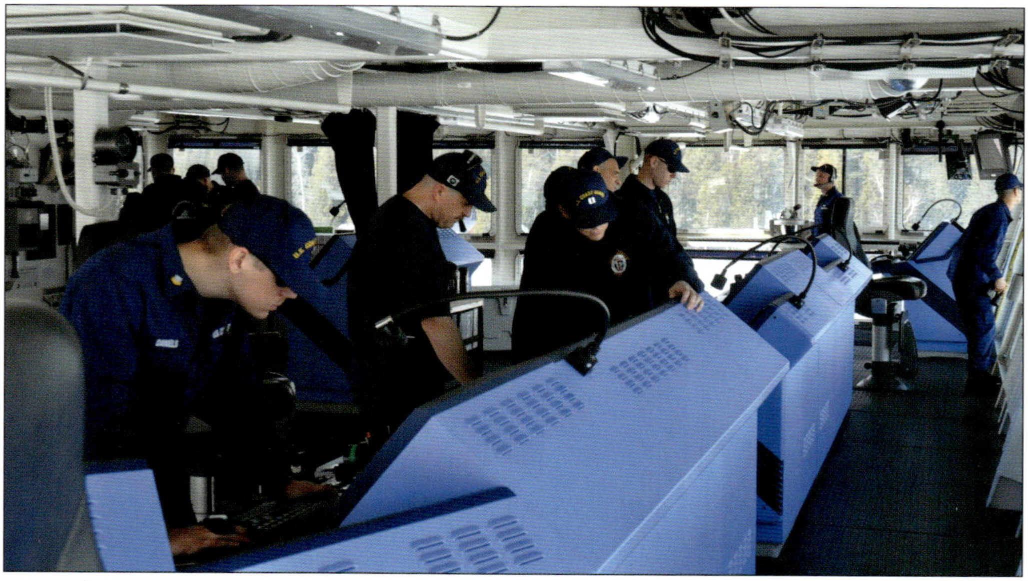

Controls for the sophisticated technology would be within an Integrated Bridge System, located on an expansive bridge deck. Navigations, communications, and ship controls would be operated with a nearly 360-degree view of positions forward, to each side, and to the port-stern and starboard-stern angles from high above the buoy deck and waterline. The view, crew capacity, and working space were vastly larger than the design of the bridge on the original *Mackinaw*. (Courtesy of U.S. Coast Guard.)

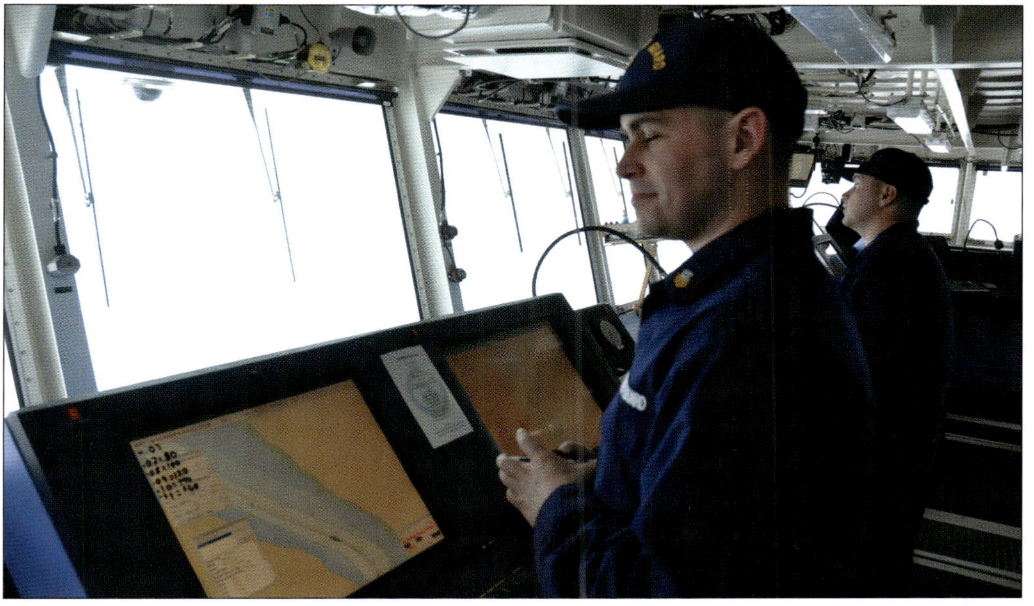

New technology was ordered to control *Mackinaw's* positioning, navigation, and propulsion. Pictured on the bridge, Storekeeper 1st Class Blake Rausch (left) and Bosun's Mate 1st Class Steve Brown are controlling three Electronic Chart Display and Information System (ECDIS) consoles, a Dynamic Positioning System (DPS) display, and a Thruster Control System (TCS). Most crewmembers reporting aboard say they have never seen a bridge with no ship's wheel. (Courtesy of U.S. Coast Guard.)

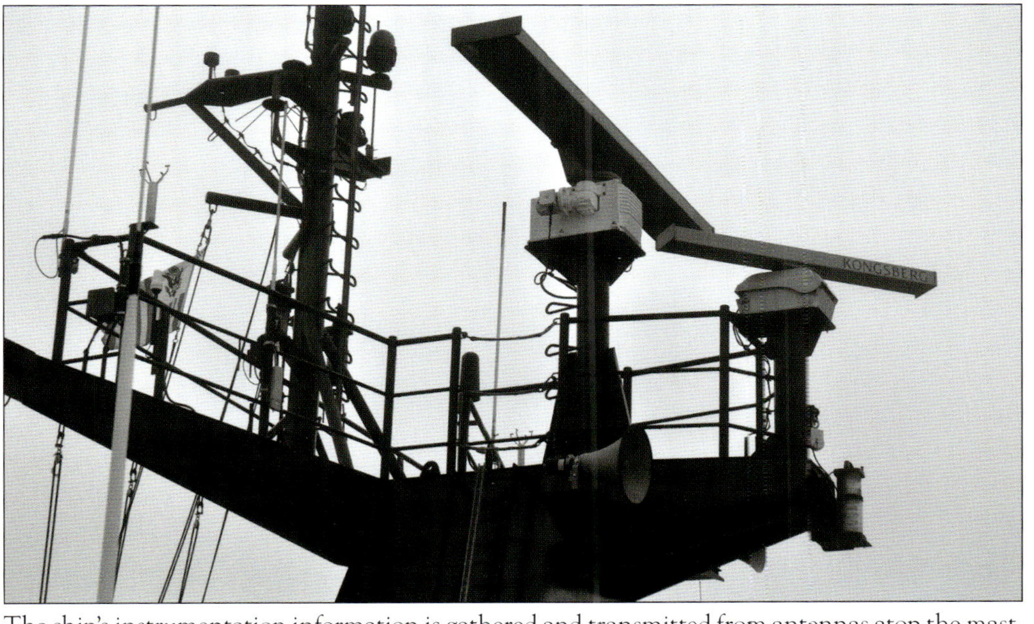

The ship's instrumentation information is gathered and transmitted from antennas atop the mast. In addition to radar, GPS, and radio communication antennas, weather data is also gathered here. *Mackinaw* has backup systems for all electronics on the mast and also operates the all-call deck communications and the ship's horn at this location. (Courtesy of U.S. Coast Guard.)

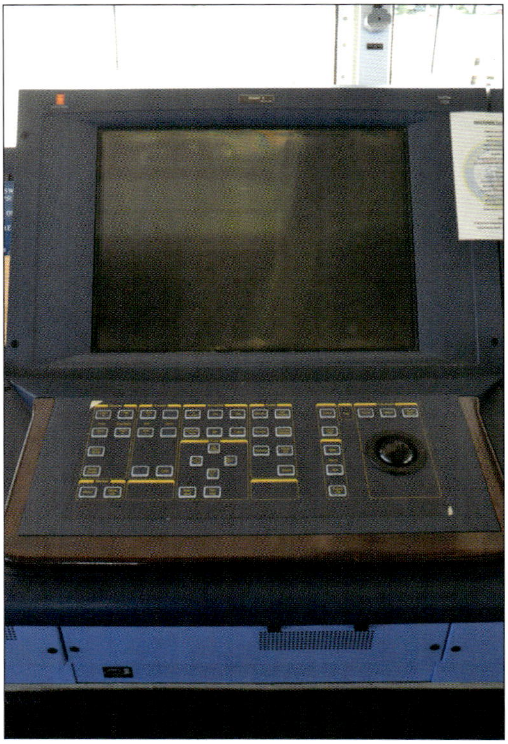

The ECDIS combines electronic National Oceanic and Atmospheric Administration (NOAA) charts, a global-positioning system, compass, and other sensors to provide an image within a chart to the bridge crew. Automatic updates every few seconds provide information accurate to within less than 10 feet of the ship's true position. Remote displays are at the port and starboard bridge wings, and remote-control panels are in the port and starboard secondary conning stations. (Courtesy of U.S. Coast Guard.)

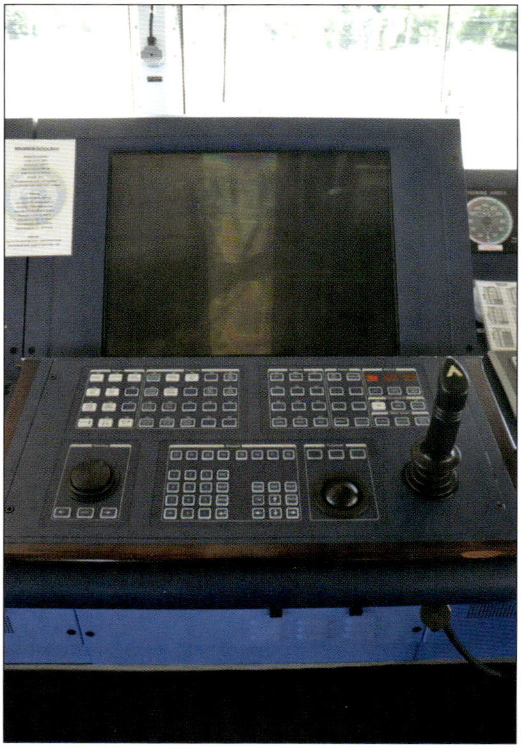

The DPS provides dynamic positioning capabilities such as auto positioning and automatic track following. The system consists of a DPS operator station, a main computer system, and two remote operator terminals. The operator station is located on the navigation workstation. The two operator terminals are located at the port and starboard secondary conning stations on the bridge wings. (Courtesy of U.S. Coast Guard.)

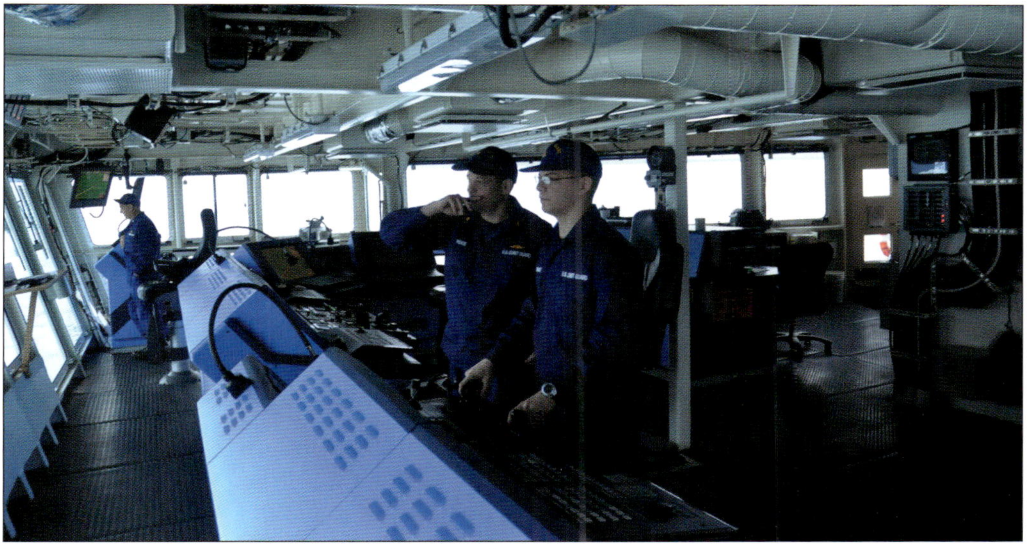

The nav station incorporates many elements of navigation into the ship's movements. In addition to electronic chart data, the conn also relies on visual-range measurements, radar observations, and radio communications. The entire bridge crew is constantly updating information that keeps the navigation precise; it then is relayed to the commanding officer. Lt. Cmdr. Eric Peace is pictured instructing Seaman Jakub Rodriguez. (Courtesy of U.S. Coast Guard.)

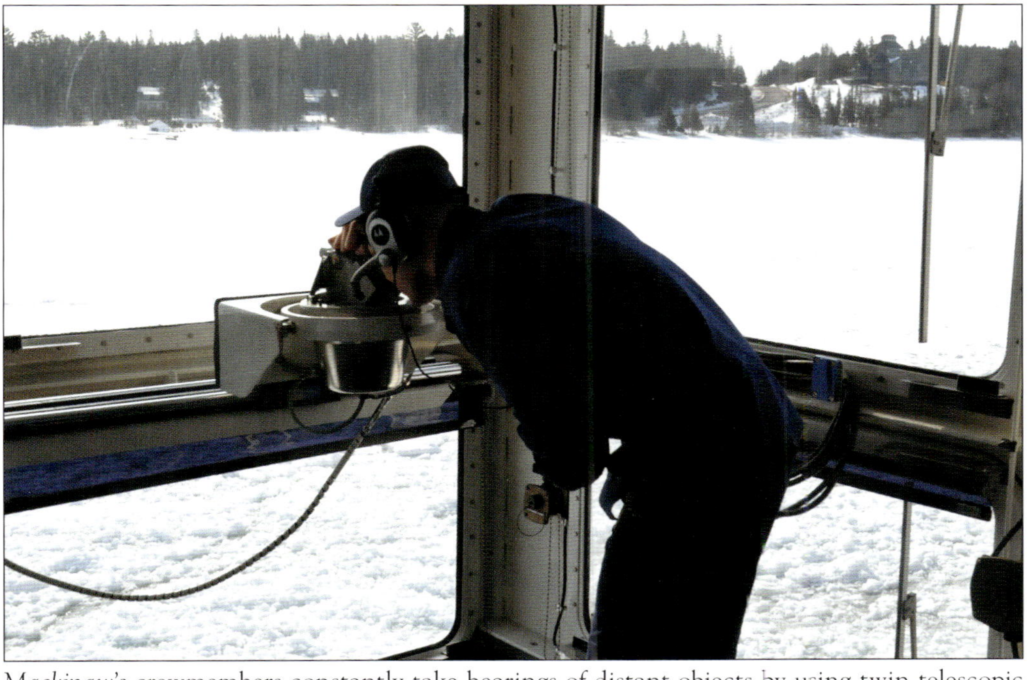

Mackinaw's crewmembers constantly take bearings of distant objects by using twin telescopic alidades mounted on each bridge wing atop a slide-mounted gyro repeater. The nav station uses readings from these instruments to check the position of the ship relative to other ships, buoys, and objects on shore. This information constantly changes the navigation picture and is kept ready as additional input to what the electronics provide. (Courtesy of U.S. Coast Guard.)

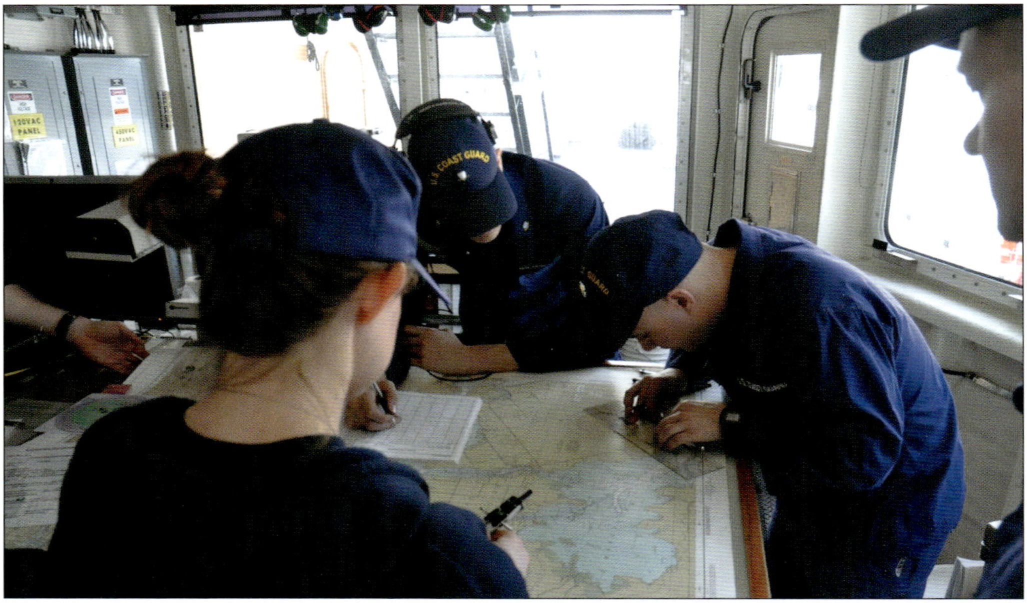

Manually plotting bearings and courses is part of navigation duties for *Mackinaw's* crewmembers. The methodology of navigation not only serves as a data backup to supplement the ship's electronics, but is essential in the event the electronics should fail. Diligent weekend sailors in small boats know this, and it is absolutely necessary to know exactly where a $110.5 million ship is at all times. (Courtesy of U.S. Coast Guard.)

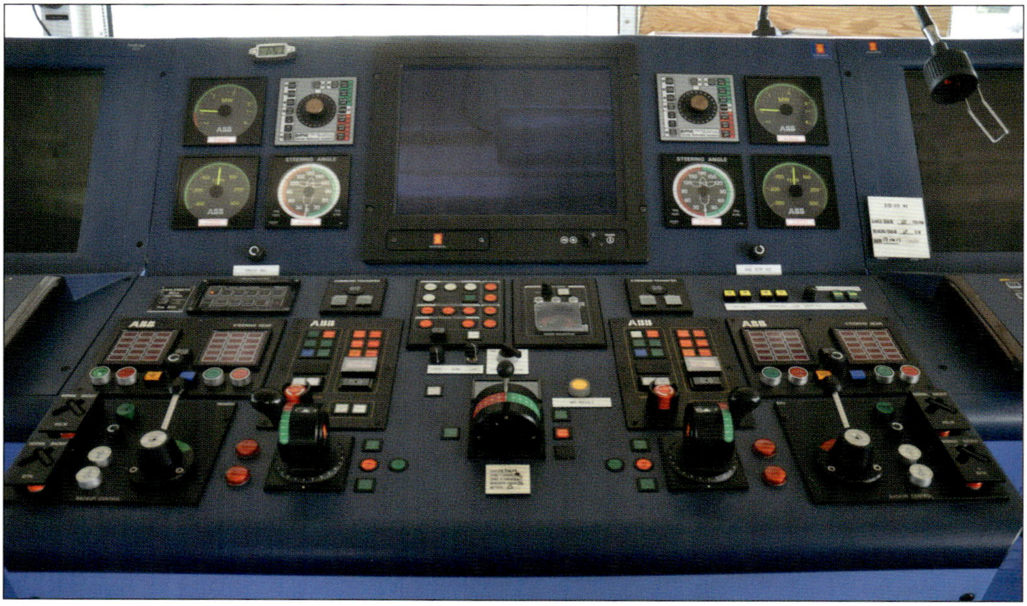

The Thruster Control System (TCS), referred to as "manual" or "main console" by the crew, has plenty of capabilities. A main computer, three fixed control-lever panels, and two portable control-lever panels provide direction to the Azipod main propulsion units and the bow thruster. The TCS controls allow the ship to literally turn in its own wake and pinpoint close drive-by icebreaking for huge ships. (Courtesy of U.S. Coast Guard.)

Mackinaw's radar screen complements the ship's navigational package by picking up images of other ships, buoys, the Mackinac Bridge, and approaching storms. Many ships in World War II were not equipped with radar until the later stages of the war, and today's commercial radar packages are light-years ahead of earlier models. (Courtesy of U.S. Coast Guard.)

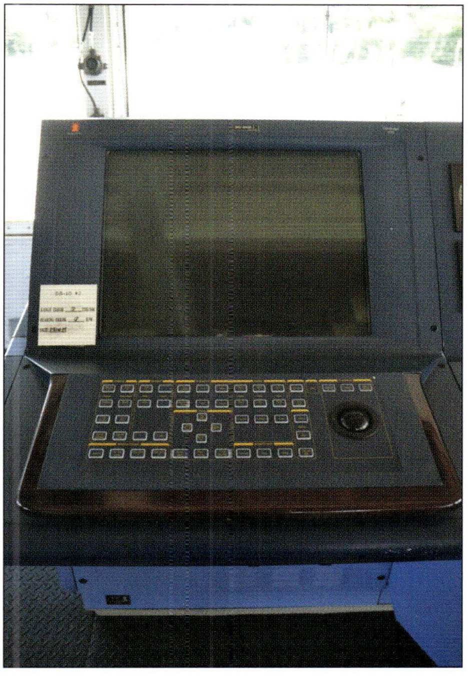

The bridge wing control stations allow for the conn to move the ship while maintaining visual contact with the immediate area next to the ship. Whether the *Mackinaw* is tying up to a dock, approaching a buoy, or assisting in a search-and-rescue mission, the approach can be made with a full view along either side of the vessel, such as conning officer Lt. (jg) Matt Perkins has here. (Author's collection.)

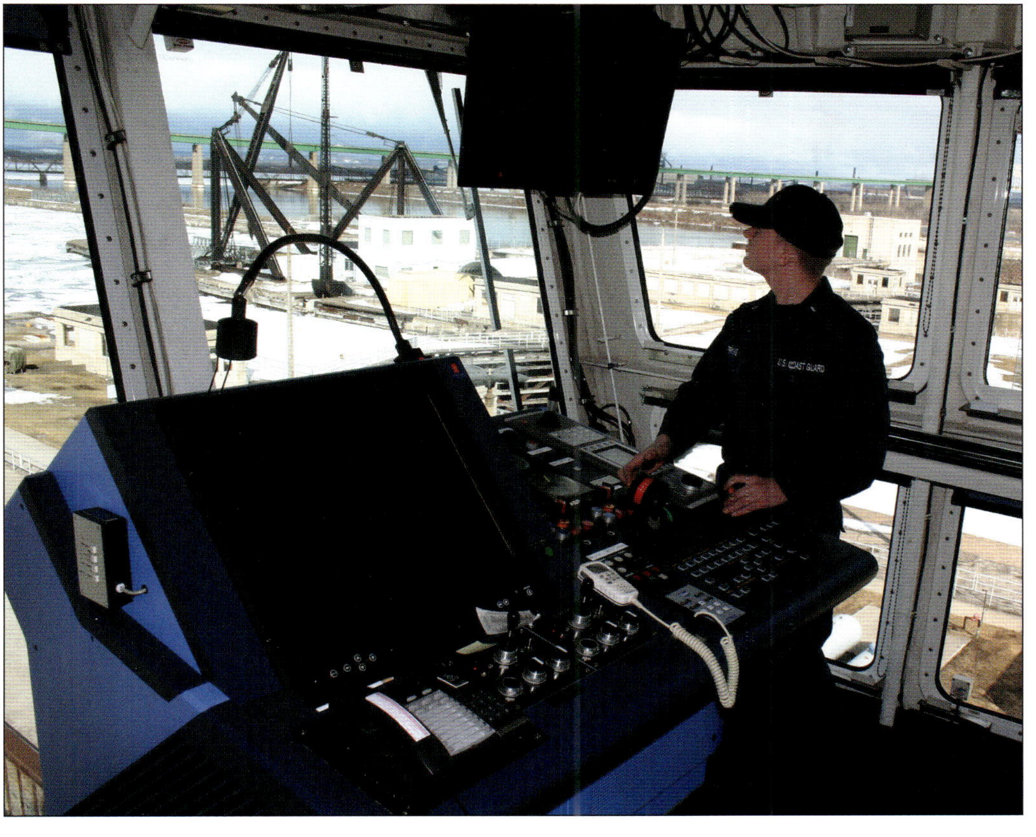

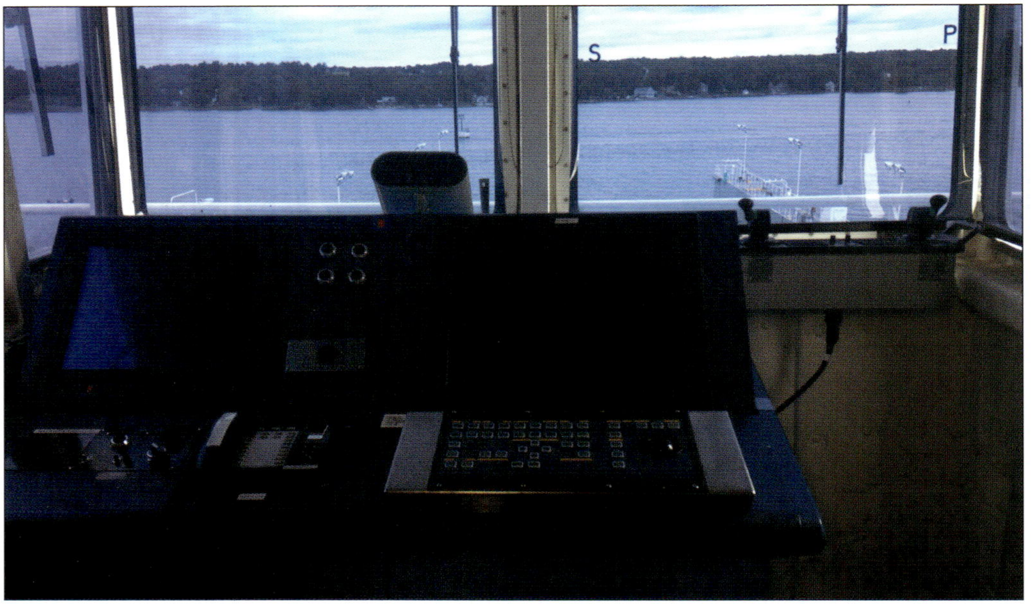

If the Azipod engines are turned around to reverse the ship's direction, a control station is needed aft. *Mackinaw* does much more than just occasionally back up. One of the ship's claims to fame is its ability to break ice in reverse, using its prop wash to flush ice away from a ship, dock, or lock chamber. The aft control station makes that job a practical and safe alternative. (Courtesy of U.S. Coast Guard.)

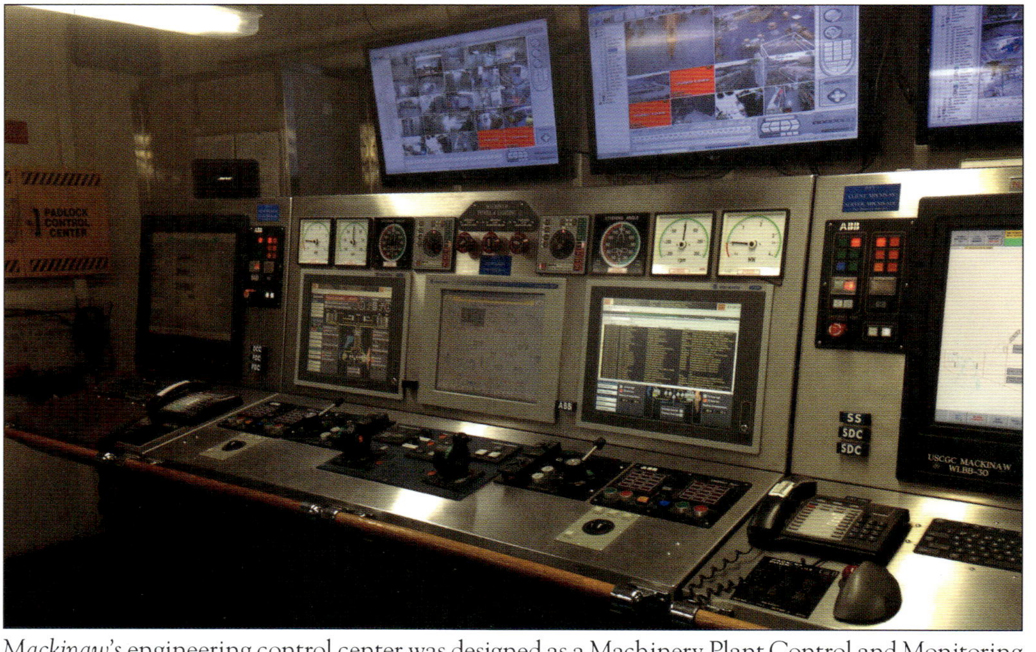

Mackinaw's engineering control center was designed as a Machinery Plant Control and Monitoring System (MPCMS) to allow control and monitoring of more than 5,800 points in the ship's various systems. From here, onboard engineers can track the trends of any monitored point over time and use that information to plan maintenance in advance. (Courtesy of U.S. Coast Guard.)

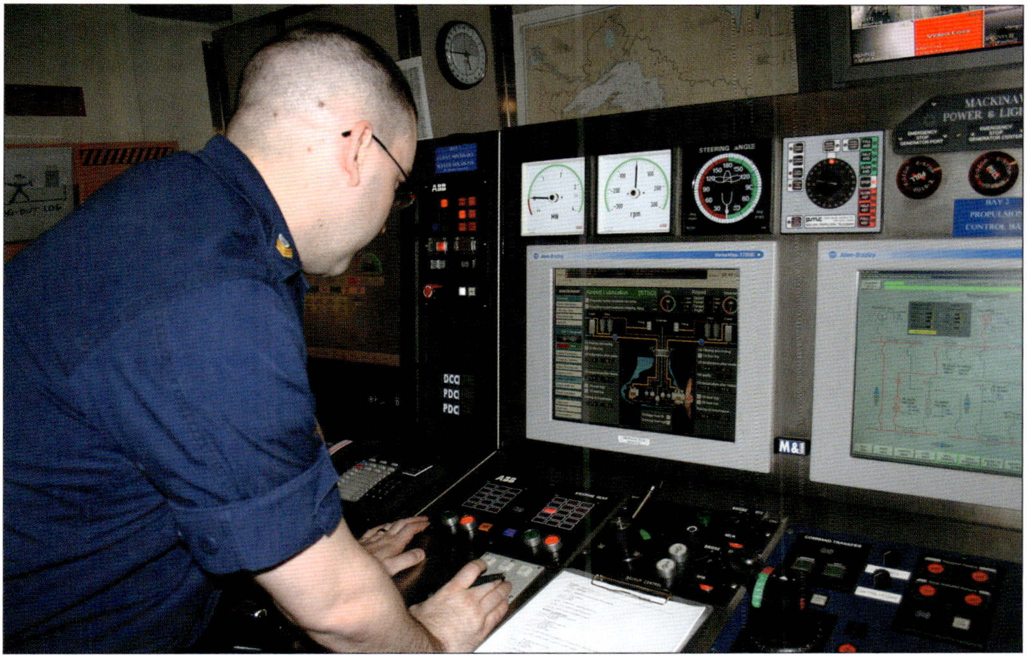

The ship's propulsion and auxiliary equipment can be controlled, monitored, and alarmed at each MPCMS station. All machinery, fire, and flooding alarms routed through the MPCMS sound an alert if not promptly answered. Engineers, such as Machinist Tech 1st Class Nick Johnson, pictured here, can monitor all entry points to the ship and other critical locations on closed-circuit television. There are even underwater views of the propellers turning. (Courtesy of U.S. Coast Guard.)

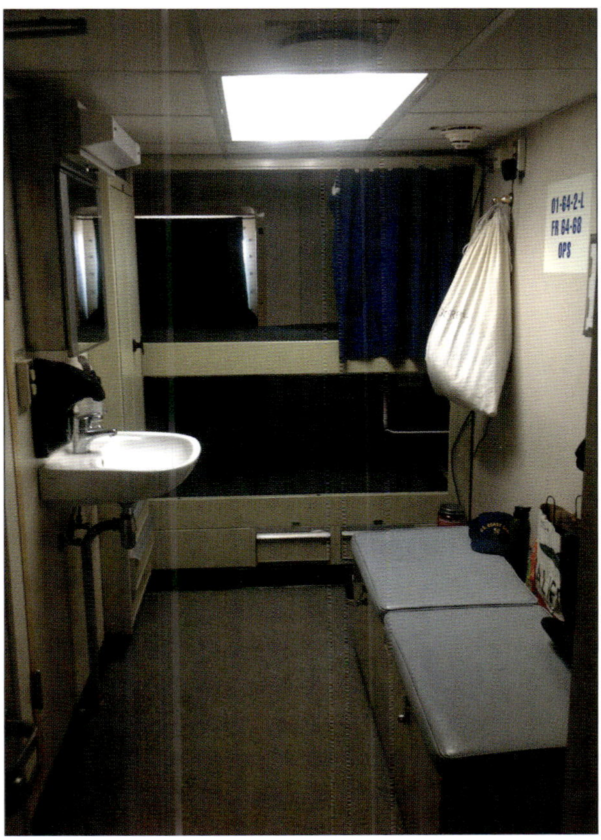

Today's Coast Guard provides sailors with far more amenities than in earlier eras, such as when the original *Mackinaw* was launched. Semiprivate accommodations, Internet connections, more storage space, and comfort were included in the new ship's design. Outside contractors bid to clean the ship in port on a regular basis, leaving personal space the only responsibility of a *Mackinaw* crewmember. (Courtesy of U.S. Coast Guard.)

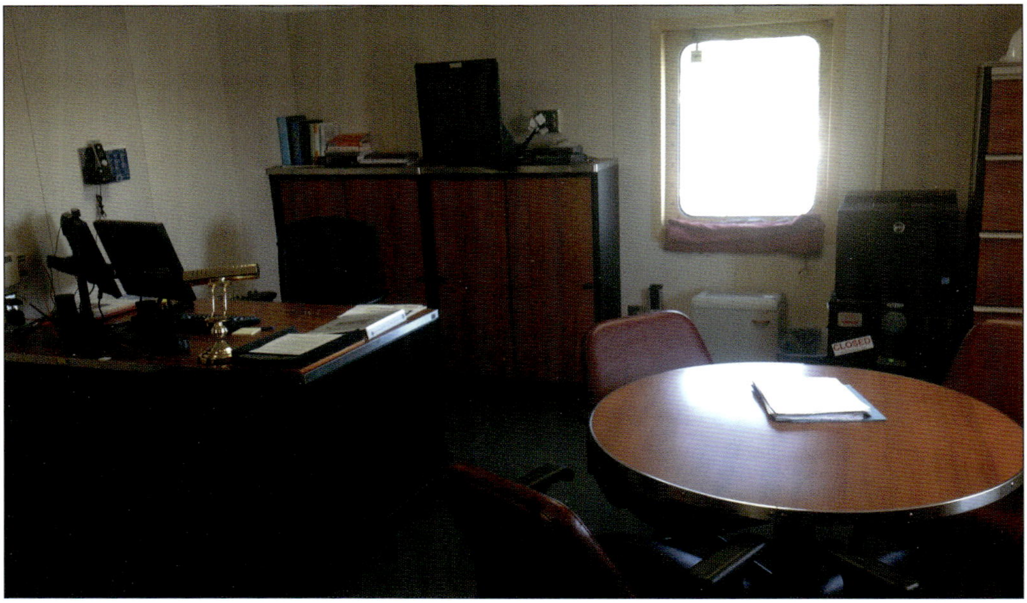

The commanding officer's quarters include a generous amount of office space, suitable for meetings and hosting guests. An adjacent cabin contains sleeping quarters and washroom space. The windows afford the best view from the entire ship, and instrumentation tells the CO the ship's course, speed, and other variables. There is also instant communication capability to the bridge and engineering departments. (Courtesy of U.S. Coast Guard.)

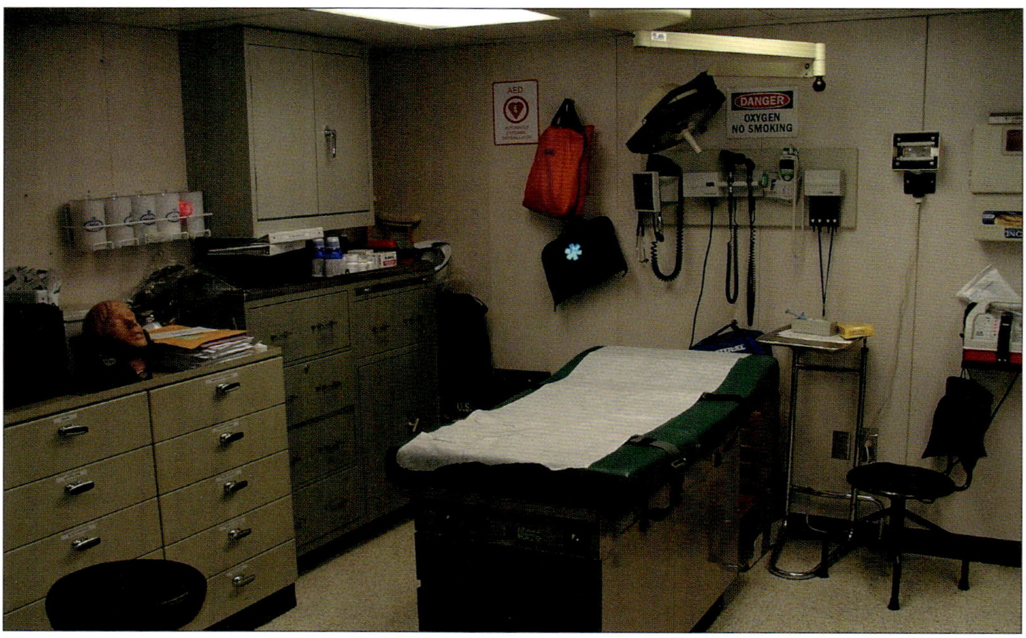

The ship is staffed with a medical corpsman, who handles patients needing anything from routine vaccinations to urgent medical care. Severe cases are stabilized aboard before being transferred to a shore-side physician. The medical suite is sufficiently equipped to handle various shipboard emergency scenarios. (Author's collection.)

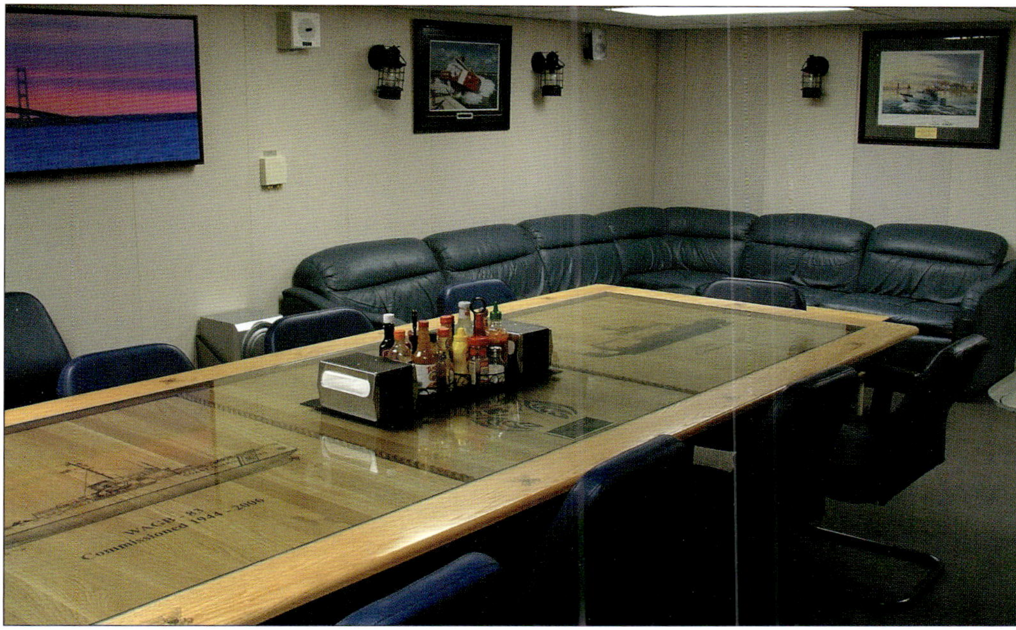

The ship's officers dine and hold meetings and planning sessions in the officers' wardroom, located adjacent to the mess deck. Placemats are designed to keep plates from sliding due to the ship's movement at sea. Officers are seated by rank, with the captain always at the head of the table. (Author's collection.)

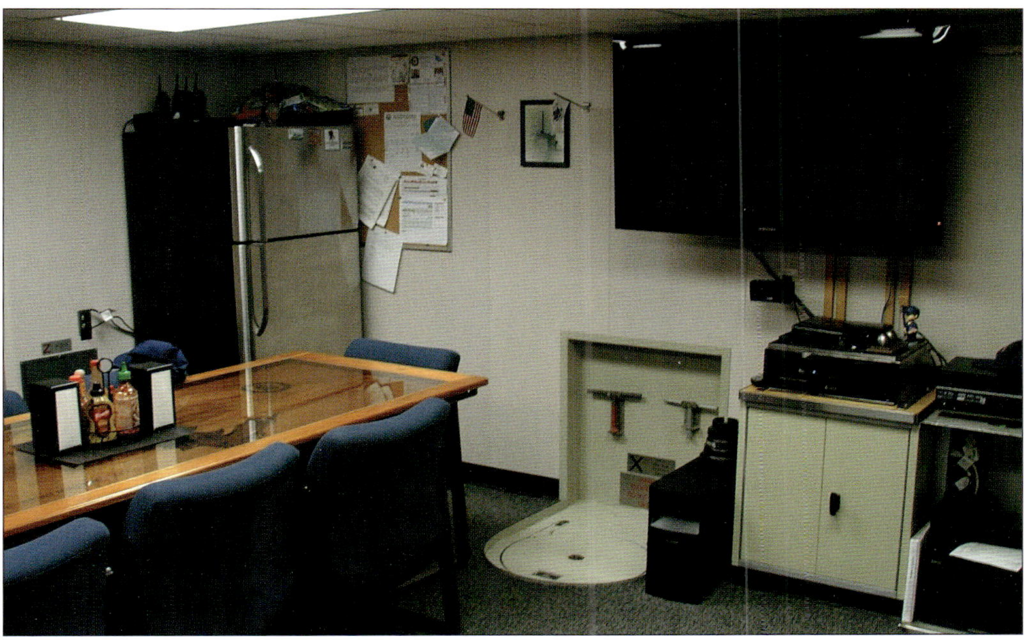

The chiefs of the ship are the senior enlisted personnel who handle onboard day-to-day operations. Their mess is located across the mess deck from the officers' wardroom. It is their own space for dining, planning meetings, and relaxation. The chiefs pride themselves as the workmen of the ship. (Author's collection.)

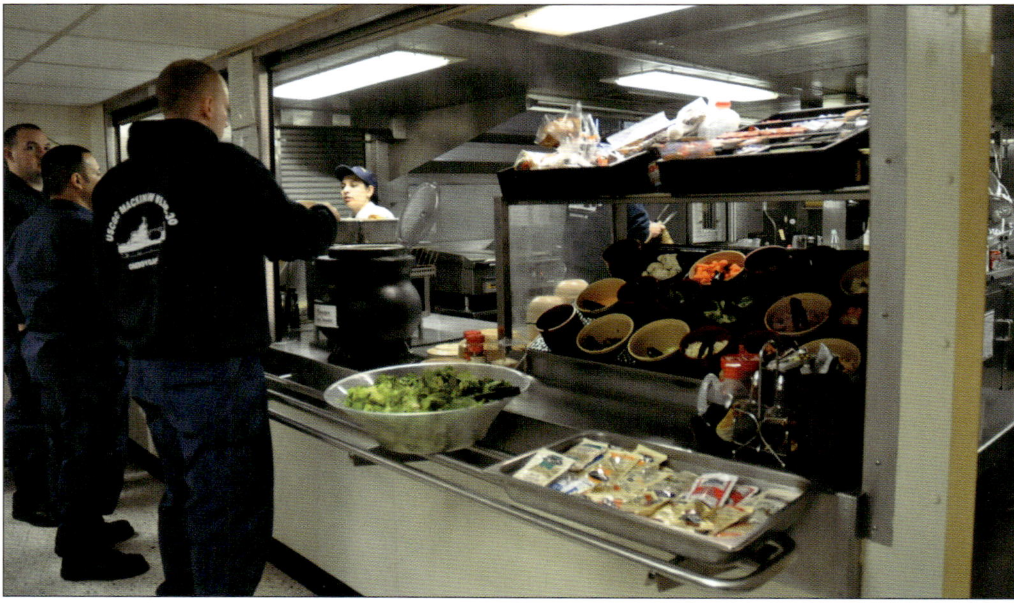

The ship's mess deck seats 32 diners at a time and includes a flat-screen television, digital music system, and a game console for crew use. Soft drink and coffee machines are available 24 hours, and the galley has ample freezer and refrigeration space for 30 days at sea. The food specialists aboard *Mackinaw* serve three meals per day, with snacks available anytime. (Courtesy of U.S. Coast Guard.)

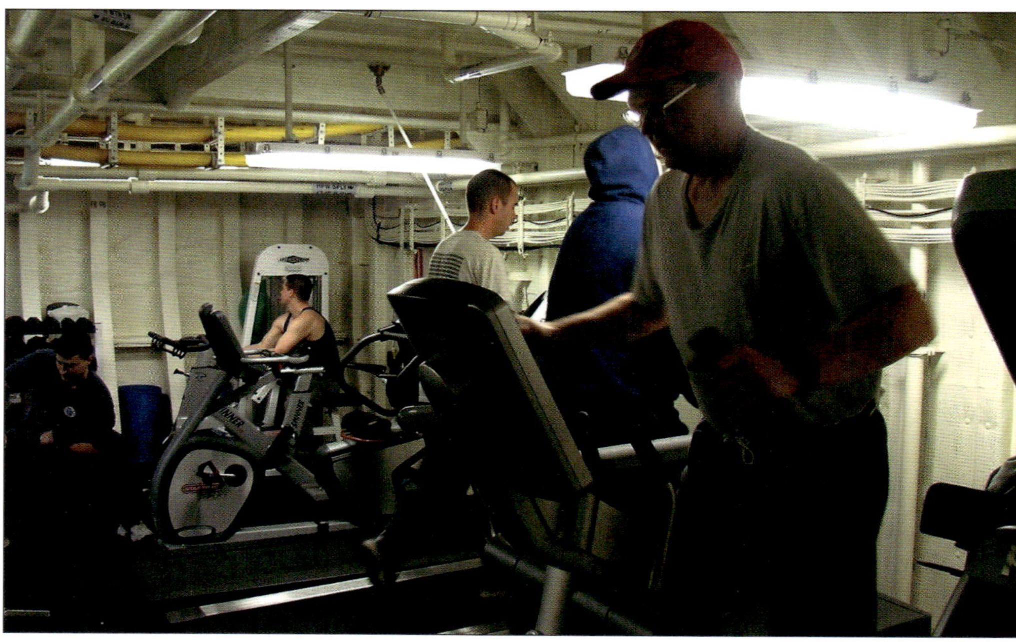

Fitness at sea is a priority when icebreaking for six weeks at a time in subzero temperatures. Some of the exercise equipment aboard was purchased with funds contributed to the *Mackinaw's* Morale Fund by citizens of Cheboygan upon the ship's arrival in 2005. In better weather, crewmembers also enjoy bicycles, kayaks, and other outdoor sports equipment. (Author's collection.)

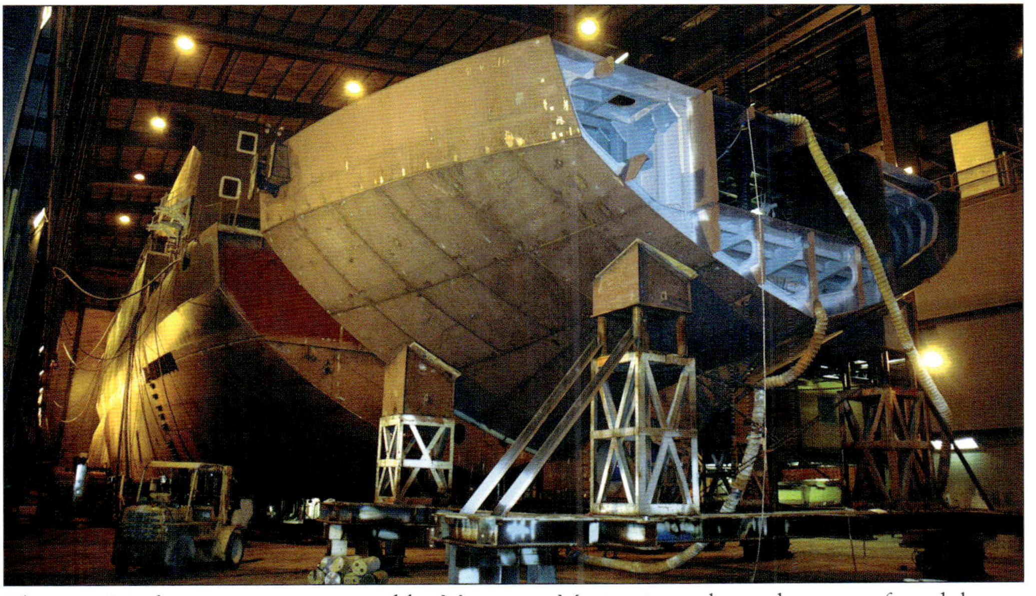

The new *Mackinaw* was constructed by Marinette Marine in a planned system of modules, or blocks, that are essentially complete prior to final assembly. The cutter was put together indoors, allowing the assembly and outfitting to take place in controlled conditions. The ship's hull was then moved outside, where the superstructure was lowered onto the deck and welded into place. (Courtesy of Marinette Marine Corporation.)

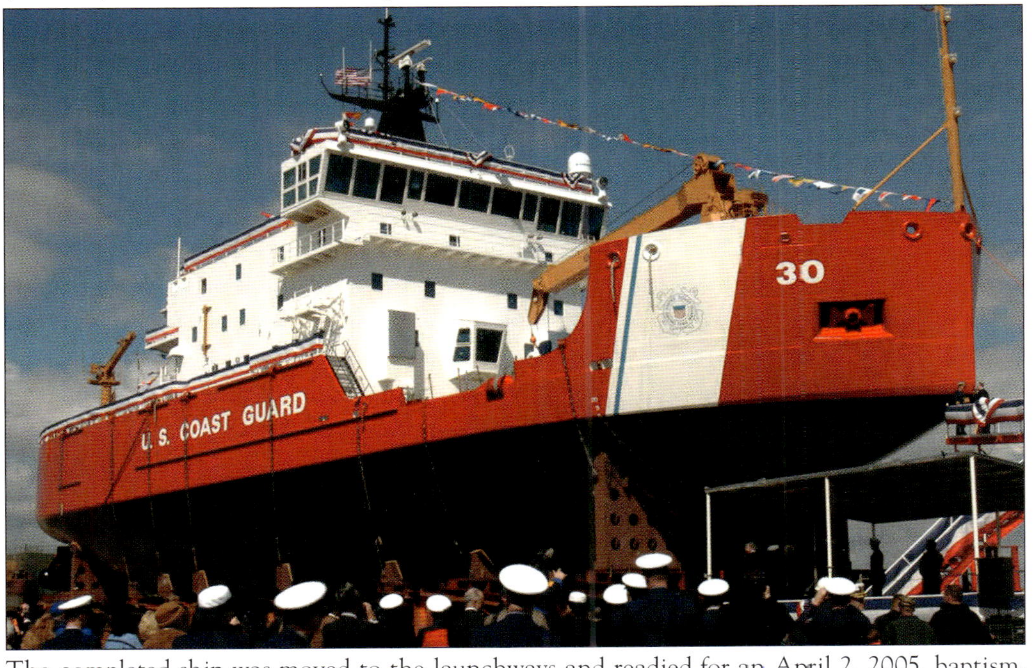

The completed ship was moved to the launchways and readied for an April 2, 2005, baptism. Angled iron support blocks allowed the *Mackinaw* to rest upright on the dock, in full view of inspectors and manufacturers' representatives, who were able to board the vessel and complete final installation and troubleshooting of newly-installed components. (Author's collection.)

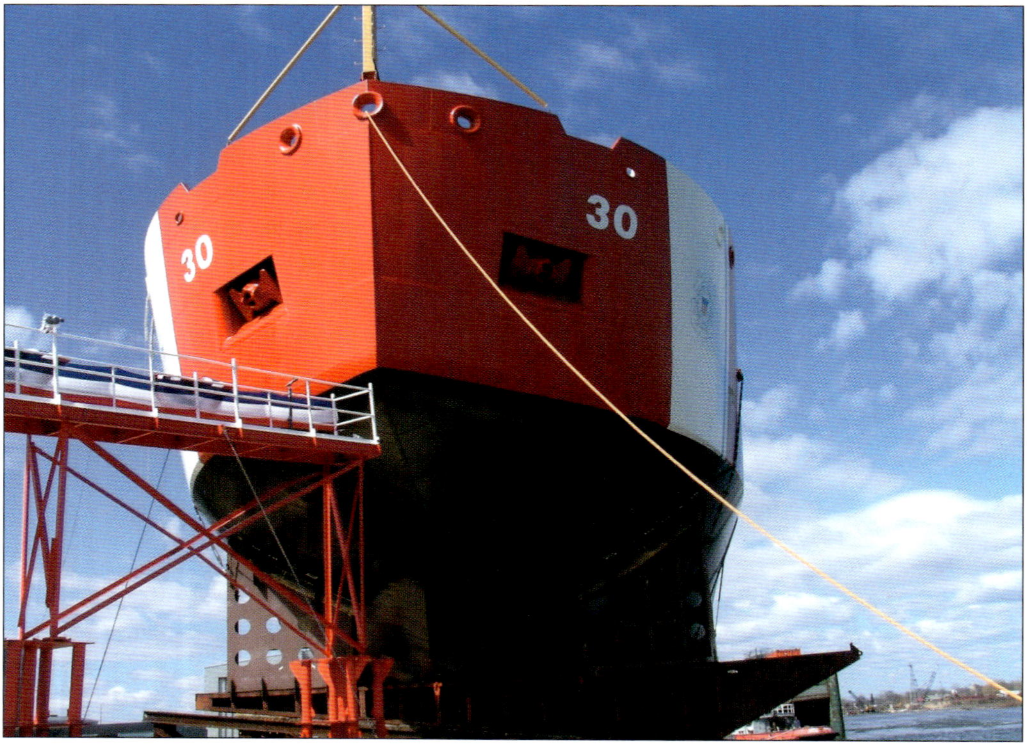

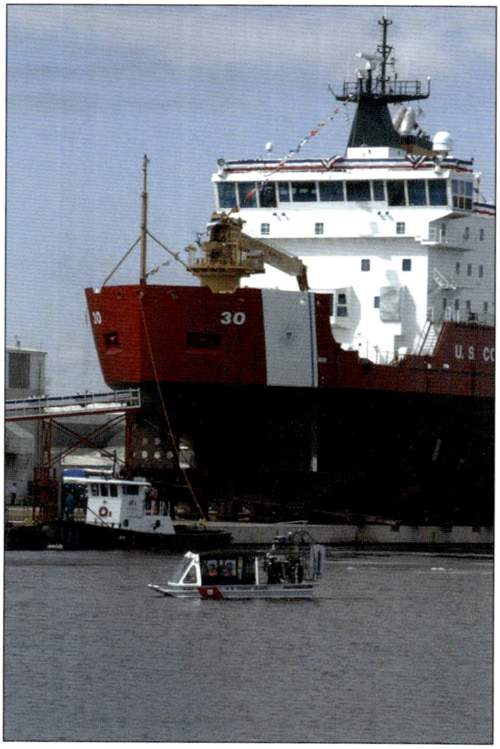

Every view of the *Mackinaw* drew gasps of awe on launch day. The view of the bow was just as intimidating as seeing the giant Azipod engines, turned inward under the stern to protect the screws during the launch. Photographers alternated between close-up photographs and far-off, all-encompassing shots of the whole ship. There was so much to see that those with cameras—practically all in attendance—were kept busy. Nobody had a bad seat. Credentials were necessary to gain entrance to the shipyard, but plenty of onlookers also had great views from the north side of the Menominee River. (Above, author's collection; left, courtesy of U.S. Coast Guard.)

The *Mackinaw's* first skipper, Capt. Donald F. Triner, came to the new vessel in his fourth command after graduating with honors from the Coast Guard Academy in 1984. His awards included two Meritorious Service Medals with operational device, three Coast Guard Commendation Medals, two Coast Guard Achievement Medals, the Commandant's Letter of Commendation, and several Meritorious and Unit Commendations, plus two Coast Guard Special Operations Service Ribbons. (Courtesy of U.S. Coast Guard.)

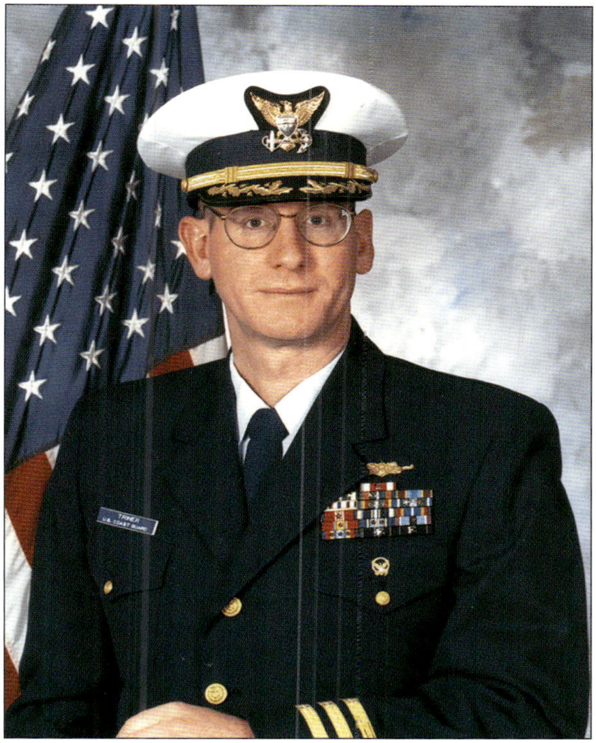

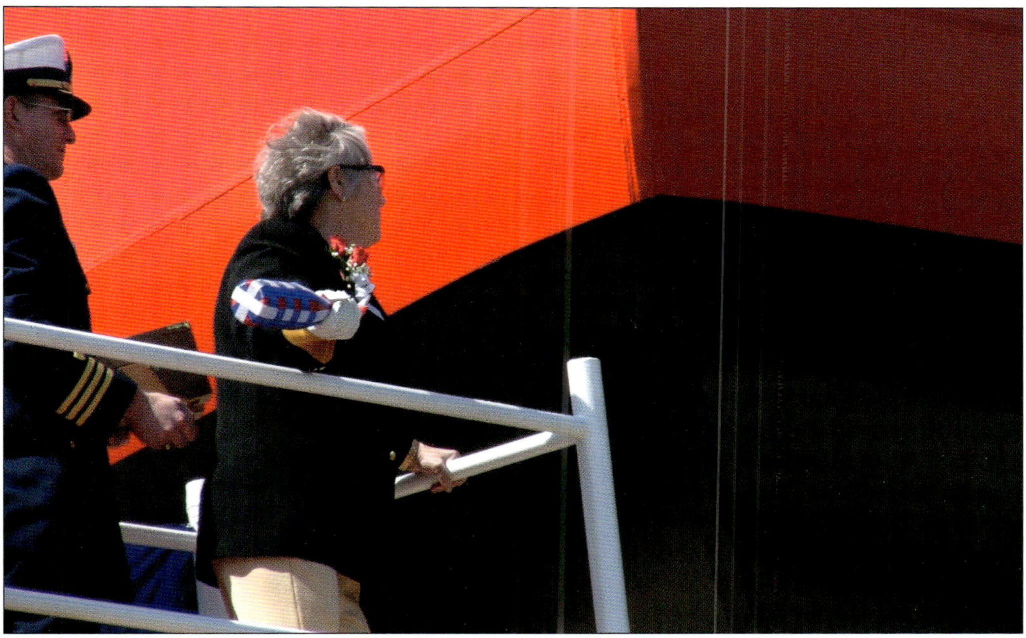

Jean Hastert, wife of Speaker of the House Dennis Hastert, was the ship's sponsor. She was present early in the construction process and regarded the cutter as a miracle that quickly grew, from so many "pieces and parts," to a huge, beautiful ship. With Captain Triner at her side, she swung the christening bottle to the bow, and the launch began. (Author's collection.)

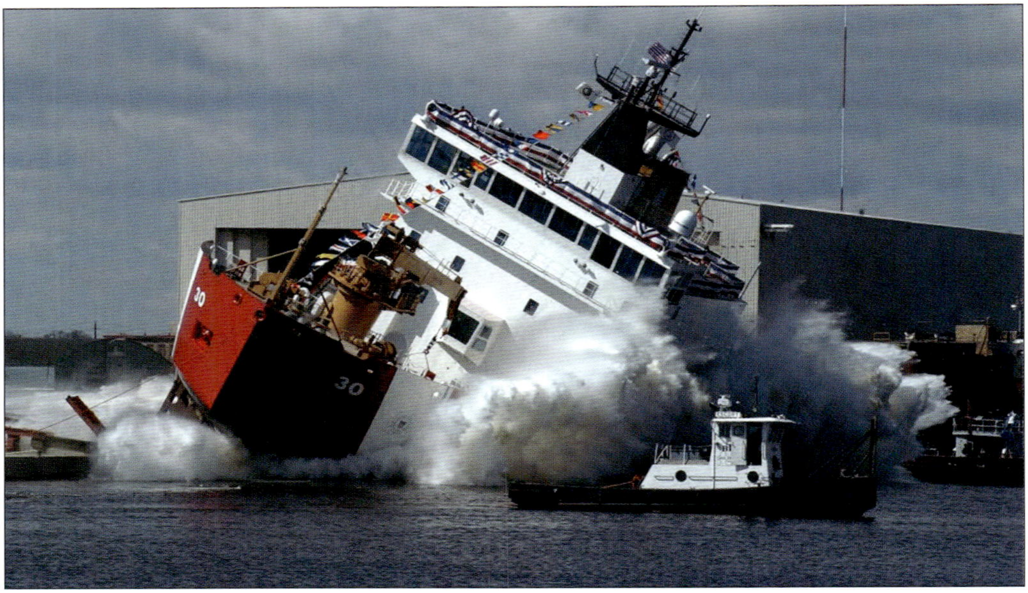

The launch of a ship can be described in many ways: impressive, intimidating, beautiful, precise, and, perhaps, even romantic. When workmen sounded an alarm and sent the *Mackinaw* on its way into the Menominee River, all of those ideas and more were no doubt in the minds of the more than 5,000 onlookers who witnessed the sideways launch. The launch was noisy; a machine-like rumble accompanied the new ship's slide to the edge of the pier, settling into a hiss and then silence. The crowd roared in approval at the spectacle. The era of the GLIB had begun. (Above, courtesy of U.S. Coast Guard; below, courtesy of Chris Winters.)

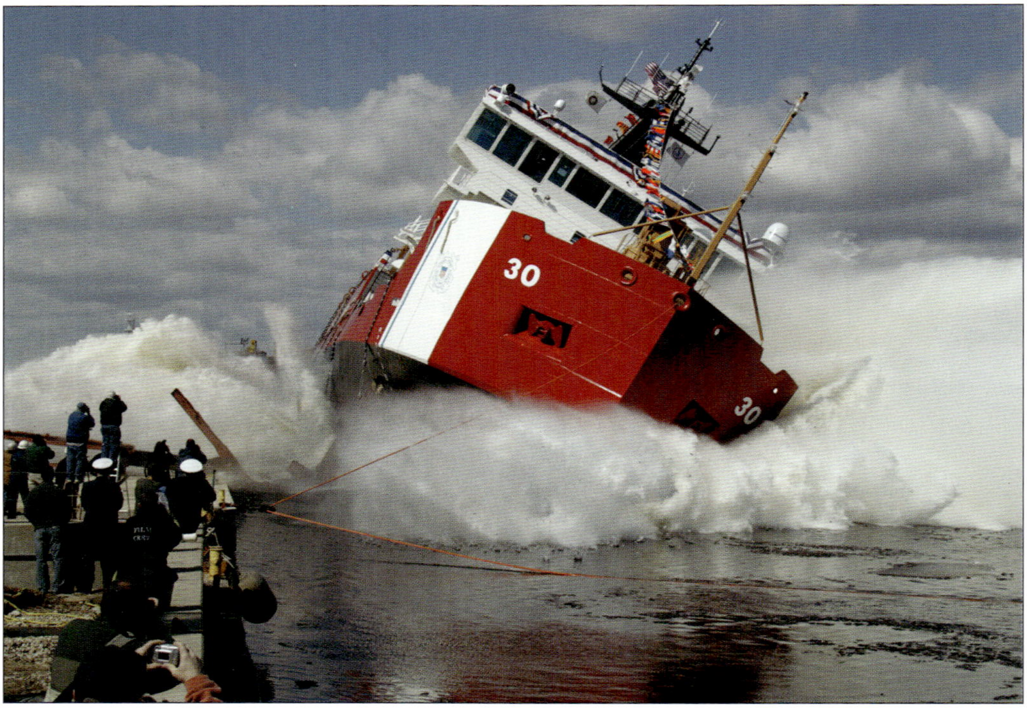

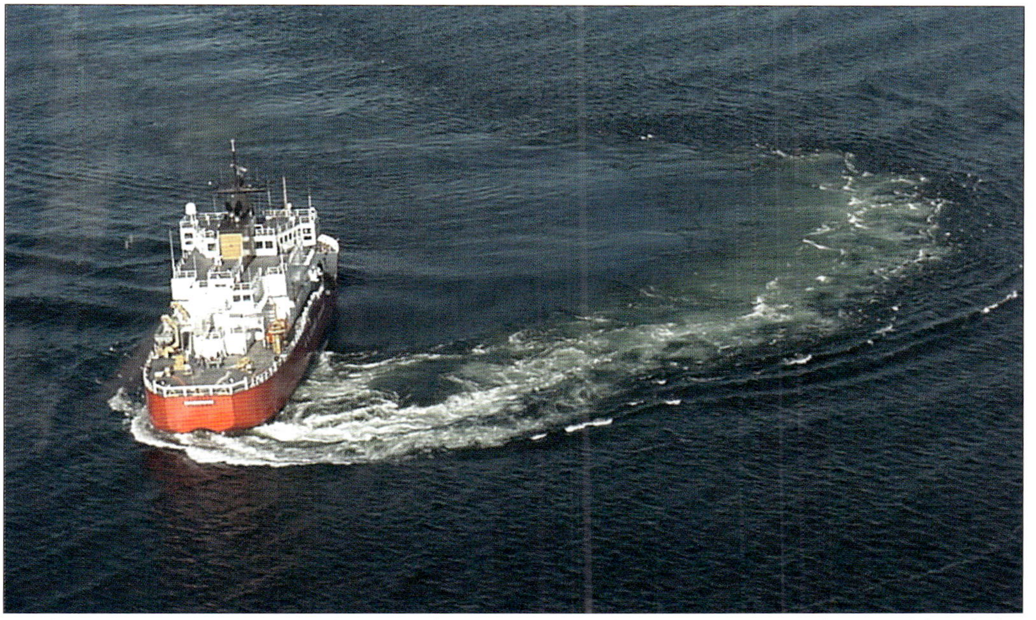

In the weeks that followed, the new ship completed those refinements that could only be accomplished in the water. A fleet of trucks, service vehicles, and skids of supplies arrived daily to begin the process of stocking the ship with tools, spare parts, safety equipment, furnishings, and all the weight that was to be avoided during the launch. Breakable items were placed in secure locations. Then, it was time to start and test engines, electronics, navigation equipment, and safety gear. Sea trials began, with the *Mac* making daily runs out of the river and into Lake Michigan to perform turns, calibrate more equipment, and test performance expectations. The Azipods delivered as promised, allowing the ship to turn on a dime. The *Mackinaw* was more than impressive. (Both, courtesy of Marinette Marine Corporation.)

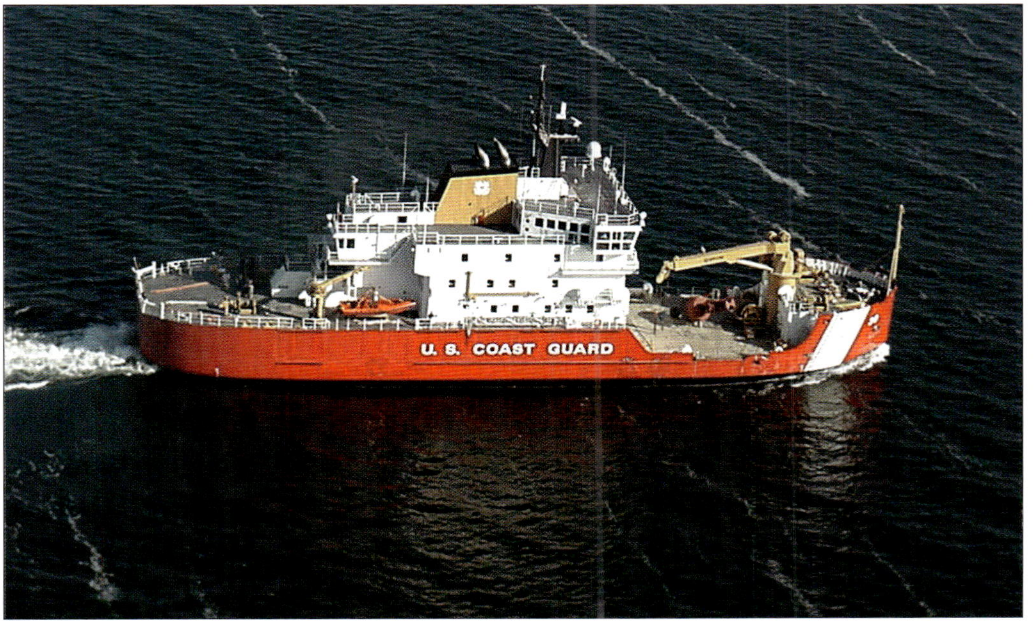

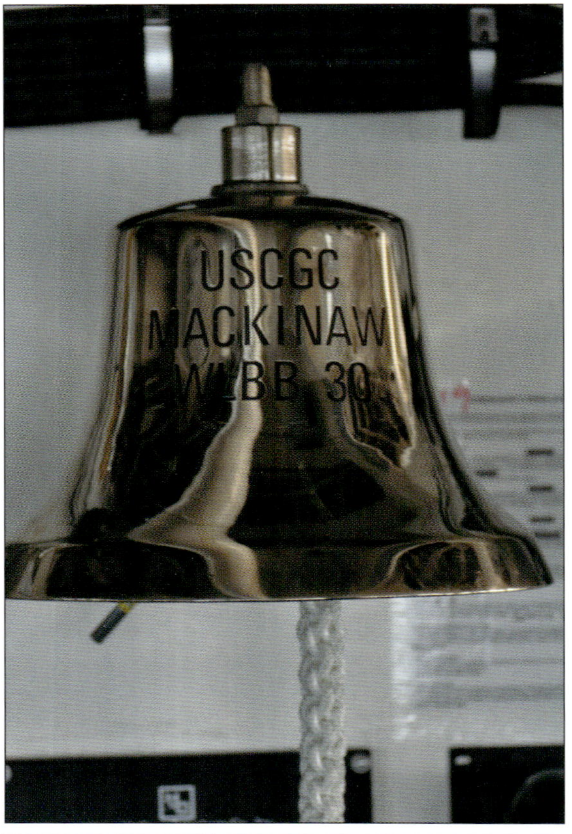

Mackinaw's ship's bell hung ready to be rung by the crew on its first missions; it was ready for real logbook entries and all that awaited. The first search-and-rescue missions, the first buoy-tending runs, the first icebreaking, and the first heavy seas all lay ahead, waiting for the newest ship in the Coast Guard. It was a story yet to be told and a legacy ready to be fulfilled. (Courtesy of U.S. Coast Guard.)

This "plankowners" plaque—listing the names of original crewmembers—is mounted in the main passageway between the engineering space and the mess deck, a highly visible location for crewmembers and visitors alike. Captain Triner, who had trained in Europe on the systems to be used in *Mackinaw's* design, handpicked the first crew for the ship. Many had served under him in past commands, and they developed a fierce loyalty to their leader. (Courtesy of U.S. Coast Guard.)

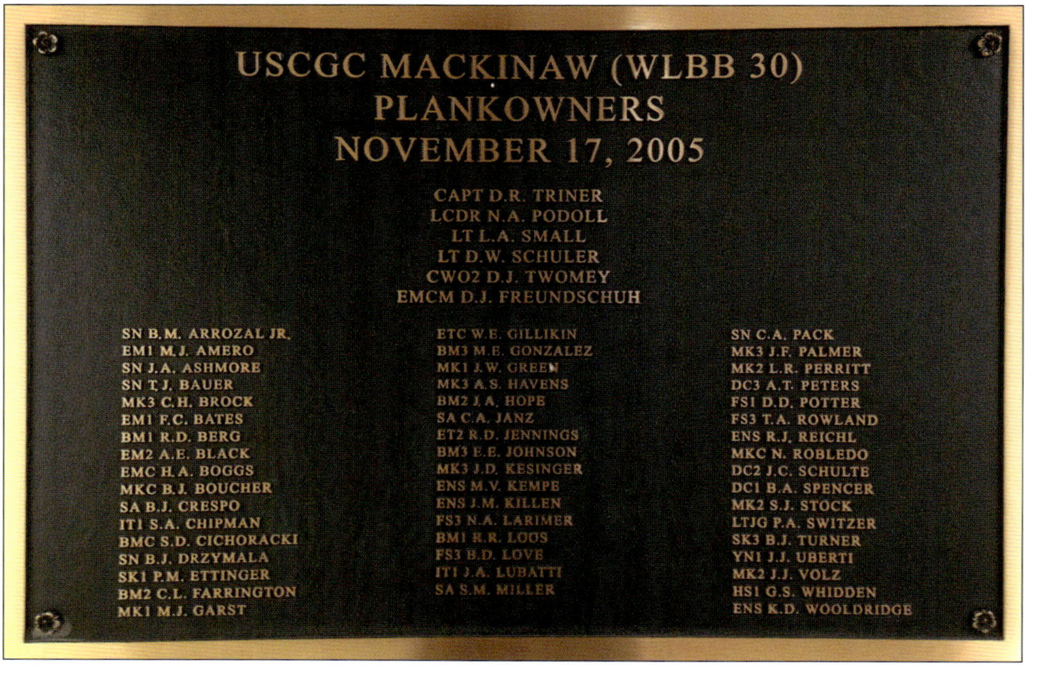

Three

A Grand Haven Allision

In a historic day that brought goose bumps to many—if the 27-degree temperatures and the wind chill had not already—the new U.S. Coast Guard cutter *Mackinaw* arrived in the Cheboygan River on December 17, 2005. Crowds had gathered along the shoreline and on the decks of the original icebreaker *Mackinaw*.

Sirens blared from fire engines parked on the west side of the channel; motorists watching from their vehicles honked horns, and throngs who lined the route along the river waved American flags and cheered the city's newest residents and their families. As the ship approached the dock, the Cheboygan Area High School Marching Band repeatedly played the Coast Guard's theme song, "Semper Paratus," with a zeal that created an indelible image for all who were there.

However, the ship's maiden voyage to its new home port was planned to include prior celebratory stops at Grand Haven (home of the Coast Guard Festival), and Sault Ste. Marie (home of the Soo Locks). In addition, the ship was to take on its first major supply of fuel at Rogers City. All that changed when the ship struck the pier on December 12 while entering the harbor at Grand Haven. Capt. Donald Triner, who was commanding the *Mackinaw*, was quoted by the Associated Press shortly after the allision (the act of a vessel striking a stationary object) as saying that a junior crewmember had moved the wrong steering controls. Damage to the cutter consisted of a dent in the starboard bow measuring approximately eight feet long by three feet high. A segment of the breakwall also required repairs.

"It's a pretty good dent with some paint scraped off," Triner told the *Cheboygan Daily Tribune*. "The Coast Guard will conduct an investigation." Then, three days later, Rear Adm. Robert J. Papp Jr., commander of the Ninth Coast Guard District, temporarily suspended Triner and ordered the cutter to sail directly to Cheboygan under the temporary command of Capt. Michael Hudson. Triner accompanied the ship's company as a "technical advisor to the commanding officer."

The Cheboygan community unconditionally welcomed Triner and the new ship with a once-in-a-lifetime celebration. Within 48 hours, Papp would relieve Triner of his command.

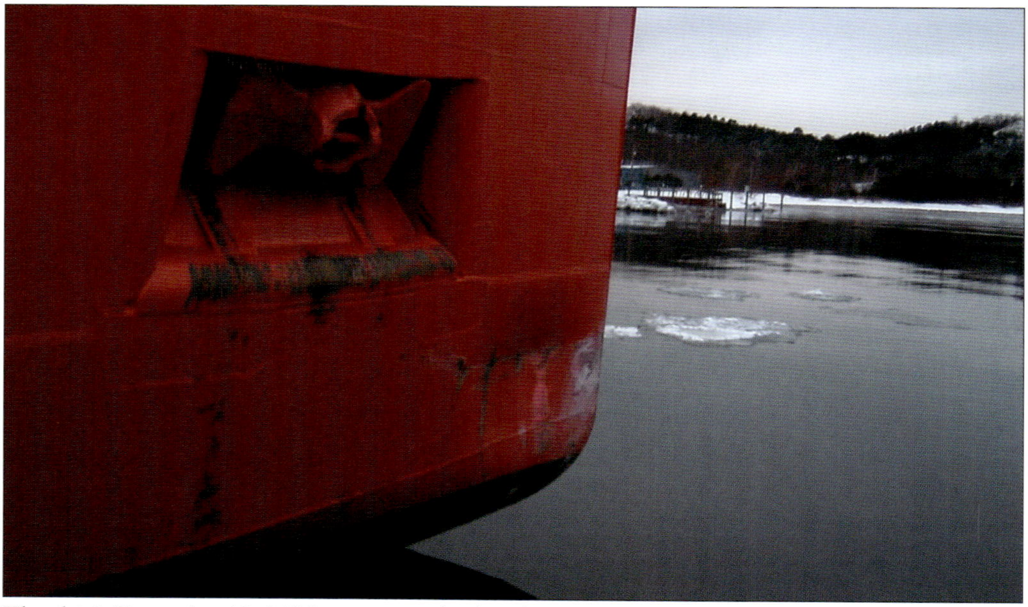

The ship's December 12, 2005, impact with a breakwall at Grand Haven resulted in Capt. Donald Triner's temporary relief, a standard Coast Guard procedure. His dismissal followed a complaint about the behavior of Triner and his crew at a downtown establishment following a formal banquet. Restaurant employees and patrons defended the captain and crew and rebuked the complaints, but the admiral's decision stood, and Triner was reassigned. Military punishment can be subjective. In later years, Triner's loss of command and the damage to the ship were questioned further by the public and some Coast Guard personnel. The photograph below shows damage that appears to be far worse to *Mackinaw's* stern, suffered during a 2012 allision with the Lime Island Pier in the St. Marys River during the watch of Cmdr. Michael Davanzo. The damage was repaired without further concern. (Above, courtesy of U.S. Coast Guard; below, author's collection.)

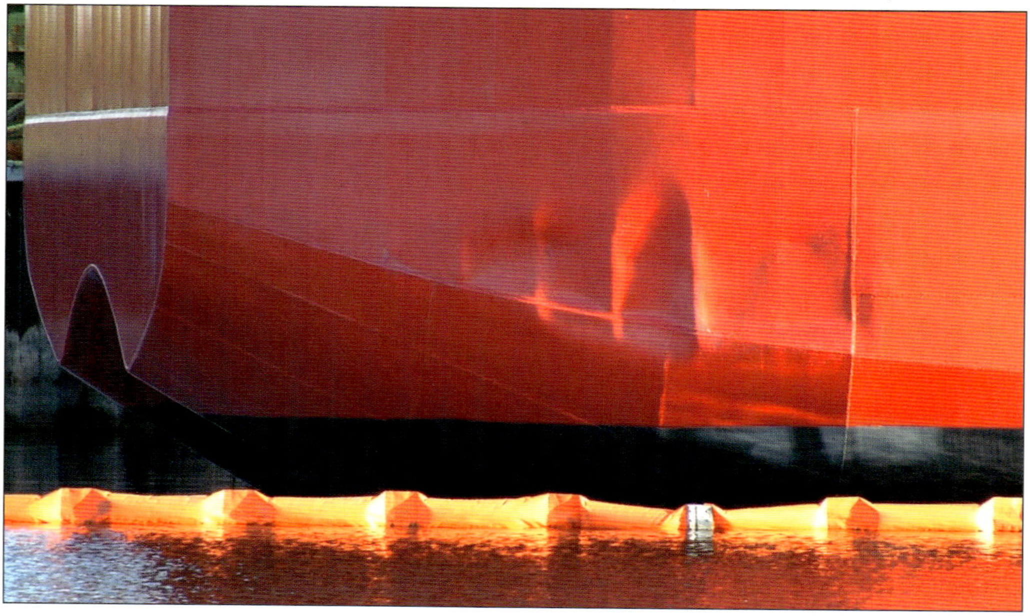

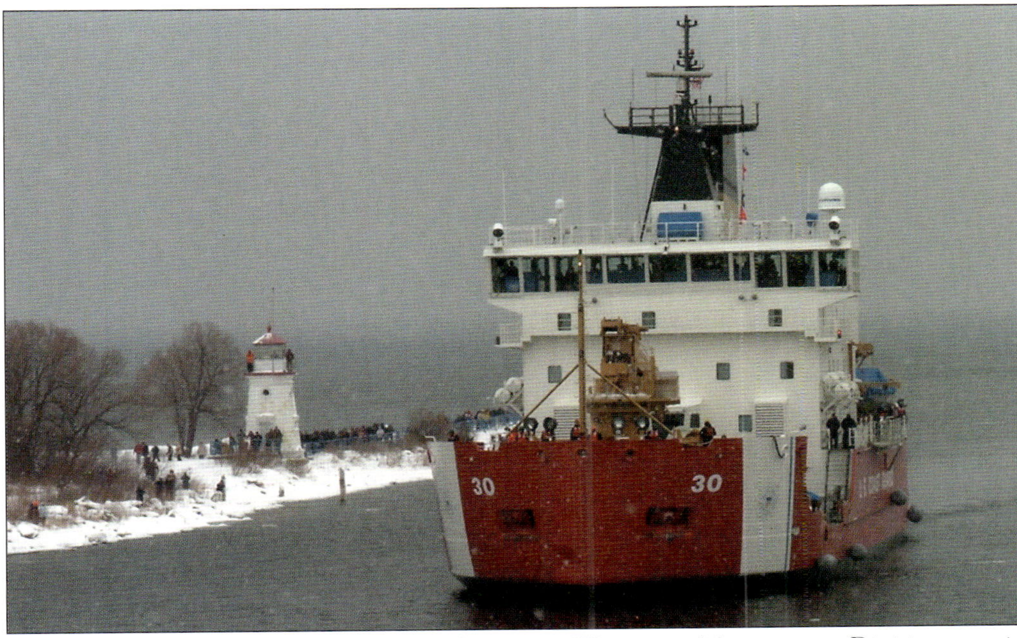

Capt. Michael Hudson, chief of the Ninth District Waterways Management Division, was in command when the *Mackinaw* arrived in Cheboygan on December 17, 2005, but Captain Triner was aboard and handled all ceremonial tasks. The vessel appeared through snow showers at 10:40 a.m., with leaden-gray skies closely replicating the scene that took place on December 30, 1944, when the first *Mackinaw* arrived in Cheboygan. (Author's collection.)

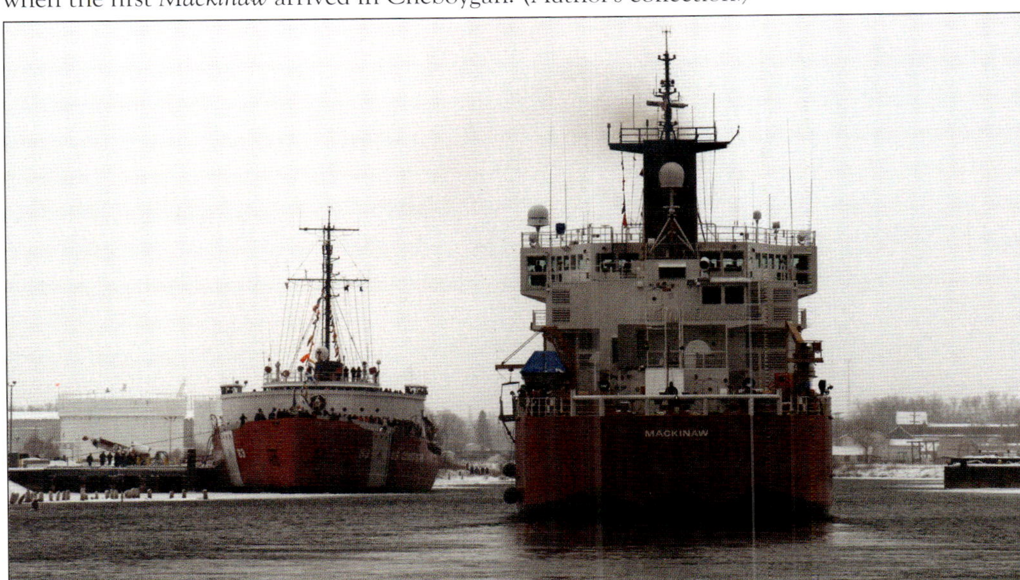

As the Cheboygan Area High School Band repeatedly played "Semper Paratus" from the deck of the original ship, the new *Mackinaw* worked its way up the channel and approached the original *Mackinaw* (left), docked in the spot the new ship would soon occupy. The new crewmembers were viewed as rivals by some on the original ship, while some newcomers regarded the old *Mac* as ancient history. (Courtesy of Jerry Pond.)

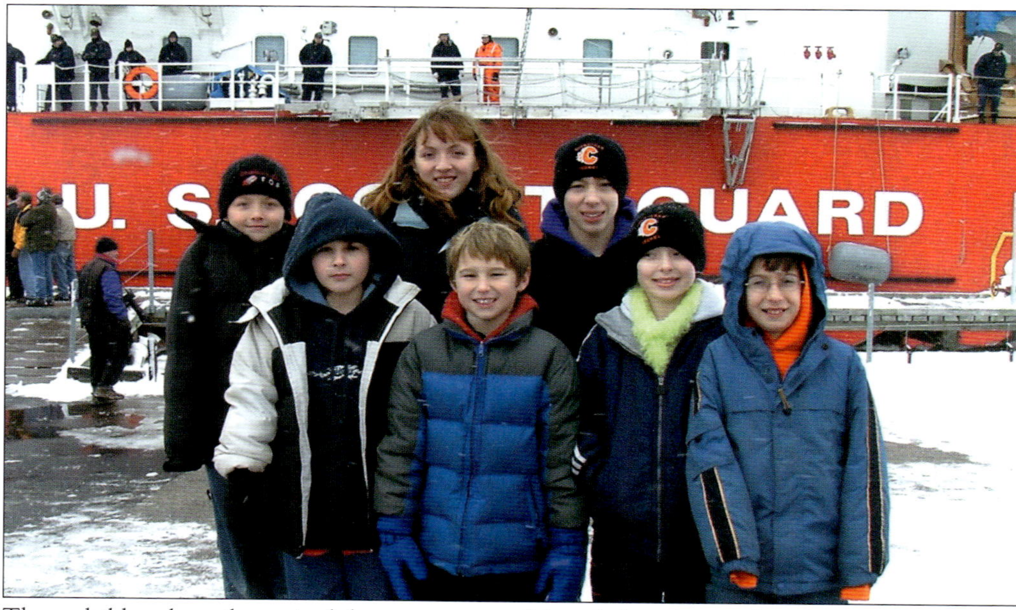

These children happily awaited the appearance of their fathers from onboard the new *Mackinaw*. From left to right are (first row) Ed Gillikin, Chandler Gillikin, Paige Boucher, and Loring Small Jr.; (second row) John Garst, Brittany Garst, and Fletcher Boucher. Most agreed that they liked their new schools; several who played hockey were overjoyed to continue the sport in their new home. (Author's collection.)

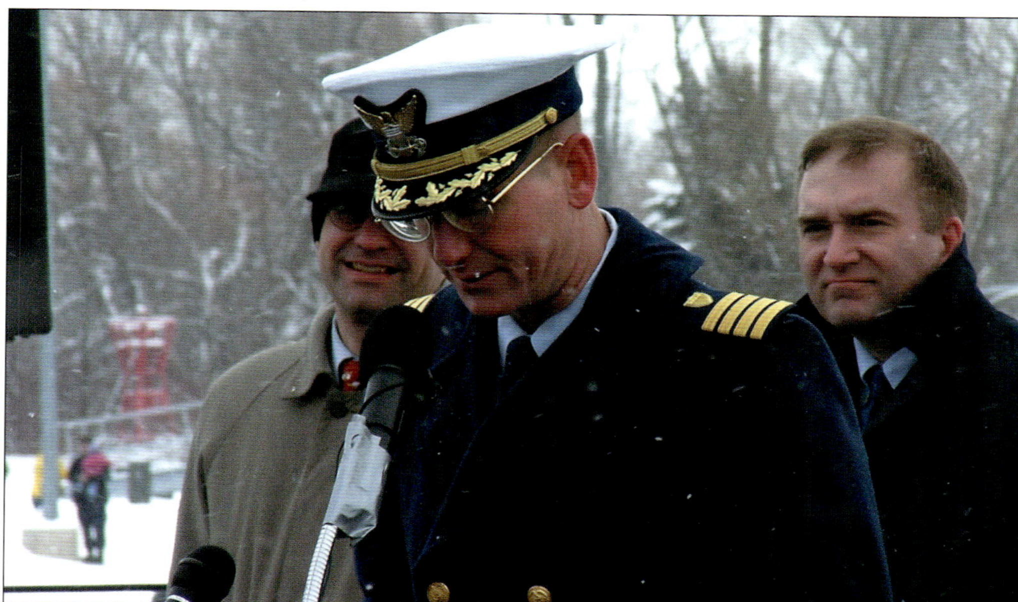

Captain Triner drew a historic link in his speech by reprising some words spoken by Cmdr. Edwin Roland nearly 61 years before, when the original *Mackinaw* arrived. "We of the new ice crusher *Mackinaw* count ourselves particularly fortunate that the ship on which we serve will have for its home port the city of Cheboygan," Triner said. "Thank you, and *semper paratus*." (Author's collection.)

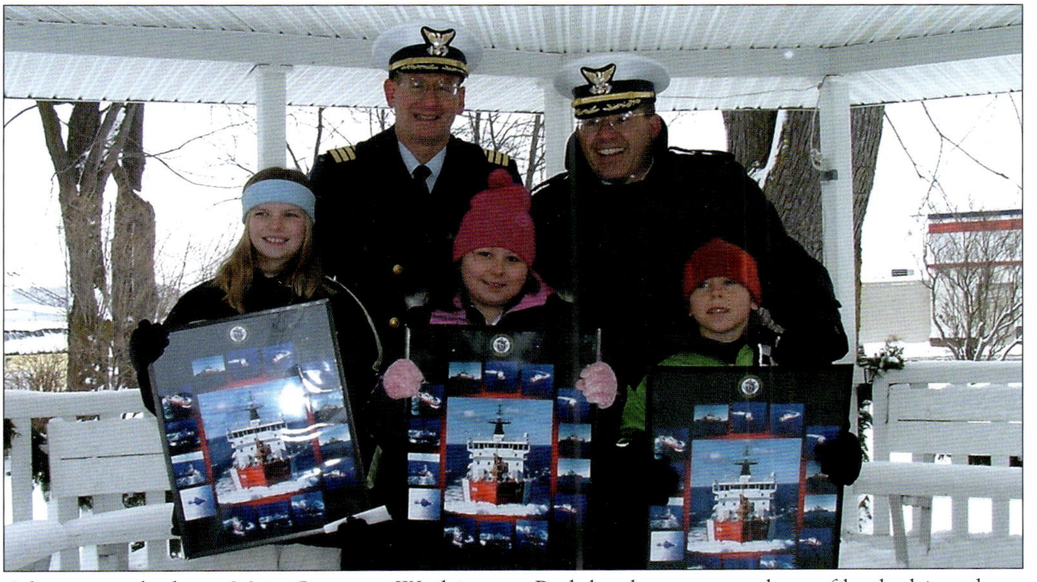

After a parade down Main Street to Washington Park by the crewmembers of both ships, three fourth-grade essay winners read their works, titled, "What the U.S. Coast Guard cutter *Mackinaw* Means to Cheboygan." Officers serving under Commander McGuiness (second row, right) judged the essays. The essay winners were, from left to right in the first row, Jena Brandt, Aubrey Ayotte, and Jacob Brown. Each student received a special memento of the occasion—a framed poster from Captain Triner (second row, left) depicting the new vessel at sea. (Author's collection.)

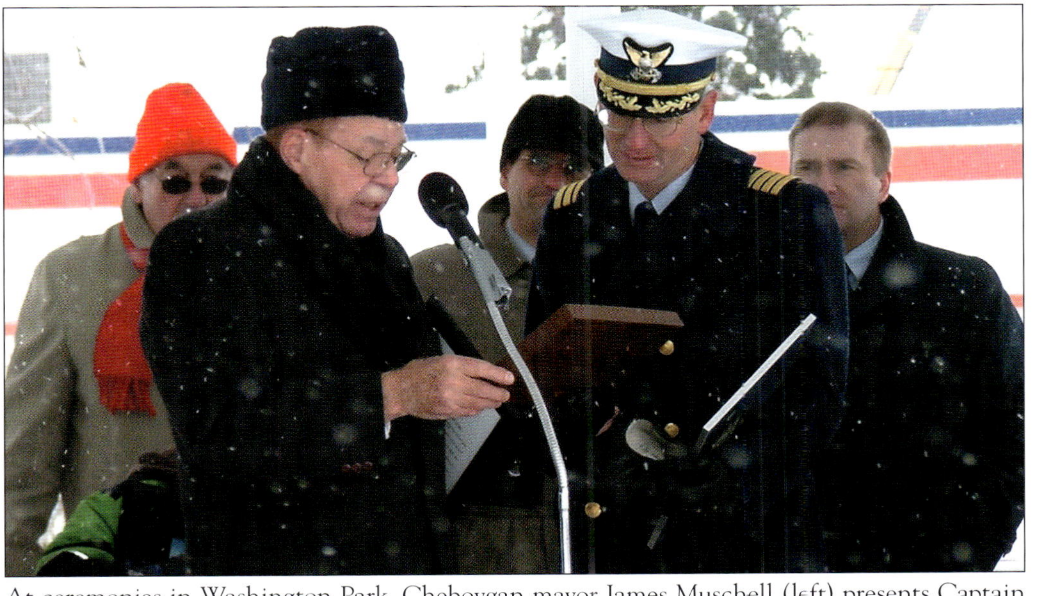

At ceremonies in Washington Park, Cheboygan mayor James Muschell (left) presents Captain Triner (right) with the symbolic key to the city. Triner was also congratulated by, from left to right in the back, Cheboygan County Board of Commissioners chairman Herb Makima, state senator Jason Allen, and state representative Kevin Elsenheimer. "Our town has had a long, outstanding relationship with the Coast Guard, and it's been an important economic factor in our community as well," Muschell said. (Author's collection.)

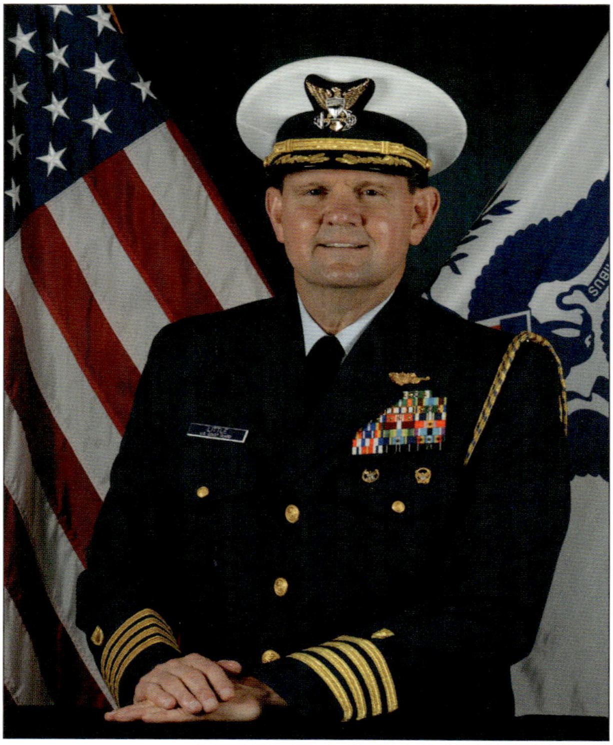

The Coast Guard could not have picked a better captain to lead the *Mackinaw's* crew in April 2006 than Cmdr. John Little. The soft-spoken, athletic man with a gentle Southern drawl was exactly the personality needed to pull the crew together from a very difficult six-month period. Little restored the *Mackinaw* and its crew to star status. (Courtesy of U.S. Coast Guard.)

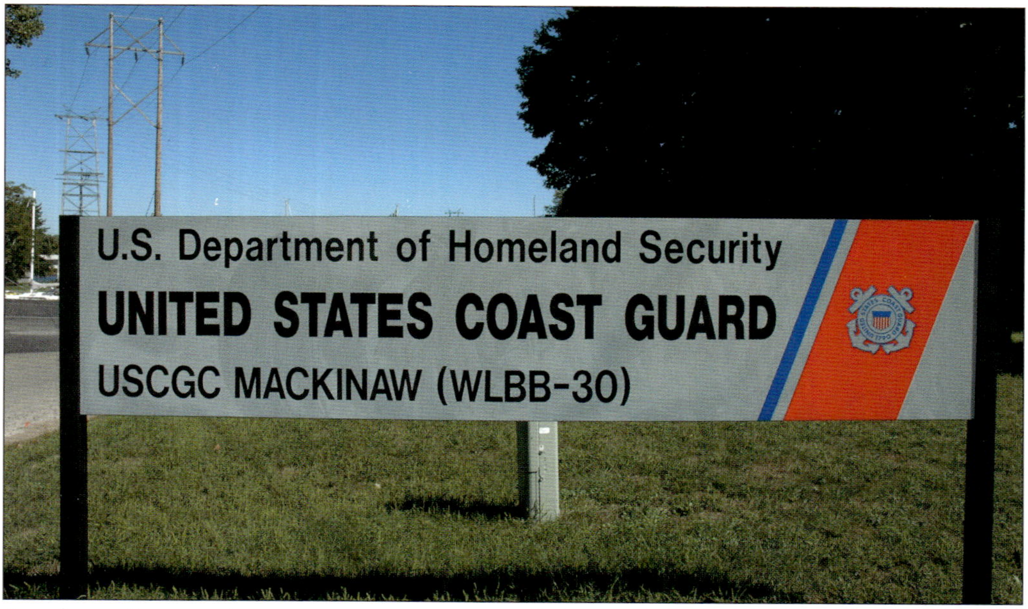

Another indication of change was a new sign installed at the Coast Guard base, proclaiming it the home of the new *Mackinaw* (WLBB-30). The Department of Homeland Security later installed fencing and video cameras around the perimeter, closing off an area where ship-watchers used to observe the *Mac* arrive and depart. Commander Little opened the vessel to tours and entertained youth with a popular "haunted ship" display at Halloween. (Courtesy of U.S. Coast Guard.)

Four

Decommissioning the Old and Commissioning the New

Never had any two Coast Guard icebreakers enjoyed a better day together in the sunshine. "In all the world, there's no place like this," quipped outgoing *Mackinaw* skipper Cmdr. Joseph C. McGuiness of the city that had hosted his vessel for 62 years. "This is a great day as we set the watch and the first log entries of this new ship," echoed Cmdr. John Little of the $110.5 million icebreaker he would take into the next chapter of Great Lakes maritime lore.

The June 10, 2006, decommissioning of the original Coast Guard cutter *Mackinaw*, followed by the commissioning ceremony for the new icebreaker that carries the same name, was everything it was expected to be. Commander McGuiness stole the show with his heartfelt comments about the ship he has skippered for the last three years. The day really belonged to his ship, though it was a celebration for both old and new. "The *Mackinaw* was the heavyweight champion of icebreaking—and still is," he proclaimed. More apparent was the love he felt for his crew, referring several times to the loyalty and dedication they displayed. "The ship is the crew, and what a crew I've been honored to serve with," he said, beaming with pride. "These men and women and the long line that came before them have brought the Mighty Mac to retirement today in as fine a form as ever."

McGuiness was not the only one with misty eyes. It was then time for Commander Little to read his orders and start a new era of *Mackinaw* icebreaking. Little's gentle and polite demeanor won the audience, many of whom toured his ship following the ceremony, as they did the retiring "Queen of the Great Lakes." "This is a great day as we set the new watch and the first log entries of this new ship," Little said. "Folks, this is your vessel and we're quite proud of her. We know this new cutter has a proud tradition to uphold and we're going to give it our all—count on it."

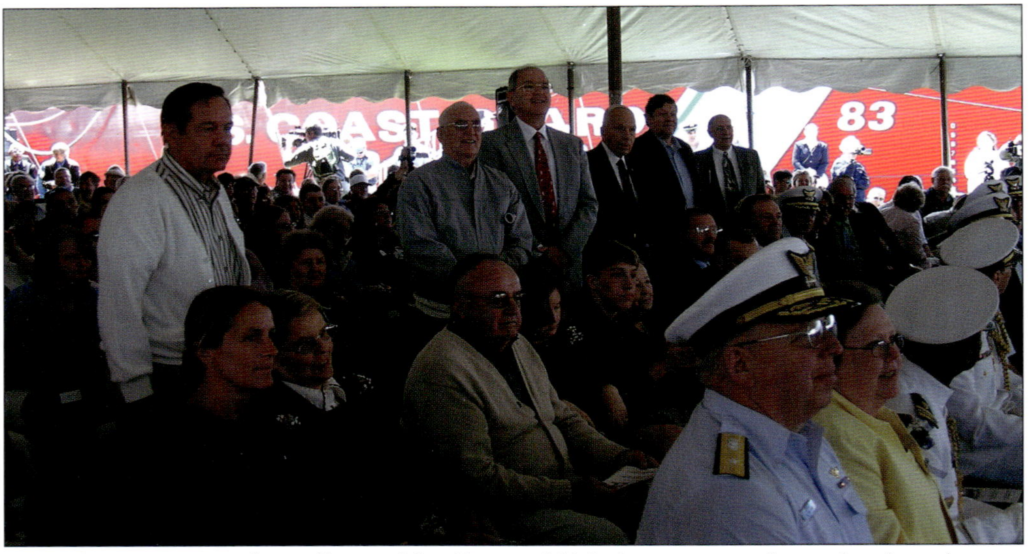

Seven former commanding officers of the 62-year-old *Mackinaw* were welcomed with applause at the ceremony to decommission the original ship before commissioning the new cutter to carry on the legacy. Approximately 100 former crewmembers attended, including one plankowner, Frank Hillus (not pictured). (Author's collection.)

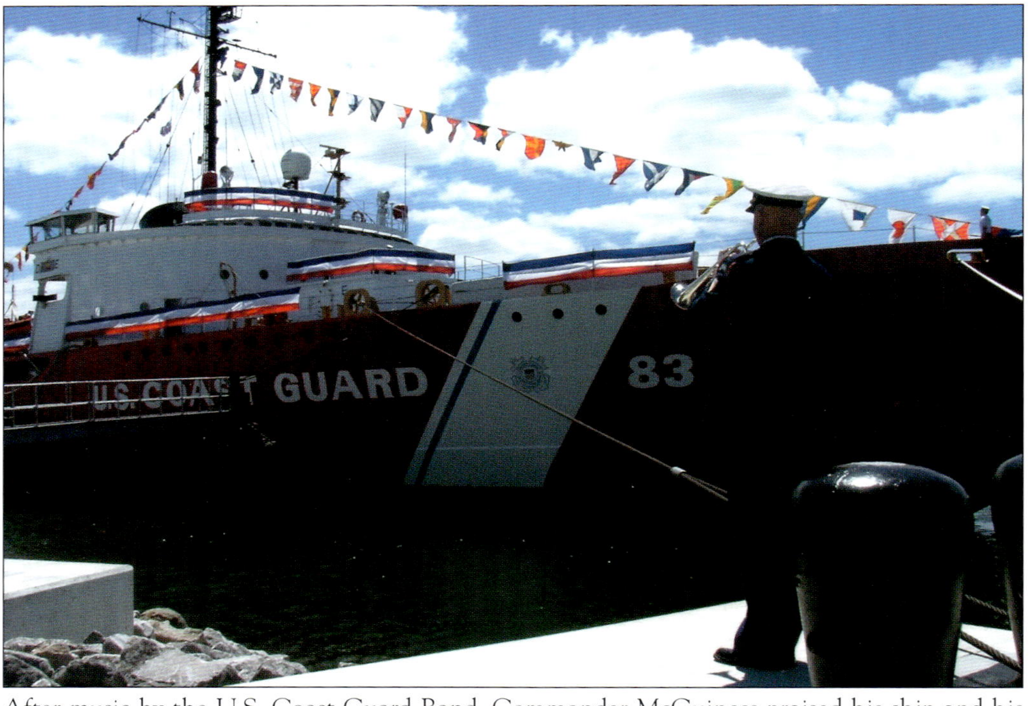

After music by the U.S. Coast Guard Band, Commander McGuiness praised his ship and his crew, noting, "All the while they continually worked to keep the ship in the condition you see today—museum ready." Then, eight bells were tolled, a perfect verse of "Taps" was played by bugler Senior Chief Carroll Potts, the pennant was lowered, and 62 years of Great Lakes service drew to a close. (Author's collection.)

Next came the passing of the long glass from old *Mackinaw's* Lt. David Schuler to Cmdr. John Little of the new *Mackinaw*. Then it was the presentation of the final commissioning pennant by Senior Chief Petty Officer David Sparkenbaugh, crewmember with the longest term of service, to McGuiness. In addition, the national ensign and Union Jack were presented from the honor guard to new *Mackinaw's* Lt. Douglas Wyatt. (Author's collection.)

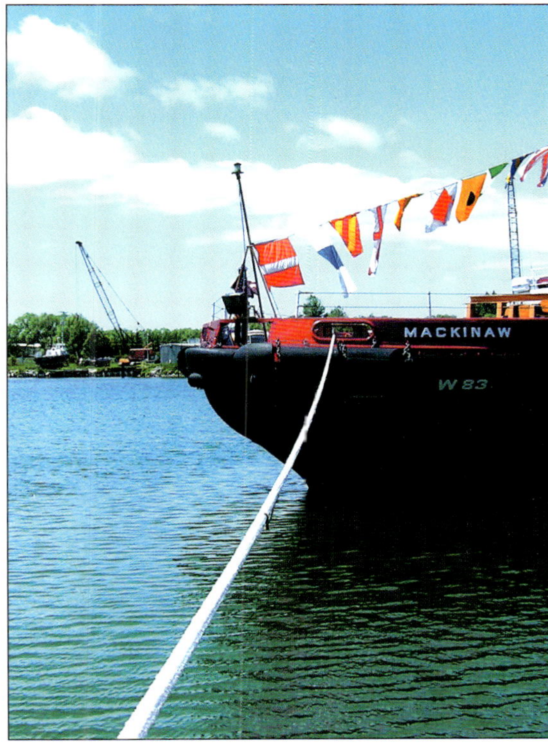

As the colors were raised on the newly commissioned ship, a 19-gun salute was fired from a small cannon aboard the new *Mackinaw*. The ship was now officially in service, and WLBB-30 became a reality. On a day of perfect weather, the historic transfer had taken place seamlessly and without a hitch. (Author's collection.)

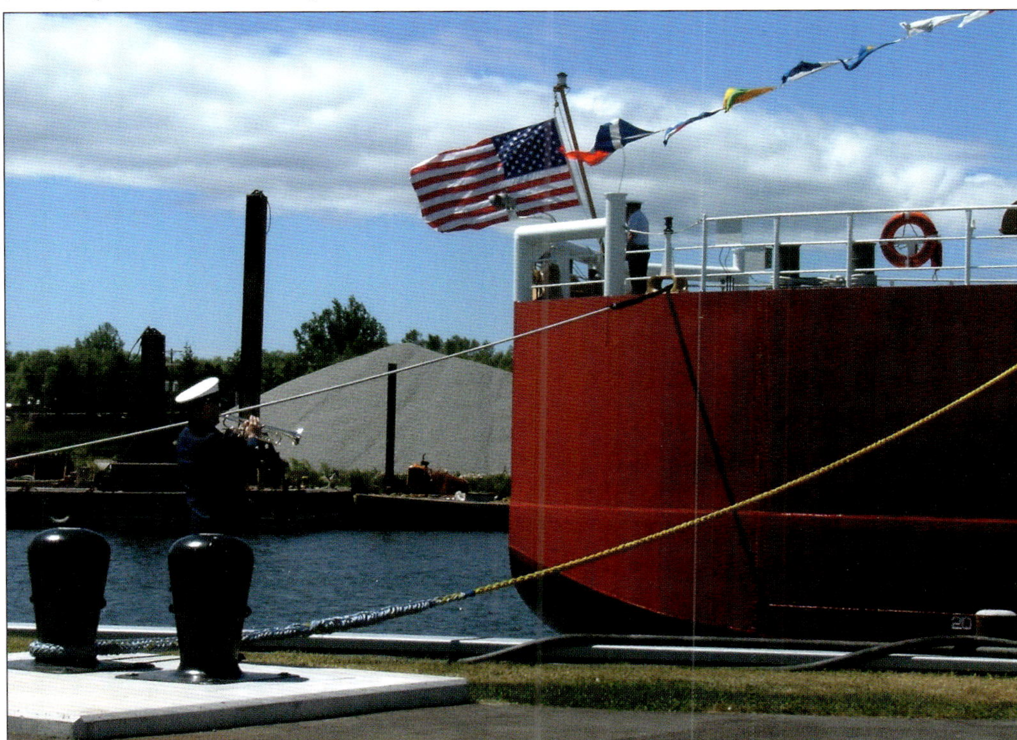

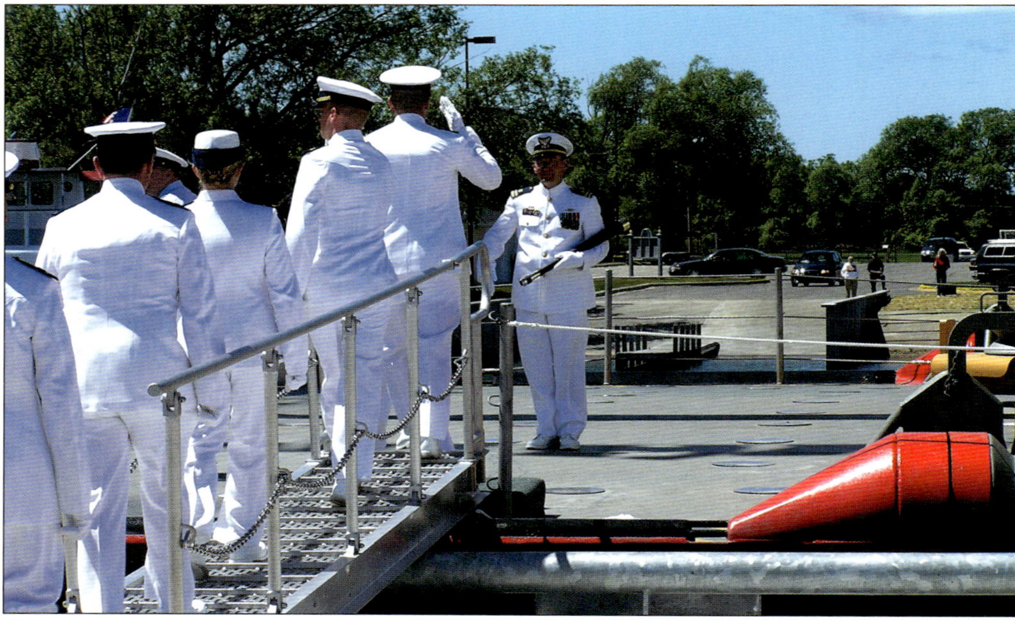

Wearing dress whites, the men and women of the new *Mackinaw* charged across the brow (gangway), officially setting the first watch. Both ships were opened to the public for tours, and many marveled at an enormous decorative cake baked by the original *Mackinaw's* food-service crew—a task that took nearly two weeks to complete. The cake was almost the size of the cafeteria table that held it for display. (Author's collection.)

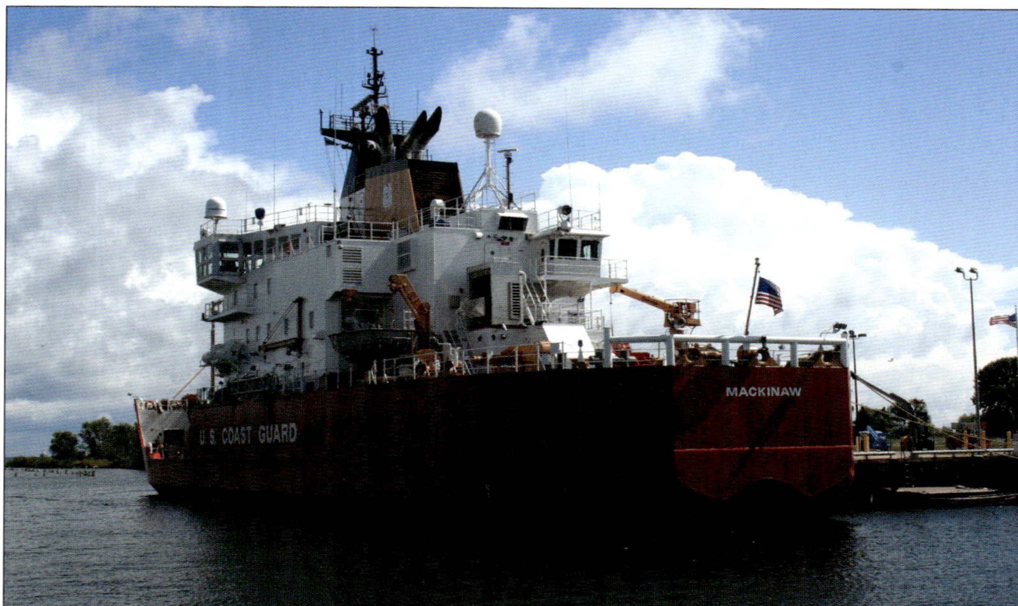

The new *Mac* now had the premiere parking spot in the Great Lakes—and all the responsibility that came along with it. Crewmembers settled into daily routines, established bank accounts, and regularly visited Cheboygan businesses, physicians, and churches. "Coastie kids" were settled in area schools, and family life became the backbone of Commander Little's command. (Author's collection.)

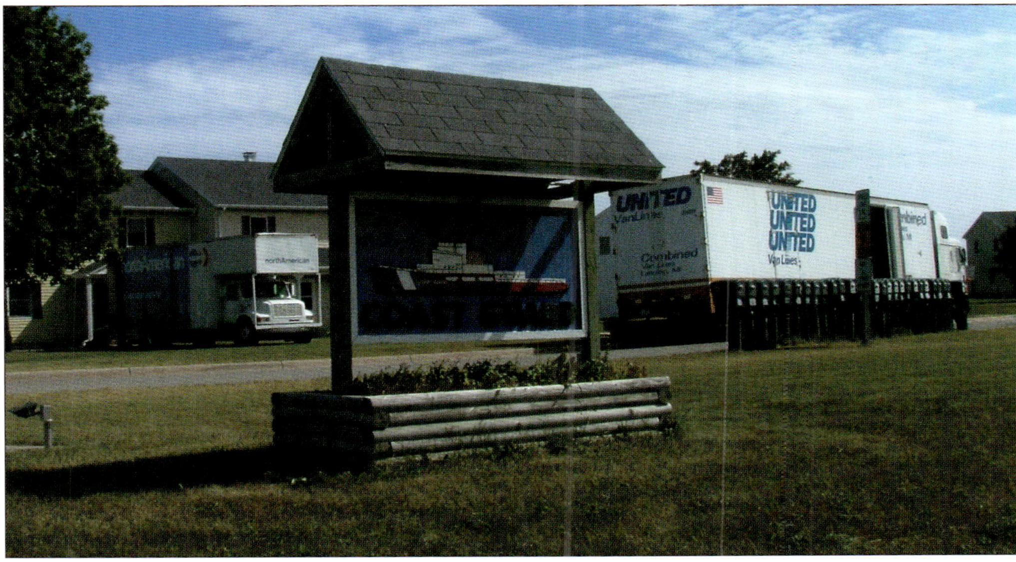

For the original *Mackinaw's* crew, moving day had come. The Coast Guard Housing Complex was a busy place, and landlords around town scurried to sign leases with new sailors as the departing ones left for new assignments. Any rivalries had been forgotten, largely due to the cooperation between commanders McGuiness and Little, coupled with the inspiring success of the decommissioning/commissioning ceremony. (Author's collection.)

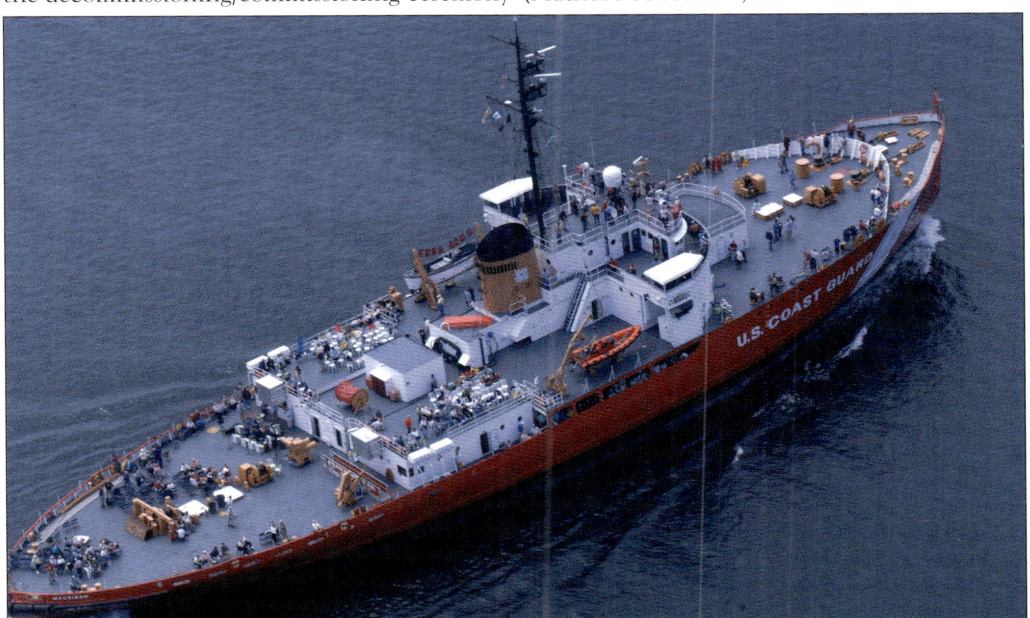

The disposition of the original *Mackinaw* (WAGB-83) was unknown until decommissioning day. A valiant effort to develop a museum site in Cheboygan failed when suitable riverfront property could not be found. With no alternative, the General Services Administration directed that the ship be prepared to sail to a Baltimore scrap yard. The charts were ordered. But Mackinaw City businessman Bill Shepler offered dock space adjacent to his ferryboat operation. (Courtesy of U.S. Coast Guard.)

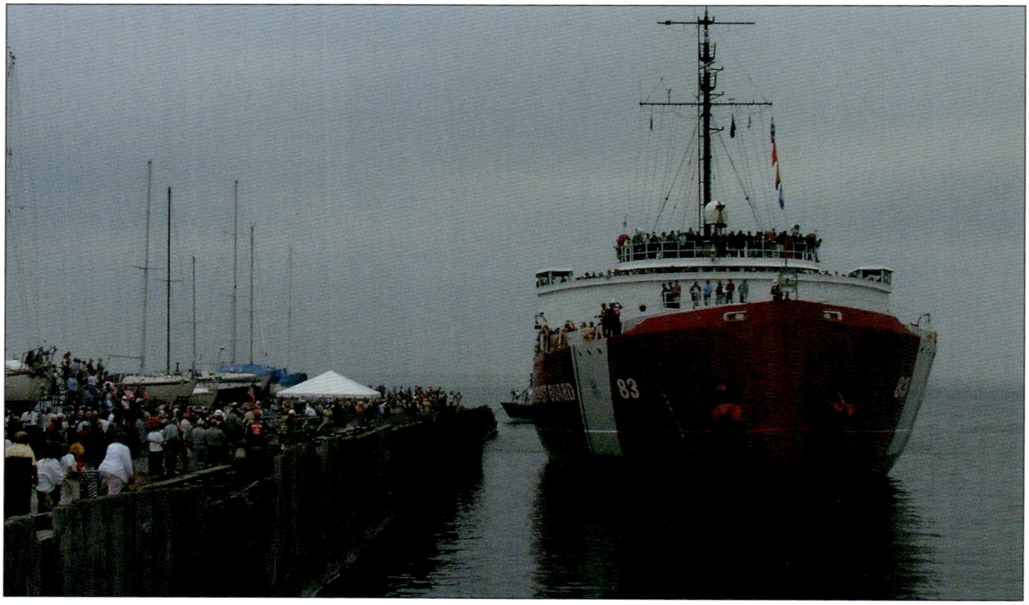

The *Mackinaw's* new custodians, the Icebreaker Mackinaw Maritime Museum, welcomed the ship on June 21, 2006, to a dock that once served the railroad ferry *Chief Wawatam*. Bill Shepler endeavored to preserve the *Mac* as it was the day it retired, with certain accommodations for visitors. Now a tourist attraction, the ship's many displays tell the story of 62 years of Great Lakes service. (Author's collection.)

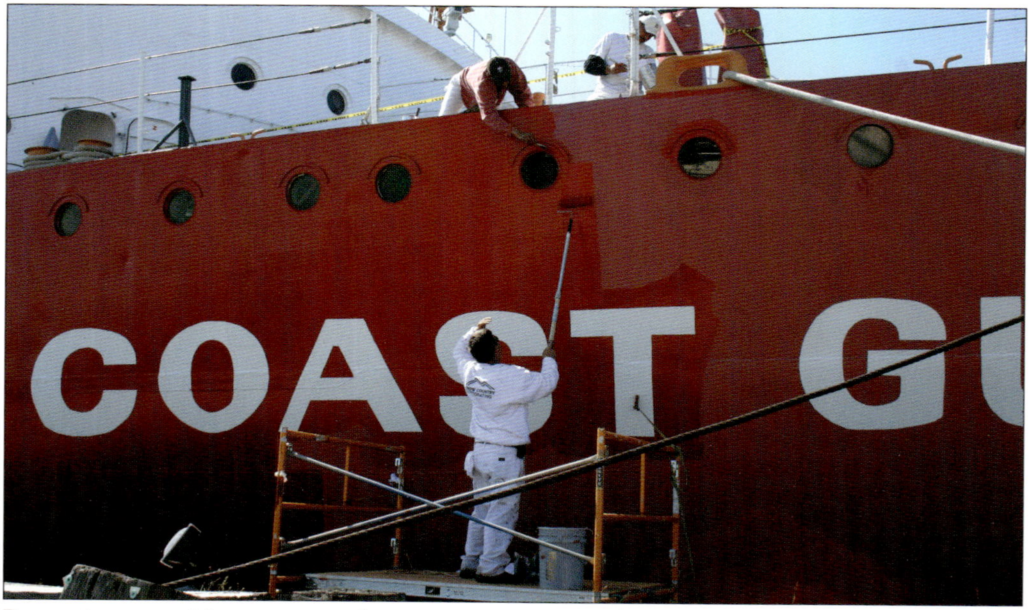

Preserving a maritime museum ship means assuming upkeep on a very large scale. Since the *Mac* had never been winterized, that task proved to be as daunting as routine painting and other maintenance chores. Although many still hope to see the ship returned to the white color it wore for 54 of its 62 years of active life, a new coat of red paint is sometimes needed to freshen up the hull. (Author's collection.)

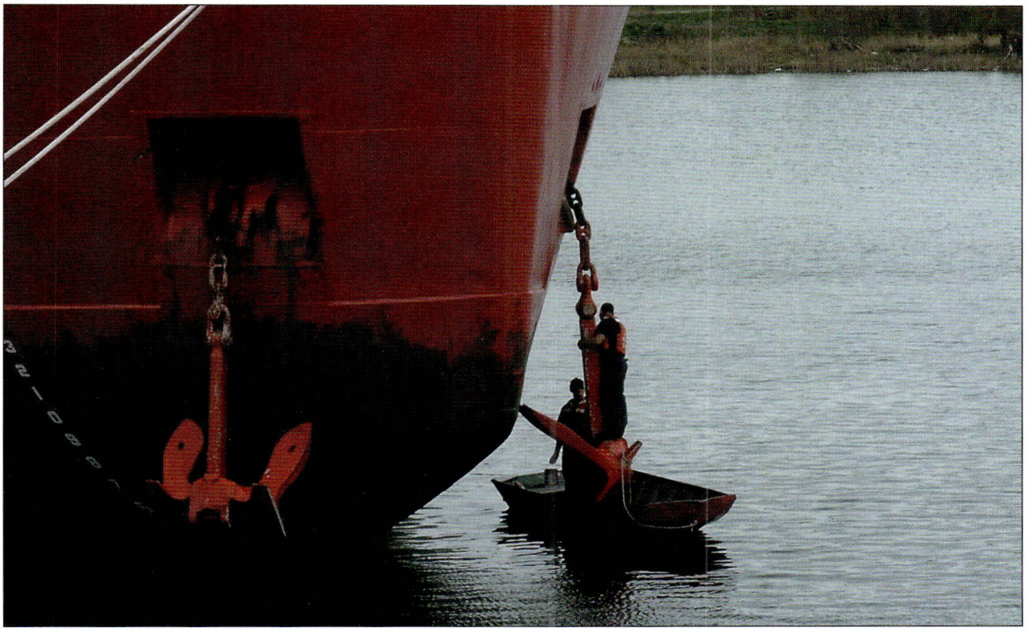

Painting the ship means painting the *whole* ship, even the twin Dunn Bower anchors, which weigh 6,000 pounds each. Fortunately for the museum crew, this task was well performed by the Coast Guard after the ship's final icebreaking season in 2006, prior to it becoming a museum ship. Each anchor is secured by 810 feet of chain, which is still aboard. (Author's collection.)

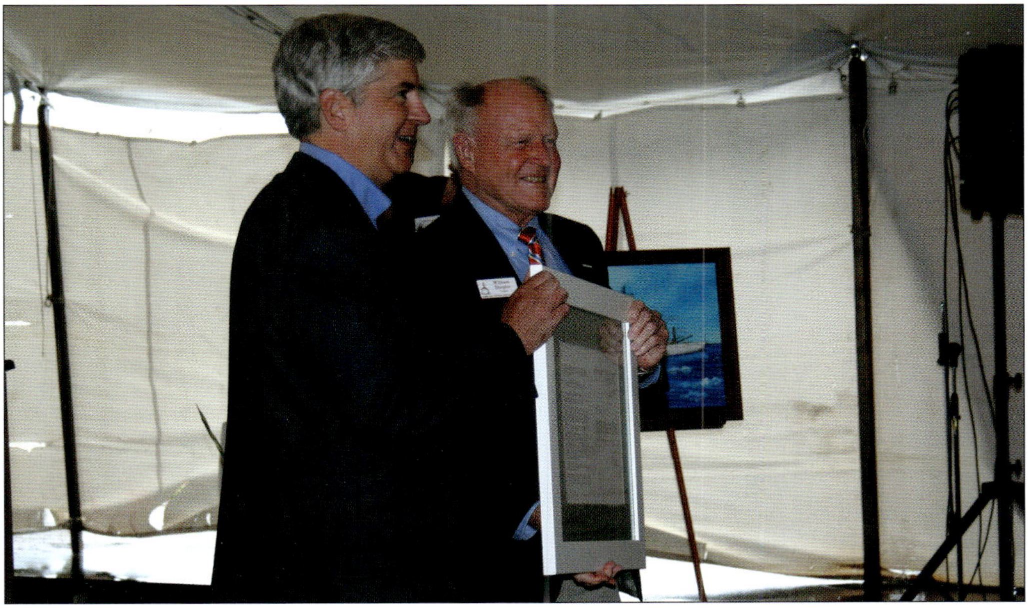

The final transformation of the *Mackinaw* from a working Coast Guard ship to a floating museum took place in 2011, when the Icebreaker Mackinaw Maritime Museum received the ship's title from Michigan governor Rick Snyder (left). Bill Shepler (right) offered a Mackinaw City dock for the ship's display in 2006, and, five years later, citizens of Cheboygan and Mackinaw City and other volunteers had proven their ability to operate the icebreaker as a tourist attraction. (Author's collection.)

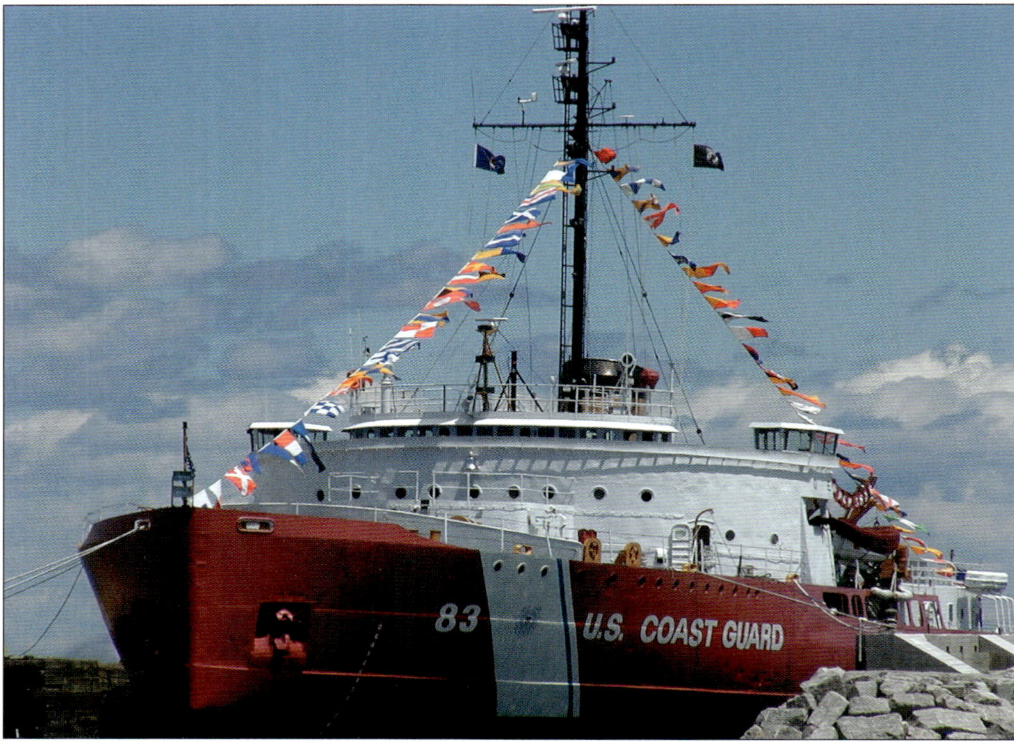

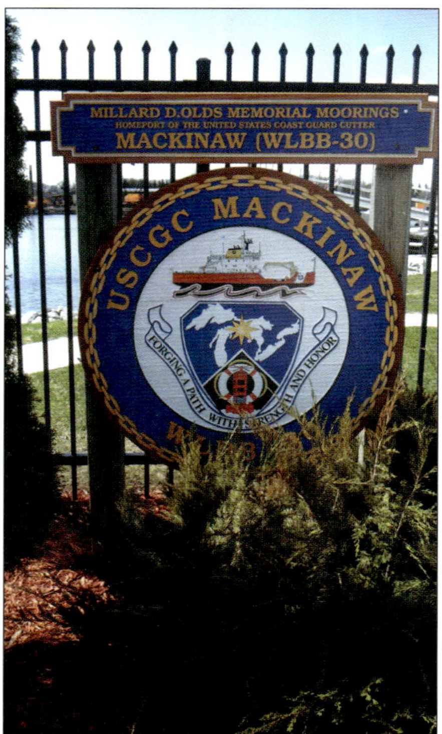

The Icebreaker Mackinaw Maritime Museum now hosts more than 20,000 visitors annually, including hundreds of Michigan schoolchildren, who get the hands-on opportunity to learn about the state's rich maritime history. Daily tours are available of the mess deck, captain's quarters, bridge, engine room, ward room, and more from late May through early October. Donations have funded the $180,000 in renovations required to turn the ship into a museum. (Author's collection.)

In 2014, a new sign at the Millard D. Olds Memorial Moorings proclaimed it as the home of the Coast Guard cutter *Mackinaw* (WLBB-30). The *Mackinaw* is very active in the community today through the people—the officers and crew—who have become such an integral part of the economy and the culture of Cheboygan. The ship's personnel are woven into the fabric of their adopted hometown. (Author's collection.)

Five

Buoy-tending

The aids-to-navigation capabilities of the new *Mackinaw* are equivalent to those installed on the Coast Guard's 225-foot Juniper class buoy tenders. The ship's buoy-handling capabilities add an impressive toolbox for dealing with Great Lakes buoys, which can weigh up to 14,000 pounds. The concrete sinkers can weigh 10,000 pounds, and the hundreds of feet of heavy-duty chain all become part of an enormous weight to carry on the deck of a ship.

Mackinaw's 4,700-square-foot buoy deck is heated to melt the ice and snow load that comes aboard when handling buoys in cold weather. There is a separate hold for chain stowage. A 40,000-pound-capacity crane can handle the heavy loads that are pulled from the lakes each fall and replaced in the spring. The ship can handle a deck load of 85 tons, tightly arranged and packed with only inches to spare. Gear installed includes cross-deck winches, a chain winch, and a powered gripping system to handle the buoys. The ship has the ability to service and maintain fixed and floating aids to navigation, up to a 9-foot-by-38-foot standard Coast Guard buoy. The entire operation is administrated at sea by a centerline-automated control station and is supported by the shore-side Cheboygan Buoy Base, capable of maintaining batteries and electronics, repairing structural damage, and meeting painting needs.

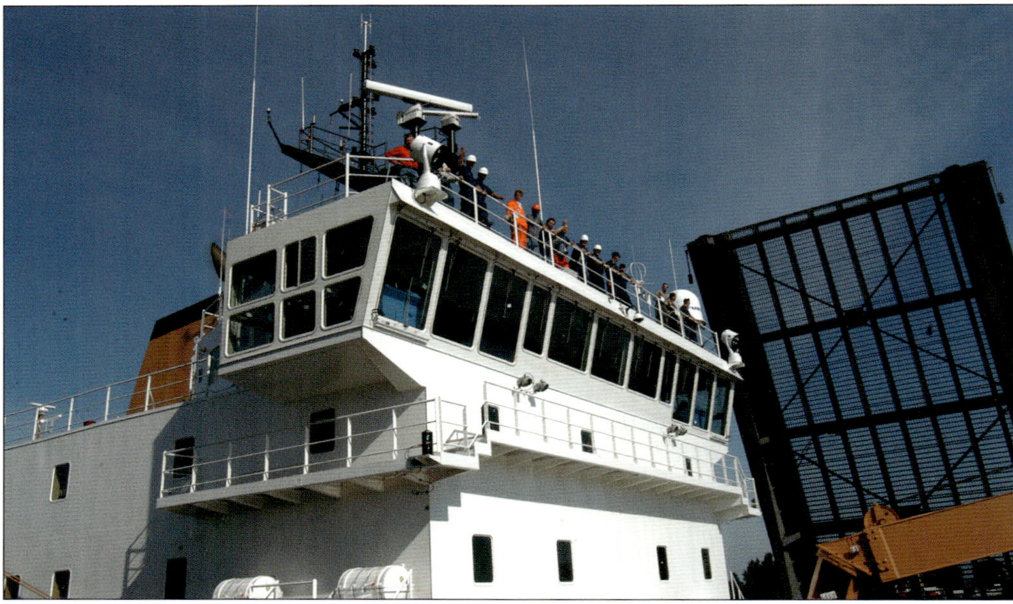

Buoy-tending involves a tremendous amount of communication and coordination among all systems and personnel of the ship. *Mackinaw's* bridge serves as the command center for all operations, whether engaged in icebreaking, buoy-tending, search and rescue, law enforcement, oil recovery, or while underway. The ship must position itself exactly where needed to restore or retrieve buoys. (Courtesy of U.S. Coast Guard.)

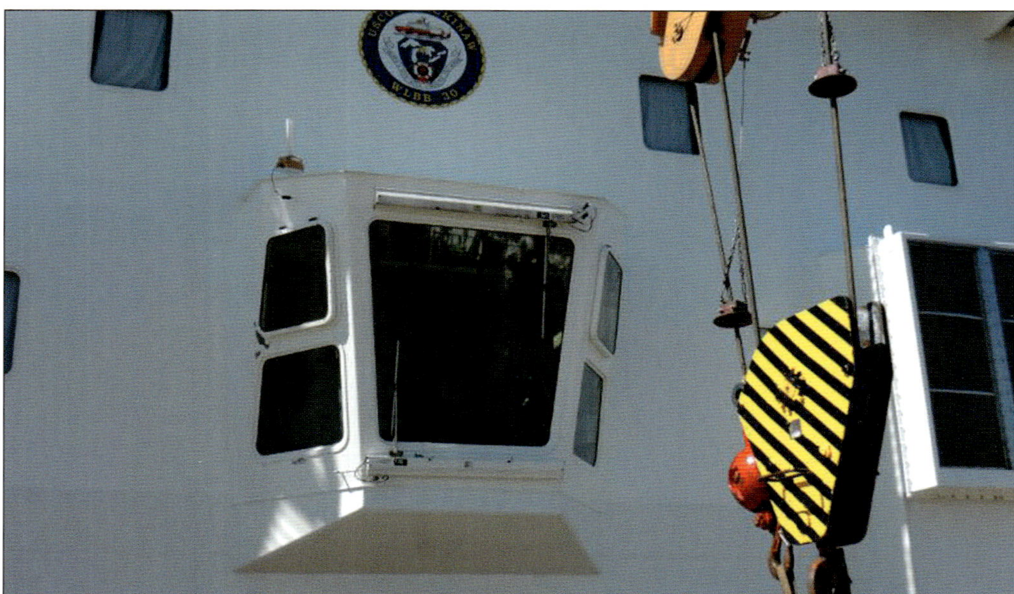

Actual operation of the buoy deck is under the command of the crane operator's control station, located with a full view of everything that happens on deck and with the buoy crane. All deck personnel can be seen from here and communications sent and received, both electronically and visually. The operator can also communicate electronically with the bridge. (Courtesy of U.S. Coast Guard.)

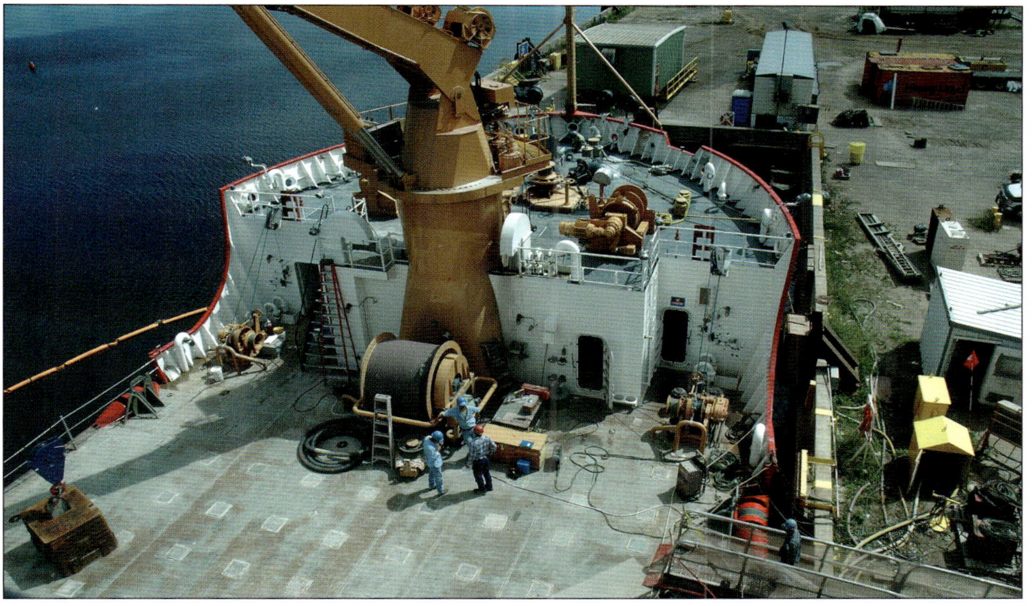

This view of the buoy deck from the ship's mast shows the 20-ton Appleton crane, the inhaul winch just below it, and the heated working surface for buoys. Deck personnel call the inhaul winch the "winch-a-saurus." This equipment saves time and strain on the main boom, once the buoy has been secured to the buoy deck, by hauling up the buoy's chain and sinker. (Courtesy of U.S. Coast Guard.)

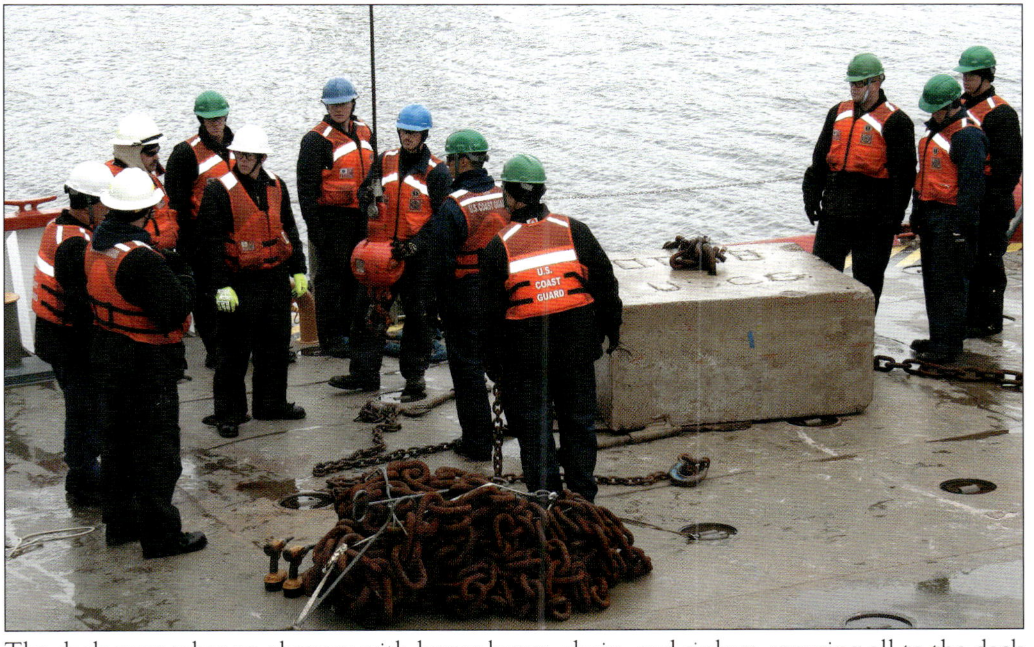

The deck crew takes no chances with heavy buoys, chain, and sinkers, securing all to the deck as soon as they are aboard. A moving ship can cause heavy gear to slide, although not as likely on *Mackinaw's* nonskid deck surface. Note the varying colors of the helmets, which indicate the jobs of personnel. (Courtesy of U.S. Coast Guard.)

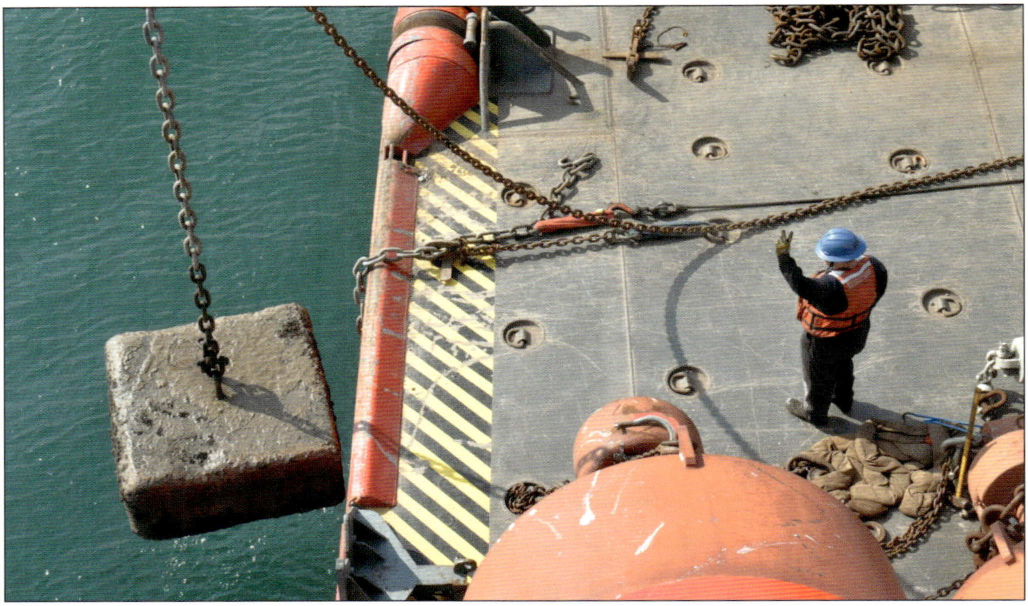

Electronic communication is essential to all personnel on the ship. However, when howling winds and noisy crane machinery affect deck operations, hand signals are very effective, standardized, and easily understood by all viewing the signalman. The danger of moving extremely heavy objects on and off the deck of a moving ship leaves no room for error. *Mackinaw's* crew trains extensively for all aspects of buoy operations and communication scenarios. Working the buoy deck requires the full concentration, coordination, and effort of all involved. Every job on the buoy deck is important and contributes to the safety and success of the mission. (Both, courtesy of U.S. Coast Guard.)

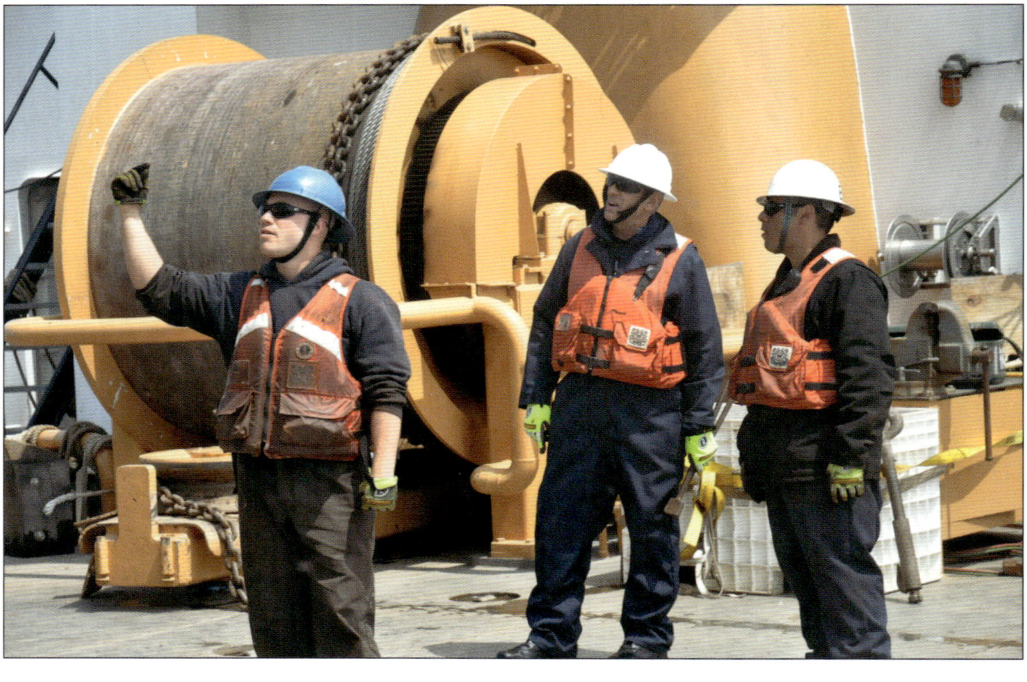

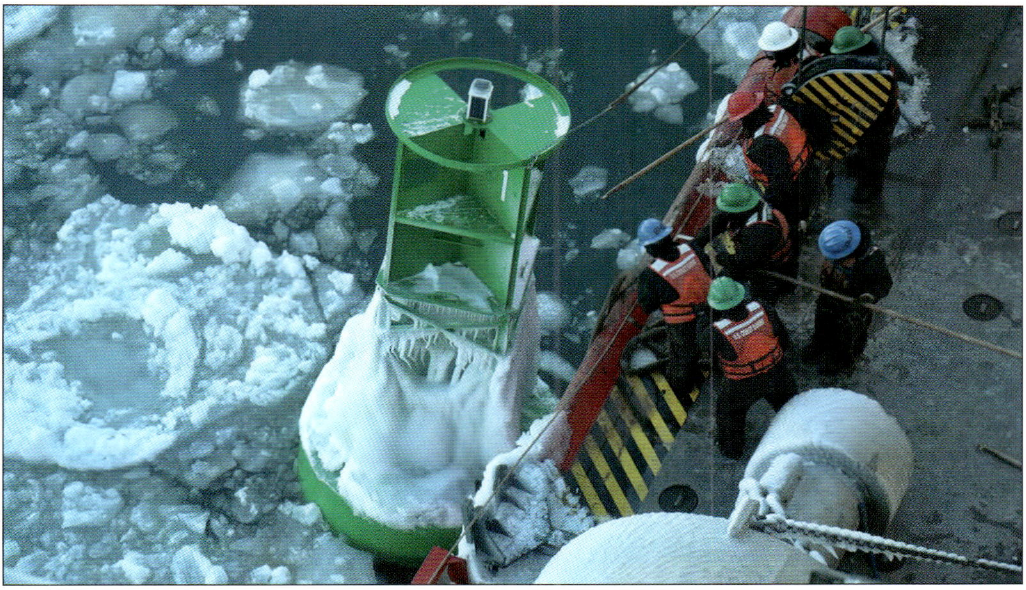

Mackinaw's buoy deck crew is pictured hooking the ice-covered Mackinac Bridge Lighted Bell Buoy No. 1 in the Straits of Mackinac in December 2013 while preparing to decommission the buoy for the winter season. An early start to the 2014 ice season meant the crew had to race to complete Operation Fall Retrieve before the ice floes set firm and damaged the navigational buoys. (Courtesy of U.S. Coast Guard.)

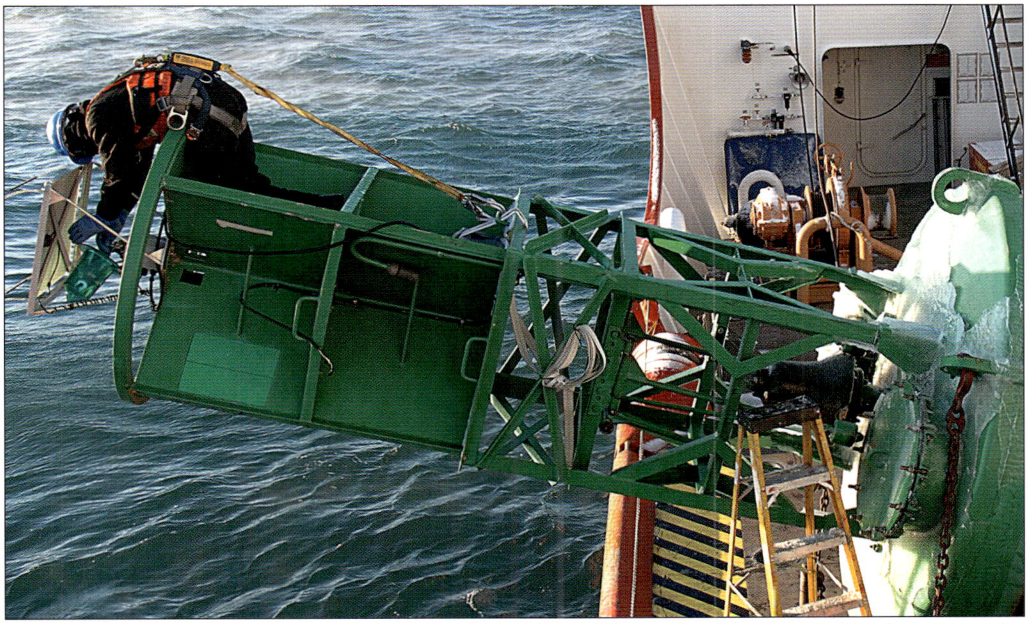

Once the buoy has been brought aboard, ice is cleared from the frame and the electronics by Seaman Bruce Cobb. Personnel working on buoys are harnessed for safety and must contend with icy, slippery surfaces. Proper clothing, shoes, and safety gear are essential to avoid injury. Deck crewmembers must allow for varying sea conditions and winds, which can cause an imbalance while working aloft. (Courtesy of U.S. Coast Guard.)

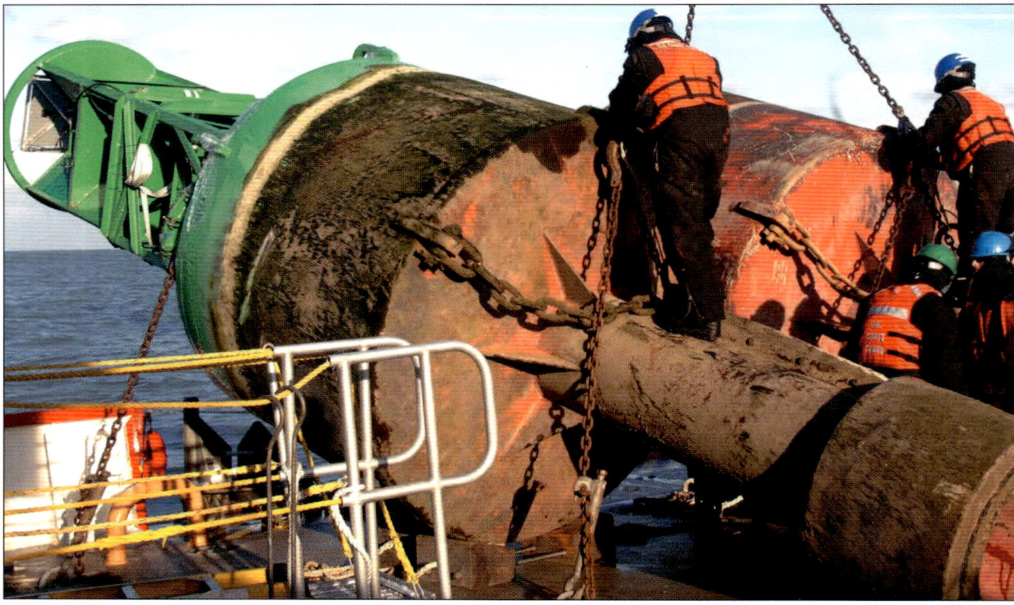

Buoys are secured to the deck to allow the greatest amount of room for more cargo. Marks of varying sizes can be in use, depending on the season. It is a challenge to make room for more to be brought aboard when other buoys still remain to be placed in a location later in the mission. Note the sediment and growth that has built up from a summer in the lake. (Courtesy of U.S. Coast Guard.)

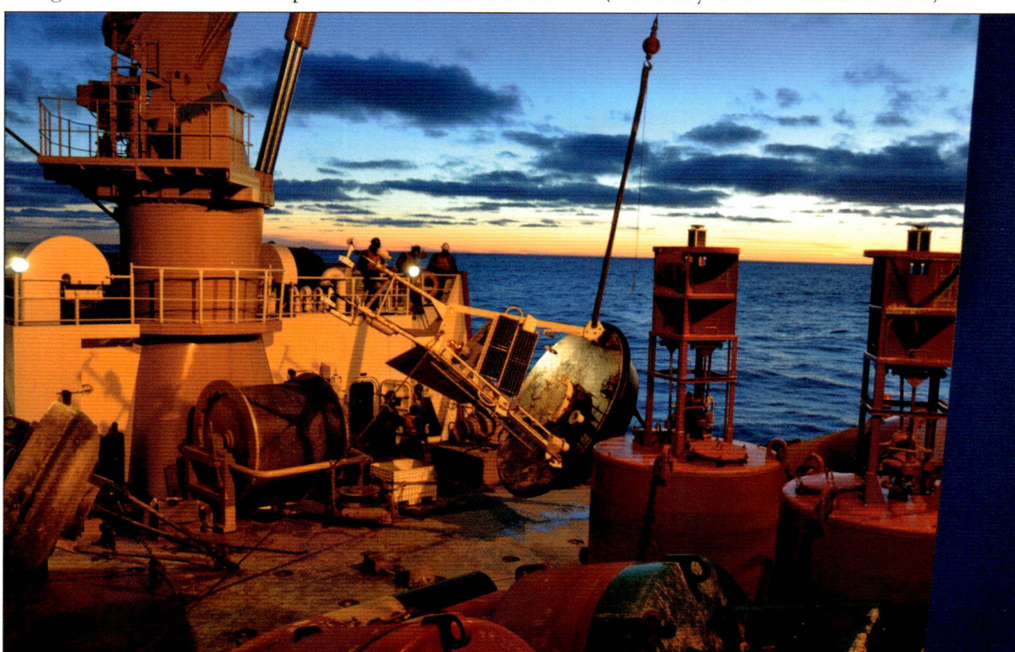

As night falls, *Mackinaw's* deck begins to fill from a long day's work. The ship's crew, working in shifts, will continue to collect buoys into the night if a particular region contains enough marks to retrieve with minimal required travel. Working space must also be allowed among the rows of buoys decommissioned for the winter. (Courtesy of U.S. Coast Guard.)

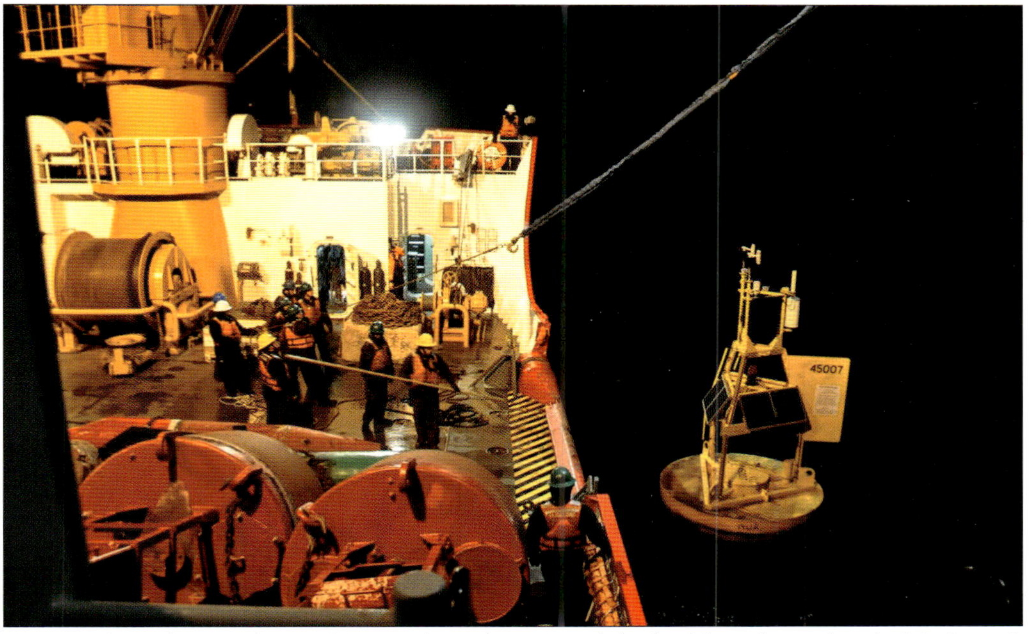

In optimal weather conditions, buoy work can be accomplished safely and expediently. *Mackinaw's* buoy deck is well lighted and equipped for work, no matter the hour. The yellow buoy being retrieved is a weather buoy, used to collect weather, wave, and current information for NOAA. (Courtesy of U.S. Coast Guard.)

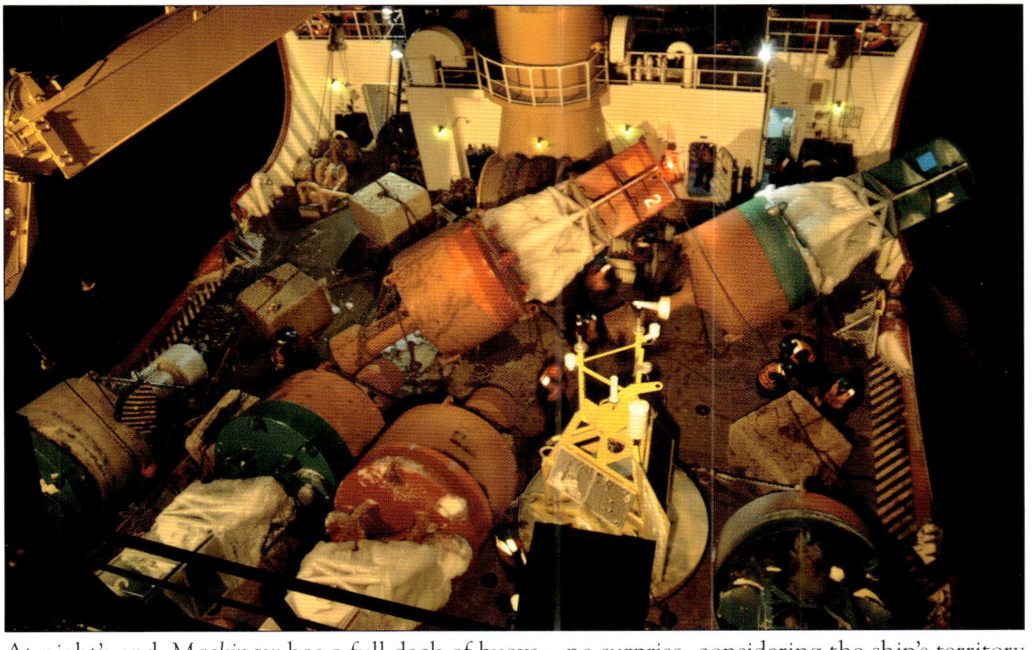

At night's end, *Mackinaw* has a full deck of buoys—no surprise, considering the ship's territory includes Lake Huron, Lake Michigan, the Straits of Mackinac, and the St. Marys River. Crewmembers say the work is similar to assembling a puzzle, but the object is to avoid handling each piece more than once. (Courtesy of U.S. Coast Guard.)

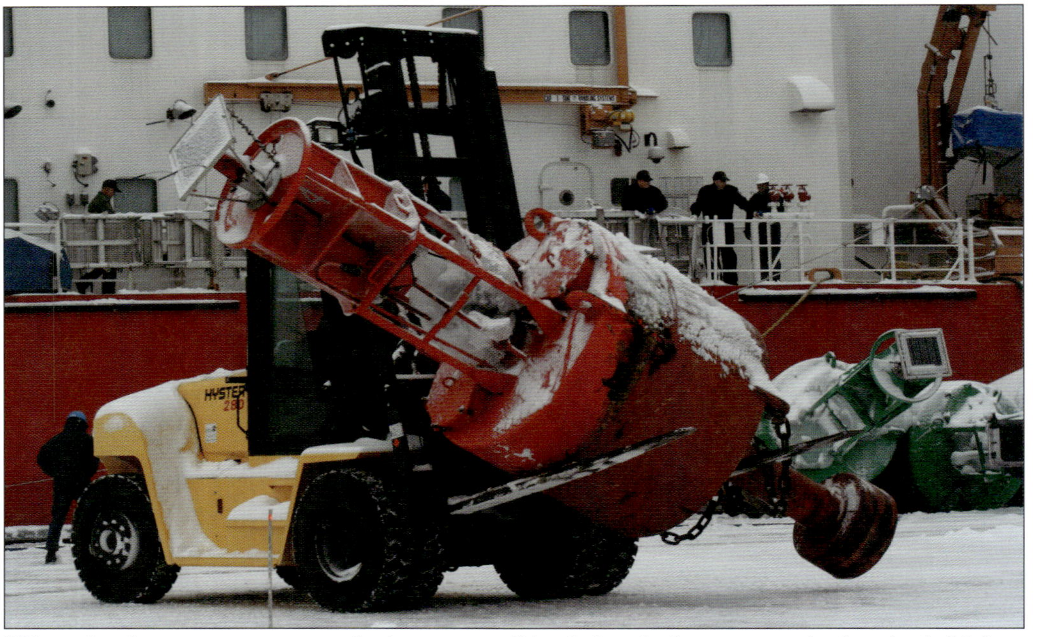

When the ship returns to port, the buoys are off-loaded with the crane and taken by forklift to the buoy yard. Weather conditions have a say in how easily this is done, for snow is usually on the ground by the time the ship returns with a buoy load. Ice is still present in the spring, when the *Mackinaw* loads them up again. (Author's collection.)

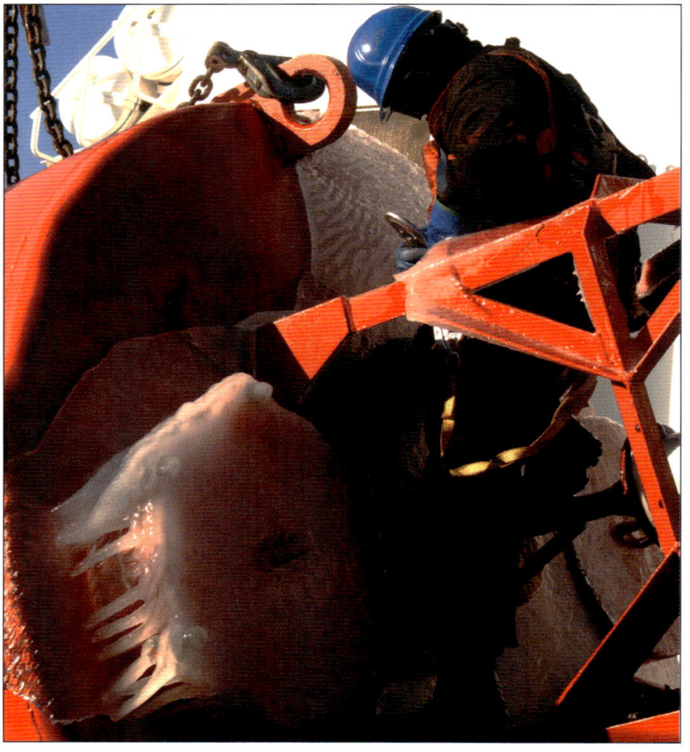

At times, despite *Mackinaw's* heated buoy deck, ice and snow gather on buoys while they are being brought back to the base for maintenance. Access to electronics, solar panels, antennas, and wiring cannot be achieved until ice is removed. So, the job must be done. *Mackinaw* crewmembers take great pride in their care of the aids to navigation they maintain at the Cheboygan Buoy Base. (Author's collection.)

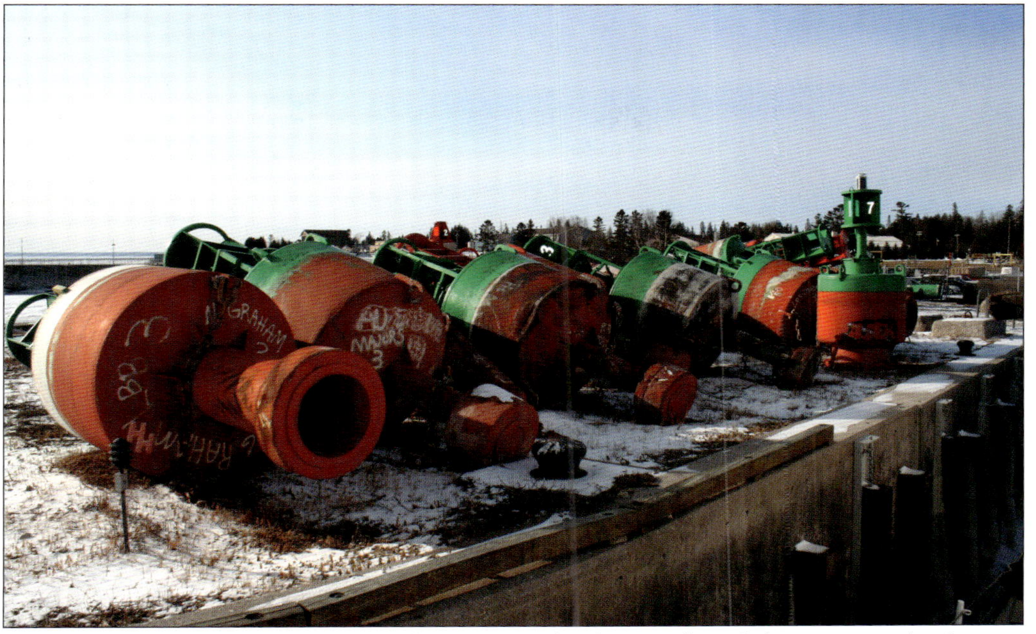

Some buoys do not need repair, and others just need to be stored until there is room for them in Cheboygan. *Mackinaw* often brings smaller buoys to Coast Guard Station St. Ignace, where an empty dock holds them for the winter. The marks can be brought to Cheboygan when time permits, or they can be picked up in St. Ignace in the spring for recommissioning. (Author's collection.)

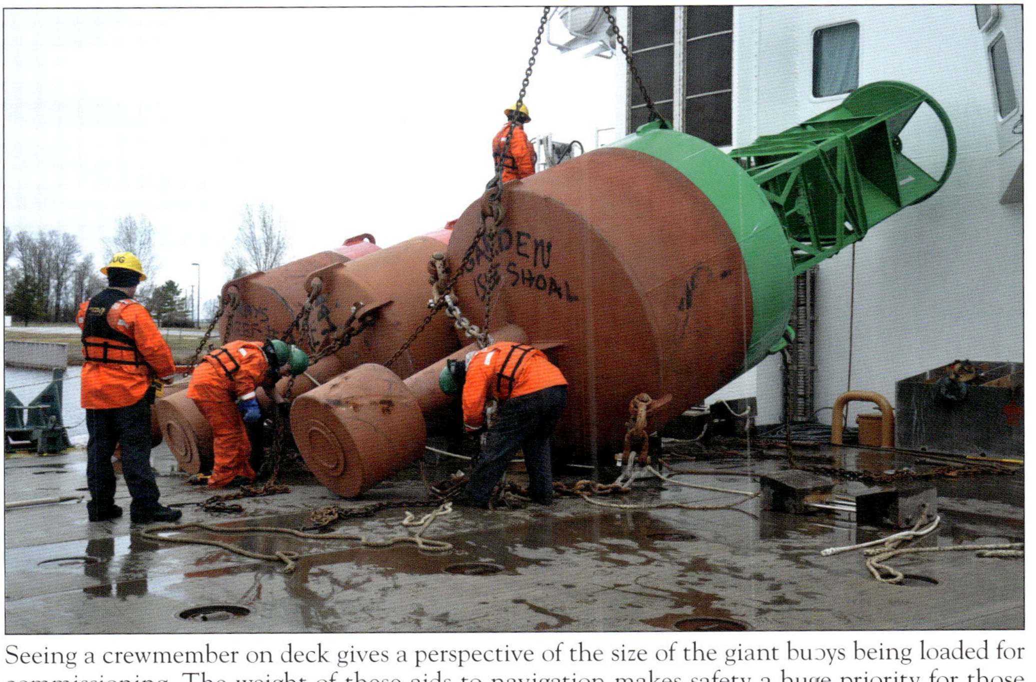

Seeing a crewmember on deck gives a perspective of the size of the giant buoys being loaded for commissioning. The weight of these aids to navigation makes safety a huge priority for those working the deck. Every move must be calculated, cleared, and executed perfectly to avoid a tragedy that could so easily occur. (Author's collection.)

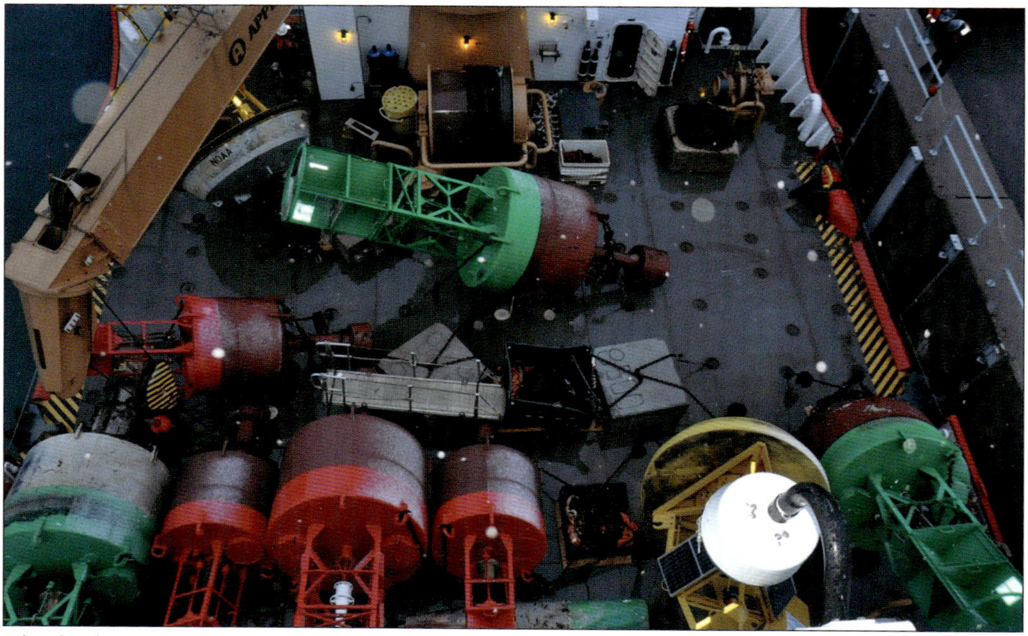

This bird's-eye view of the buoy deck, taken from atop the *Mackinaw's* bridge, shows a collection of various types of buoys ready for Operation Spring Restore. Large and medium lake buoys are mixed in with NOAA weather buoys, sinkers, and chain. Note that every item is tied down and placed to maximize available space. (Courtesy of U.S. Coast Guard.)

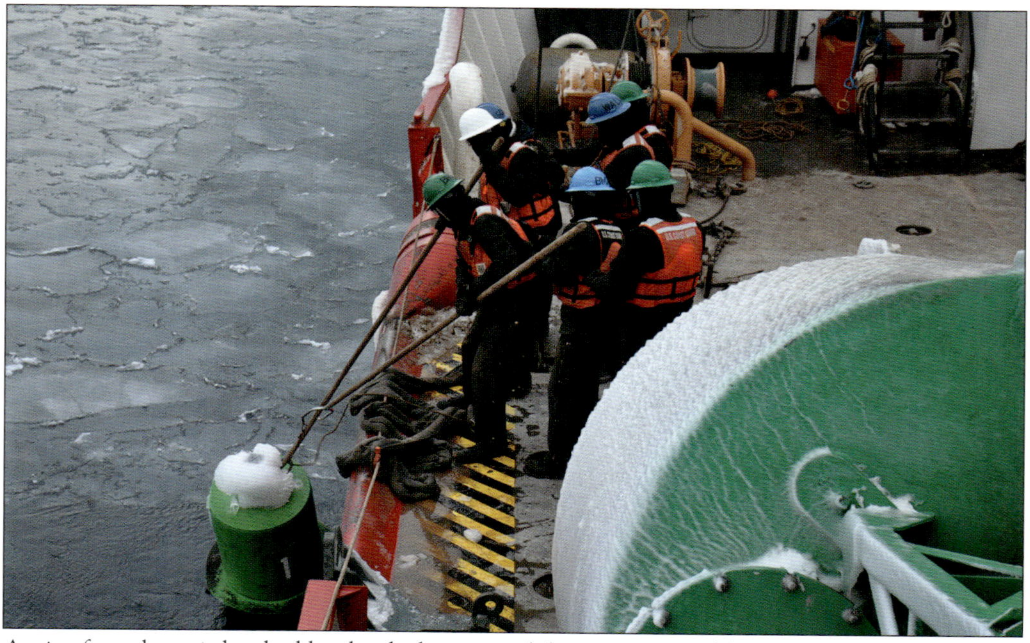

An icy foam buoy is hooked by the deck crew and decommissioned for the season. Roughly half of the aids to navigation throughout the Great Lakes region are taken out of service in the winter months during Operation Fall Retrieve in order to minimize damage caused by ice and inclement weather, and because of reduced vessel traffic. (Courtesy of U.S. Coast Guard.)

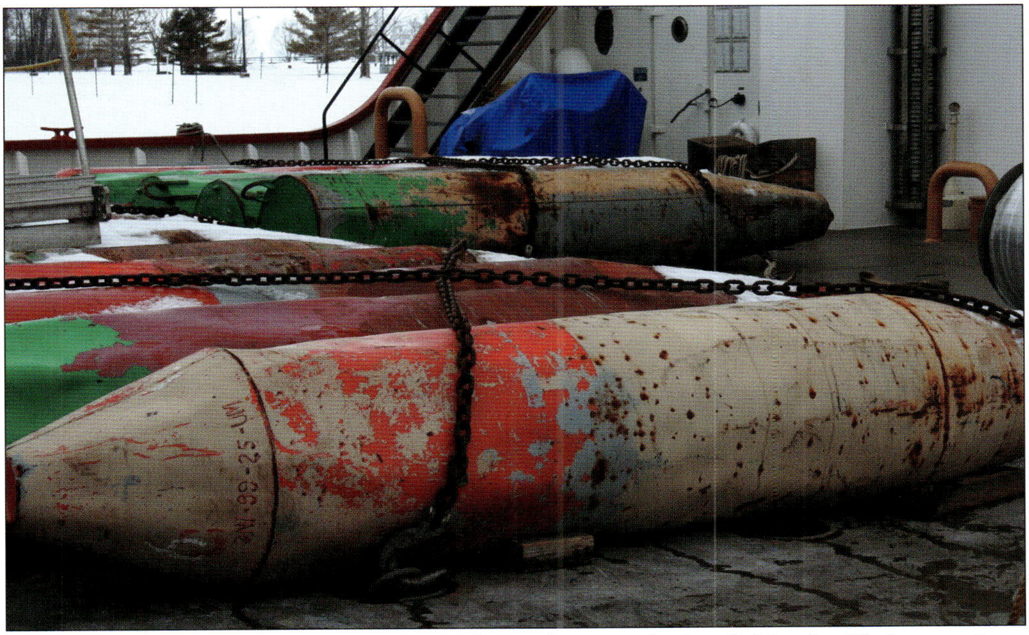

This nun buoy has had a rough winter in Lake Michigan and is headed for the Cheboygan Buoy Base for maintenance. The ice takes a toll on everything in the Great Lakes; the scraped paint and dents show how rough it can get in the ice-clogged waves. By spring, the buoy crew will have them looking like new again. (Courtesy of U.S. Coast Guard.)

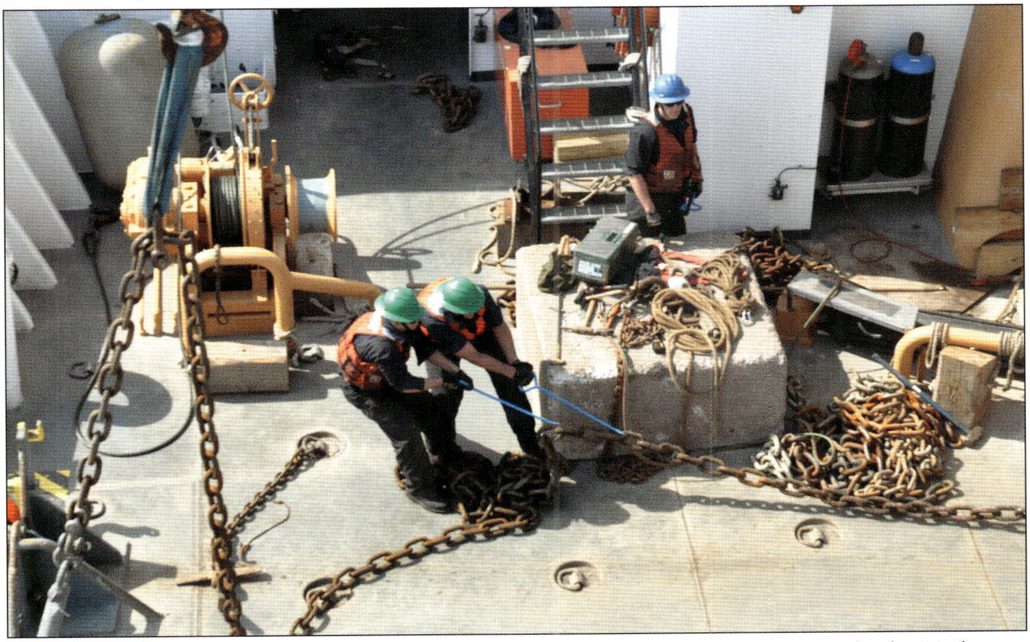

Deckhands move a section of chain to prepare it for a speedy trip to the bottom of Lake Michigan, along with the sinker it will follow. The lengths are carefully calculated to keep the buoy on station, but to allow for wave action and storms. Chain lengths are routinely inspected for wear and are replaced when necessary. (Courtesy of U.S. Coast Guard.)

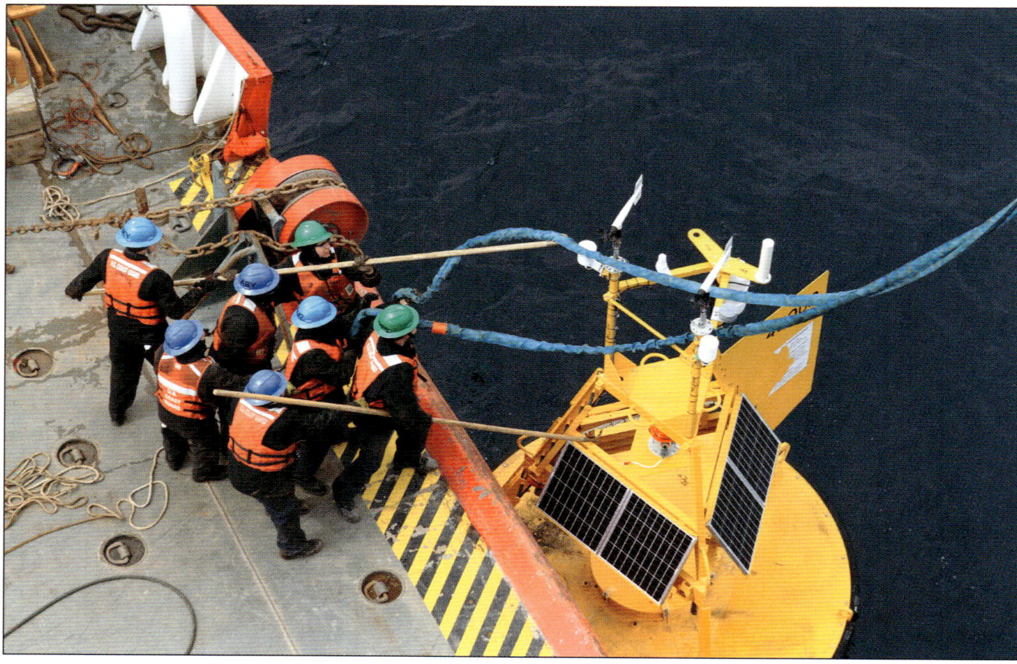

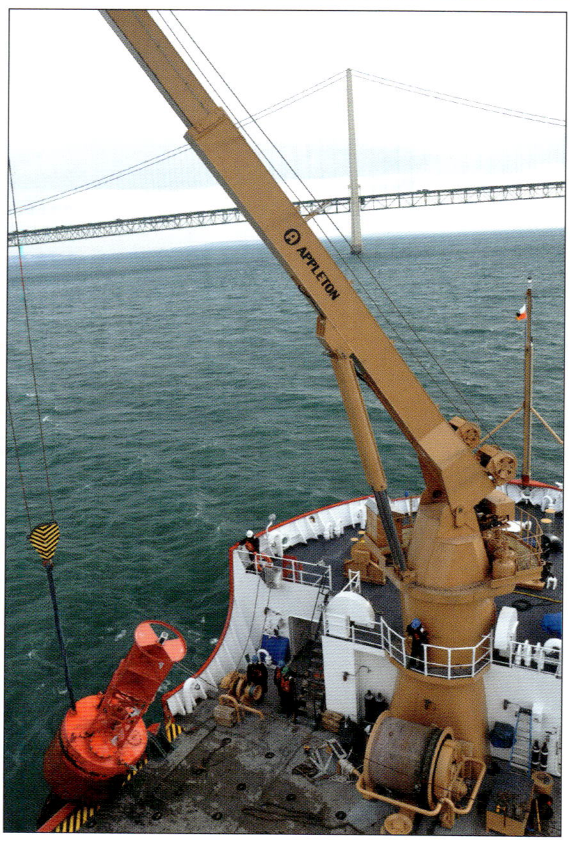

A team effort was required to corral this NOAA weather buoy after returning it to Lake Michigan as part of Operation Spring Restore. Crewmembers must release the straps that connect to the crane and avoid damaging any of the sensitive instruments on the buoy. On the bridge, the ship's navigation equipment is used to make sure the buoy will remain in the exact spot in which it is dropped. (Courtesy of U.S. Coast Guard.)

One of four Mackinac Bridge buoys is decommissioned as part of Operation Fall Retrieve. The channel markers keep ship traffic on course to safely pass under the five-mile span. Of the four buoys, two are located east of the bridge in Lake Huron, and two more are on the Lake Michigan side, to the west. (Courtesy of U.S. Coast Guard.)

Six

Icebreaking

The biggest task assigned to the *Mackinaw* is, of course, heavy icebreaking. The ship's legacy is founded on keeping the Straits of Mackinac and surrounding waterways clear of ice to facilitate commercial shipping, especially the flow of iron ore from Minnesota and Wisconsin to Lower Great Lakes steel mills.

The 1944 version of the ship accomplished its icebreaking chores through brute force. A monster of a ship, the first *Mackinaw* was an ice crusher of undisputed renown. Technological advances suggested that the job could be combined with other missions to include aids to navigation and still use far less manpower. A key improvement would be significantly more maneuverability in ice via the Azipod engine design, enabling a 360-degree turning radius.

Like its predecessor, the new *Mackinaw* faced only light ice duty in its early years, due to "soft" winters. The winter of 2014 proved to be one of record-setting levels of snow, ice, and extreme temperatures. When it ended, the ship's crew stood tall, knowing they had fought through the worst winter in 50 years and had done the job. Most agreed that the ship had been tested to its furthest capabilities, but the harsh winter had not stopped the *Mackinaw*.

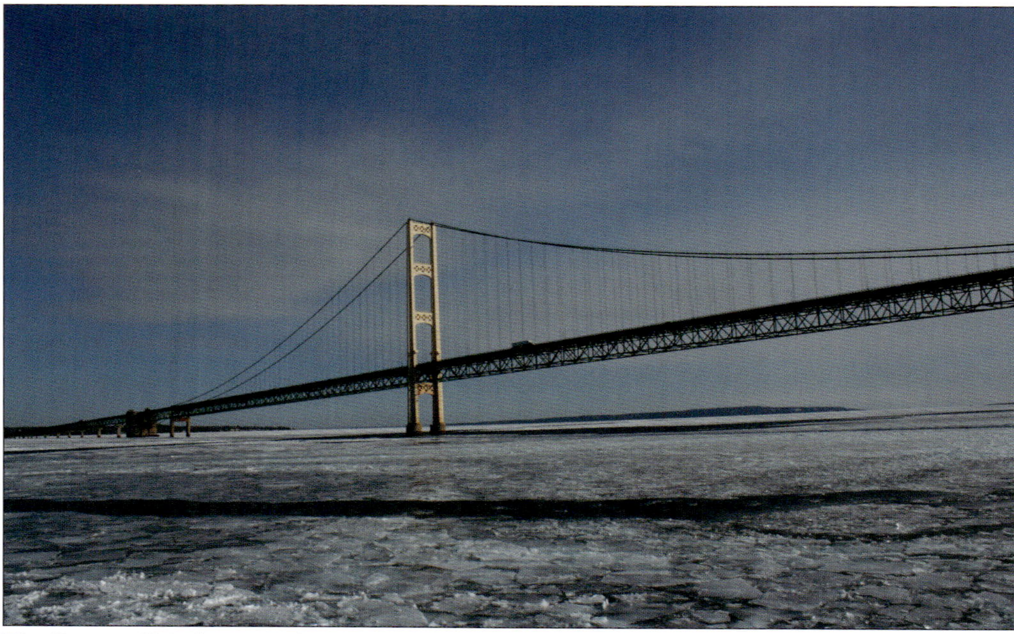

The Straits of Mackinac is a key assignment in icebreaking duties. Just five miles wide, the waters of Lake Michigan and Lake Huron interchange here with a heavy current flow that is unpredictable. Ice jams have caused many ships to sink in these waters. The Mackinac Bridge stands as an icon of the region, spanning deep water and dangerous conditions. (Author's collection.)

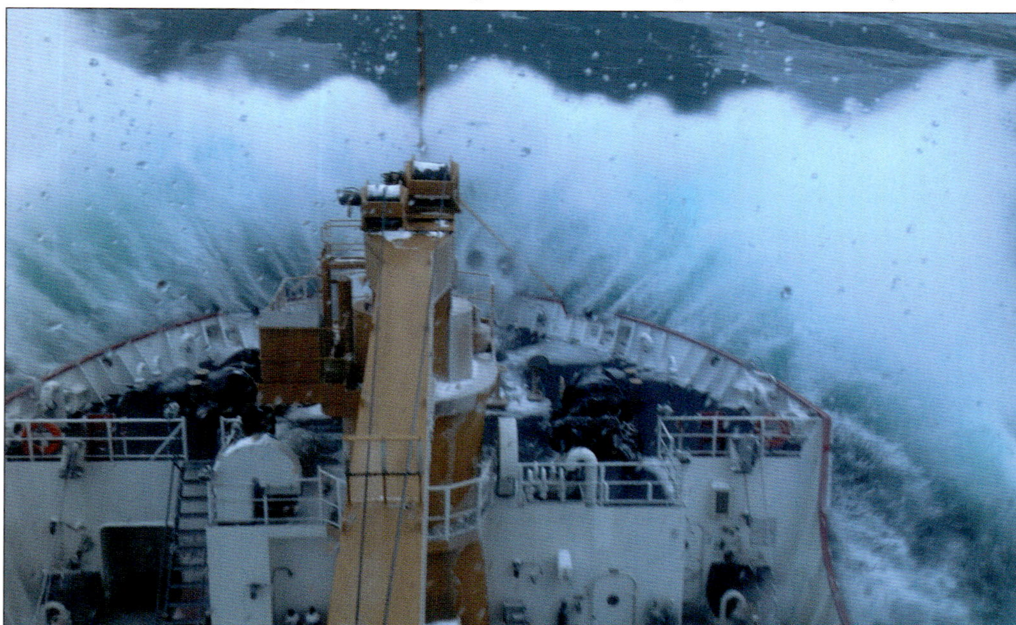

The fabled "gales of November" often unleash all their fury before the ice forms on the big lakes. *Mackinaw's* bow is seen here greeting the surf after riding down a huge wave in Lake Huron. Completely seaworthy in these conditions, the ship can handle more than some crewmembers, who tell tales of upset stomachs while riding high seas. (Courtesy of U.S. Coast Guard.)

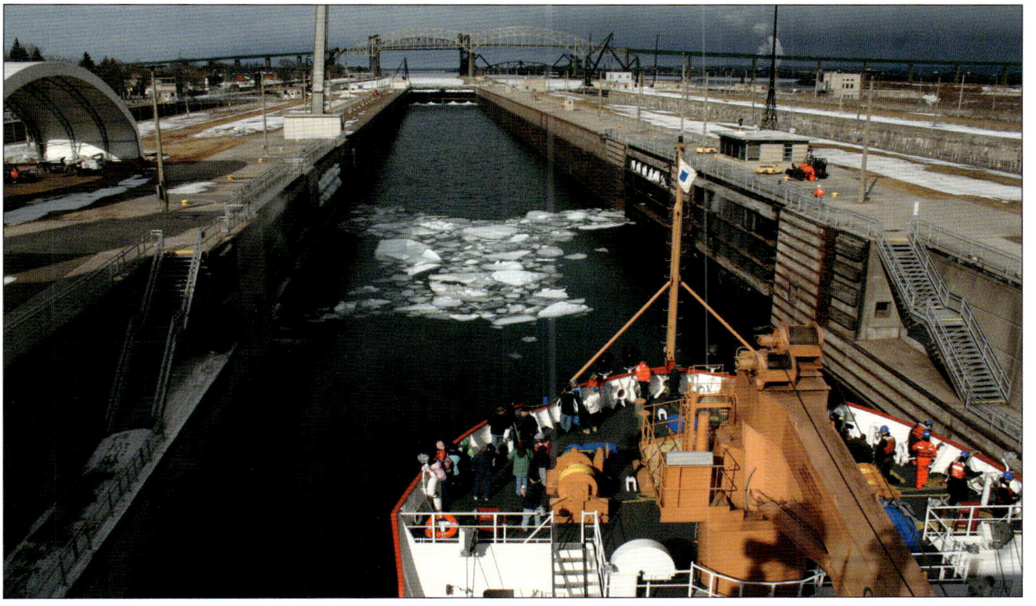

The Soo Locks are drained for maintenance from January 15 until March 25 each winter. Before they reopen, the *Mackinaw* is called to break any ice that has formed when the locks are filled with water and readied for shipping. Here, the *Mac* enters the Poe Lock and is greeted by several small ice floes that will be flushed out by the ship's bow thruster and stern Azipods. (Author's collection.)

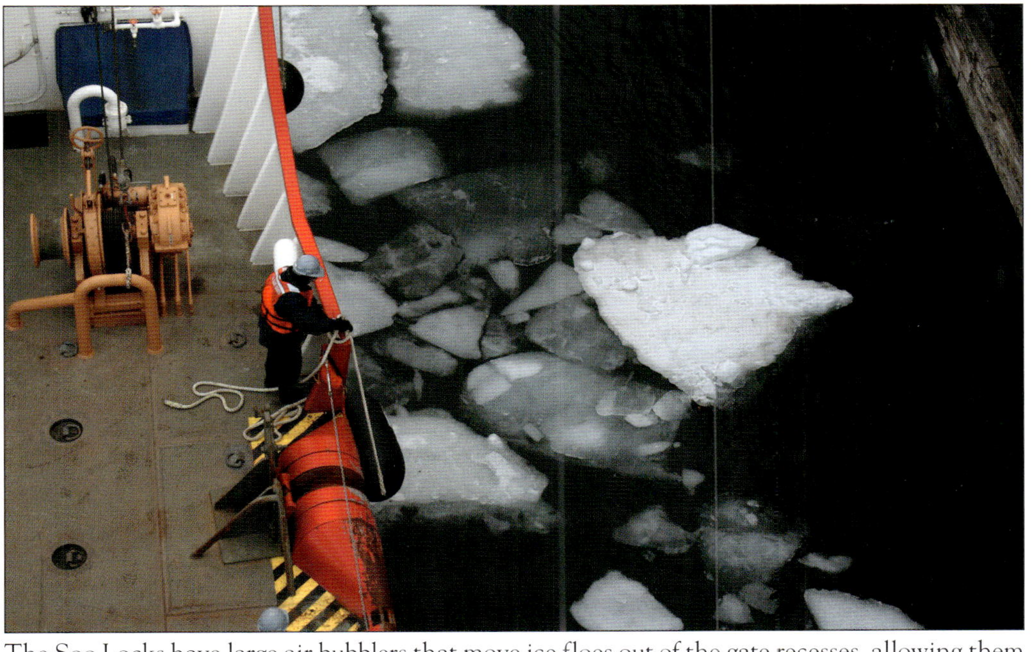

The Soo Locks have large air bubblers that move ice floes out of the gate recesses, allowing them to open and close. In heavy ice, ships are brought partially into the lock chamber, pushing ice ahead of them, then are backed out of the lock. The load of ice is then pushed into the lower river, the lock is raised, and the ship is brought back into an ice-free lock. (Author's collection.)

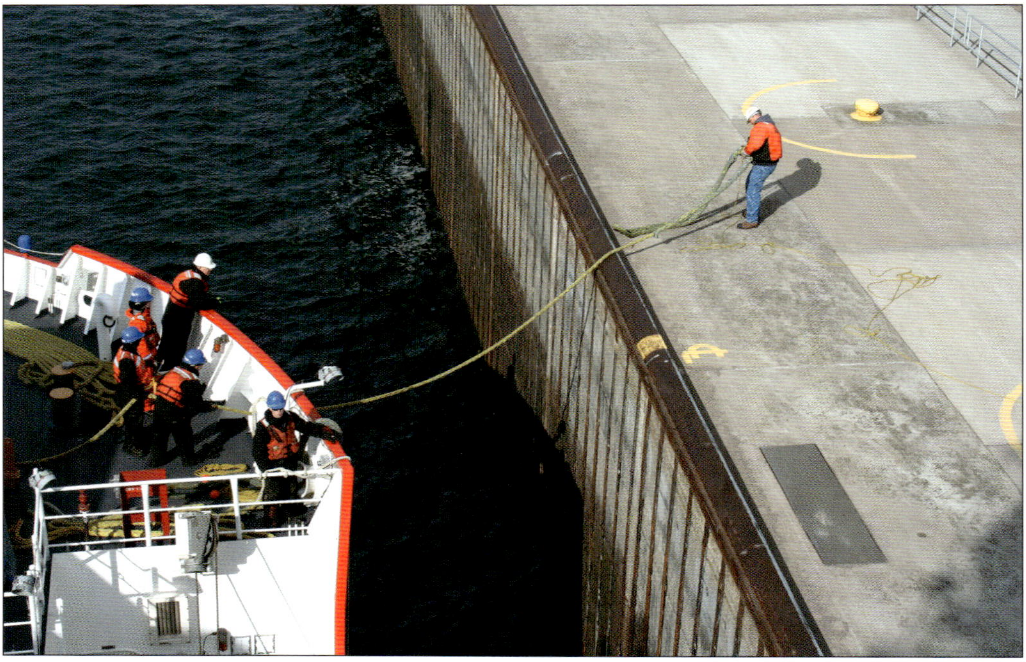

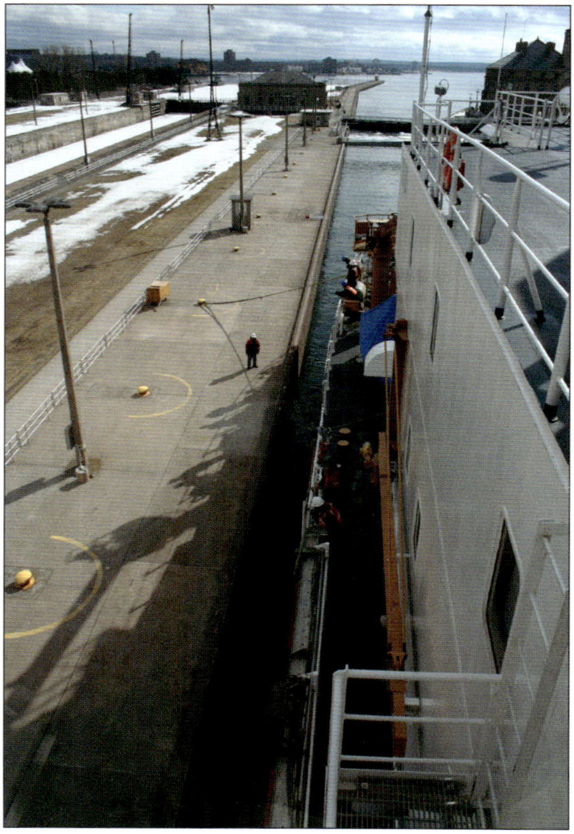

No toll is charged for any vessel of any nationality to transit the Soo Locks, operated by the U.S. Army Corps of Engineers. Workmen at the locks catch a shot line, thrown by a crewmember of the *Mackinaw*, that leads to a larger mooring line. The ship's lines are then walked along the lock wall in a process called "nursing" the vessel, while the water level is either raised or lowered 21 feet to the height of the ship's destination lake. More than 80 million tons of freight pass through the Soo Locks each year, mostly taconite iron ore pellets from the mines at the western end of Lake Superior. Low-sulfur coal, wheat and other grains, and crushed limestone are also common freight loads. It takes 22 million gallons of water to raise a ship to the lock's upper level. (Both, author's collection.)

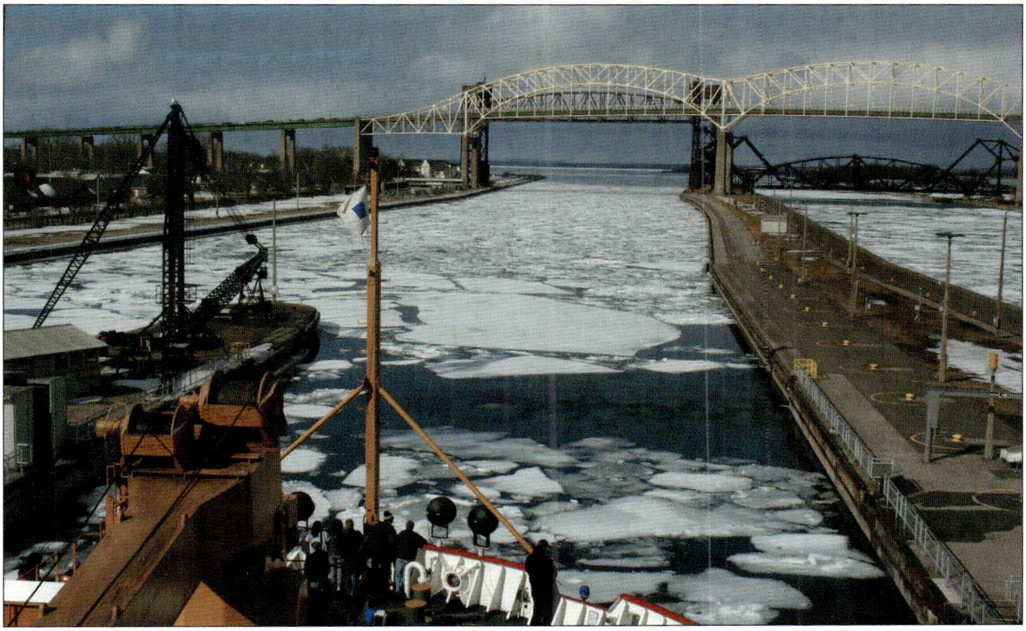

Heading west into lower Whitefish Bay, *Mackinaw* is immediately greeted by ice that has backed up to the locks from Lake Superior. Considerable work will need to be done to flush this brash ice away from the entrance to the Soo Locks. There are usually two to five feet of ice on the St. Marys River and the lower portions of Lake Superior in the winter months. As the ice begins to move in the spring, it collects at the bottom of Whitefish Bay and into the Upper St. Marys River. The *Mackinaw* teams with smaller icebreaking cutters to clear a path for ships to follow through the ice. (Both, author's collection.)

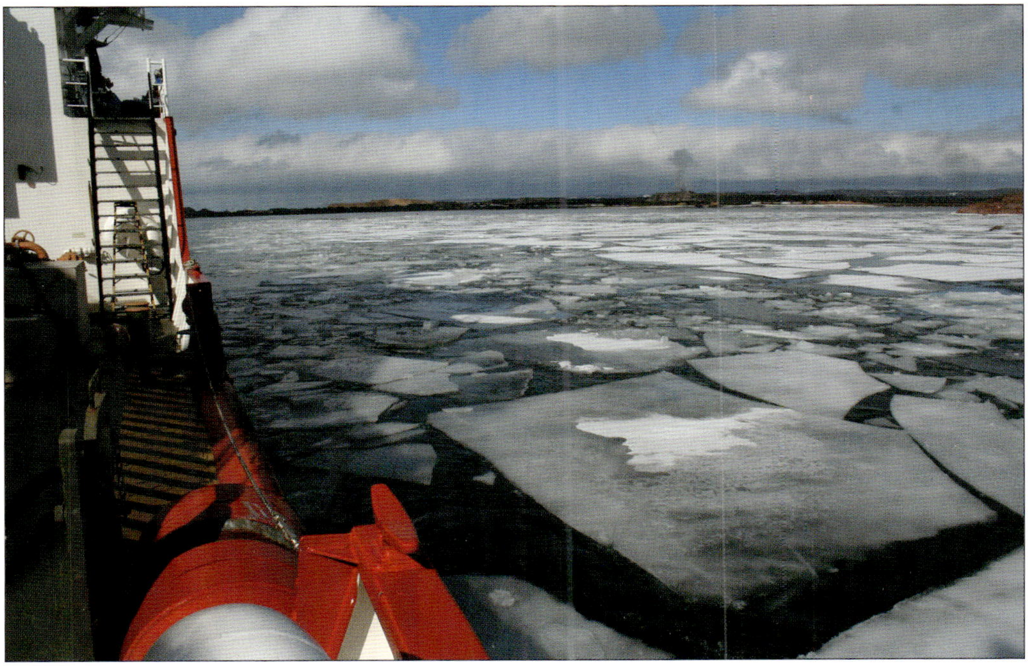

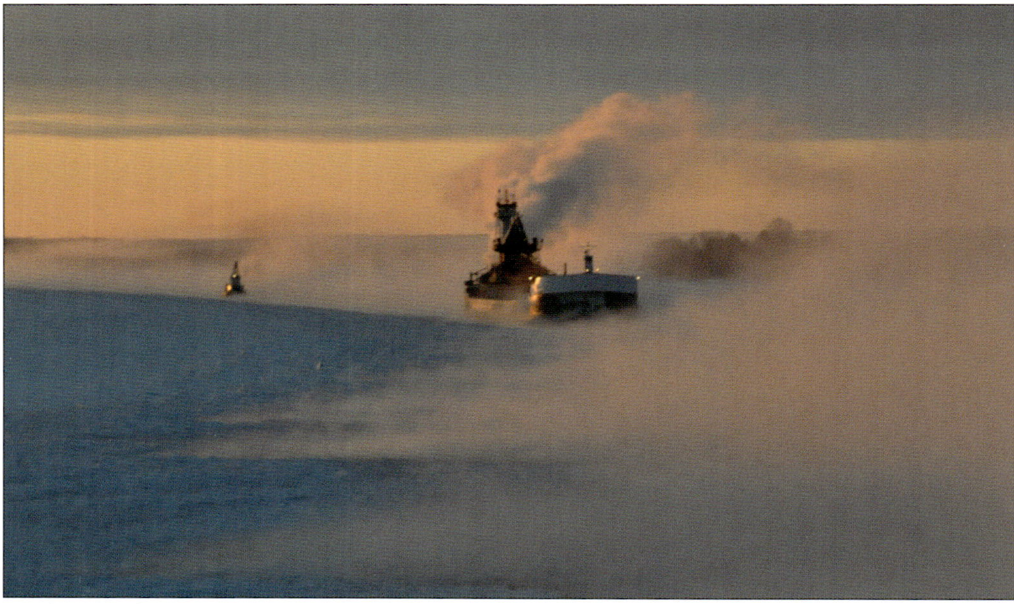

Farther north, temperature extremes can add a ghostly component to dead reckoning and visual navigation. This freighter appears to be sailing out of the early-morning snow fog in Whitefish Bay through a field of pack ice. The going is slow, and the ship will assume *Mackinaw's* track once it passes by. Windrows of ice can build up from stormy conditions, often stretching for miles and thickening to 15–20 feet. (Courtesy of U.S. Coast Guard.)

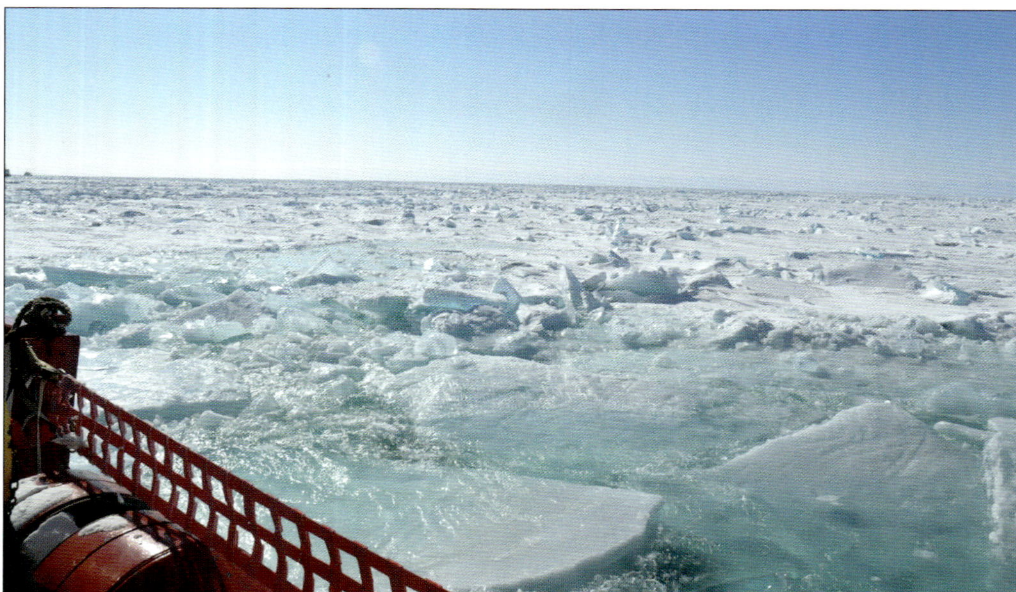

Once the *Mackinaw* passes Whitefish Point and reaches Lake Superior, ice conditions quickly become more difficult. Depending on the winter, varying degrees of ice coverage exist on the big lake. In 2014, there was extreme coverage, causing ships to wait out the spring thaw in winter layup or risk traveling a circuitous route along the northern shore to find a strand of open water. (Courtesy of U.S. Coast Guard.)

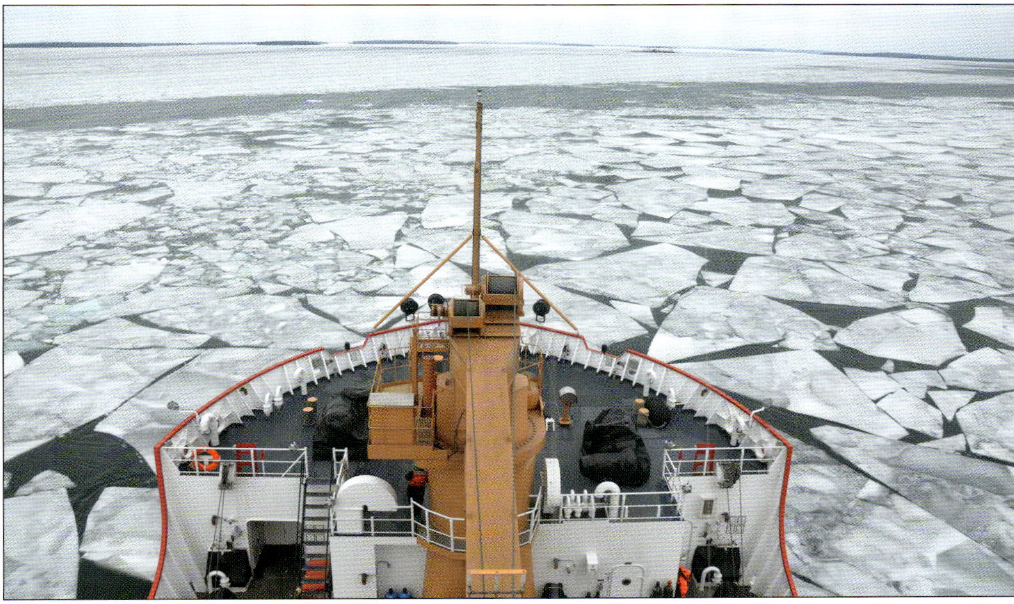

The ship is capable of "outsmarting" ice by backing down and using the powerful Azipods to break ice apart and flush it away. It is a different approach than the original *Mackinaw's* game plan of brute force. Lake Superior ice is legendary for its thickness, and the old *Mac's* logbooks contain references to breaking windrows 30 feet thick. The new *Mackinaw* handles the ice in a different, more efficient way. (Courtesy of U.S. Coast Guard.)

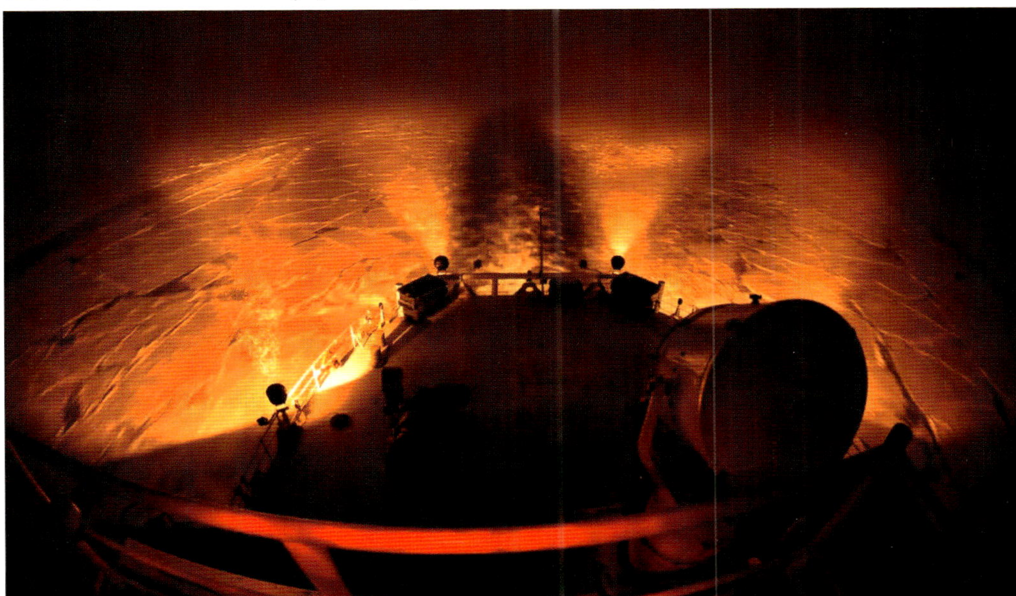

This stern view of night icebreaking operations in western Lake Superior near Duluth, Minnesota, shows the *Mac's* high-intensity flood lamps at work, illuminating the ice field. The ship, here unencumbered, is ready to back down to clear the way for the freighter *Manitowoc*. The icebreaking business knows no set hours, and when ships get stuck, the *Mackinaw* is on the job in daylight or at night. (Courtesy of U.S. Coast Guard.).

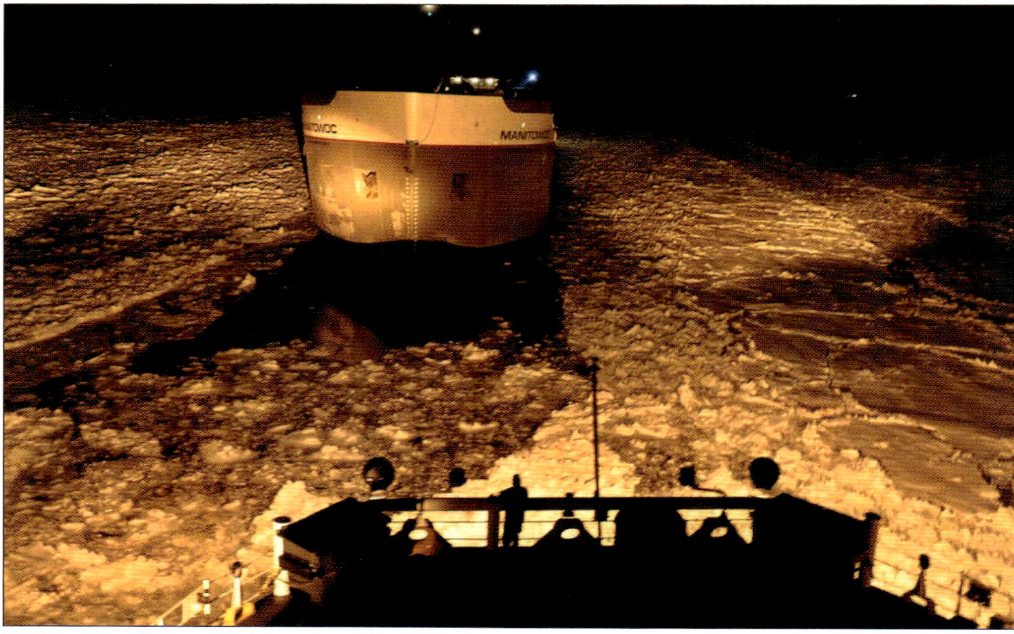

Backing up allows the Azipods to flush ice from near the *Manitowoc's* bow, affording a clear lane of travel for the freighter to follow. The flushing process allows the icebreaker to operate within a better safety margin of the distressed vessel, with no need to crack ice right up to its bow with sheer weight. (Courtesy of U.S. Coast Guard.)

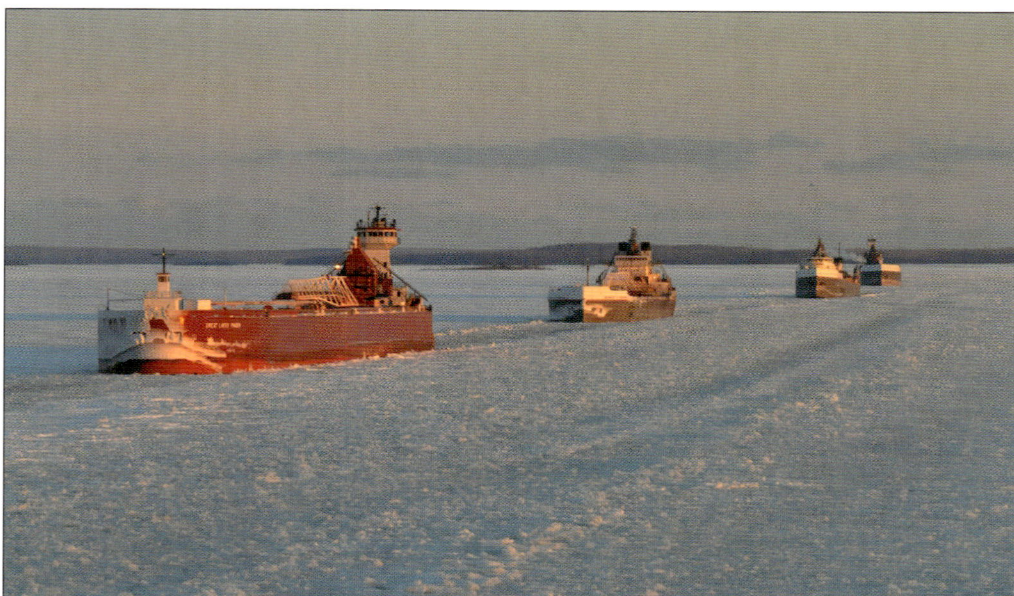

A convoy of ships made its way across Lake Superior as the 2014 navigation season began, following one of the worst winters on record in terms of ice. The ships had spent the winter in the shipyards and began their first ore-carrying loads in extreme conditions with the Soo Locks still closed. Captains hoped to time their journeys to arrive at the Sault just as the locks opened on March 25. (Courtesy of U.S. Coast Guard.)

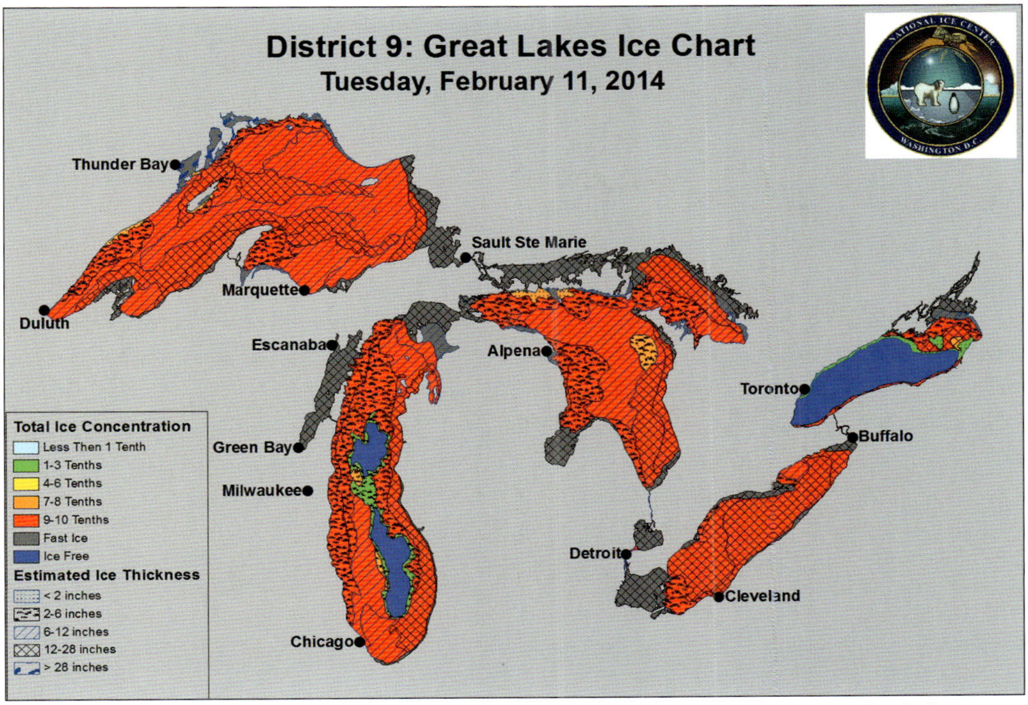

According to the Coast Guard's District 9 Ice Chart, the February 11, 2014, outlook for spring breakout was not good. The only open water on the chart is shown in blue, with the red areas representing territory a freighter would need an icebreaker to get through. The gray areas represent fast ice, such as that in Green Bay or the Straits of Mackinac. (Courtesy of National Ice Center.)

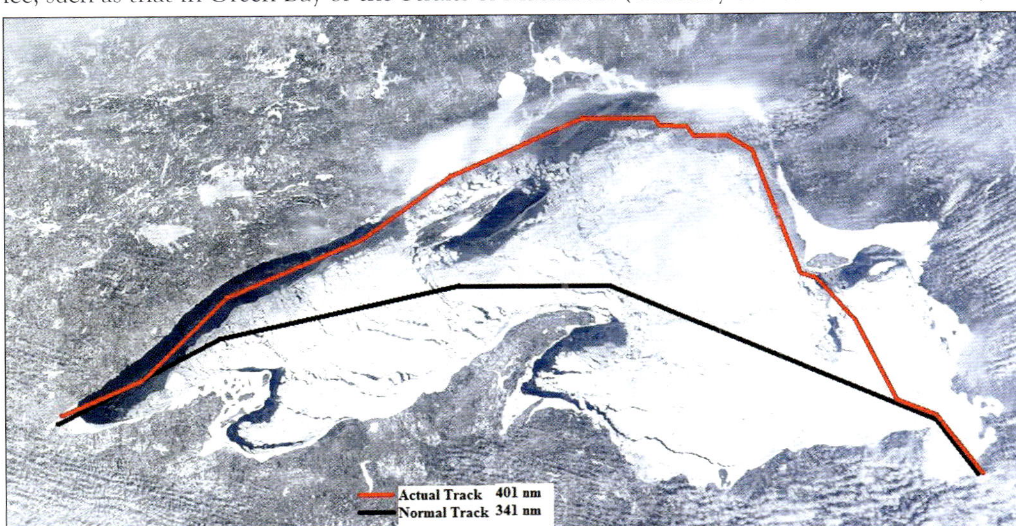

This satellite view of Lake Superior shows ice coverage when the shipping season was preparing to begin near mid-March. The black track illustrates the normal shipping route past Whitefish Point and the Keweenaw Peninsula, a trip of 341 nautical miles. The red track shows the route that *Mackinaw* led the convoys on instead, near Thunder Bay, Ontario, a distance of 401 nautical miles. (Courtesy of National Oceanic and Atmospheric Administration.)

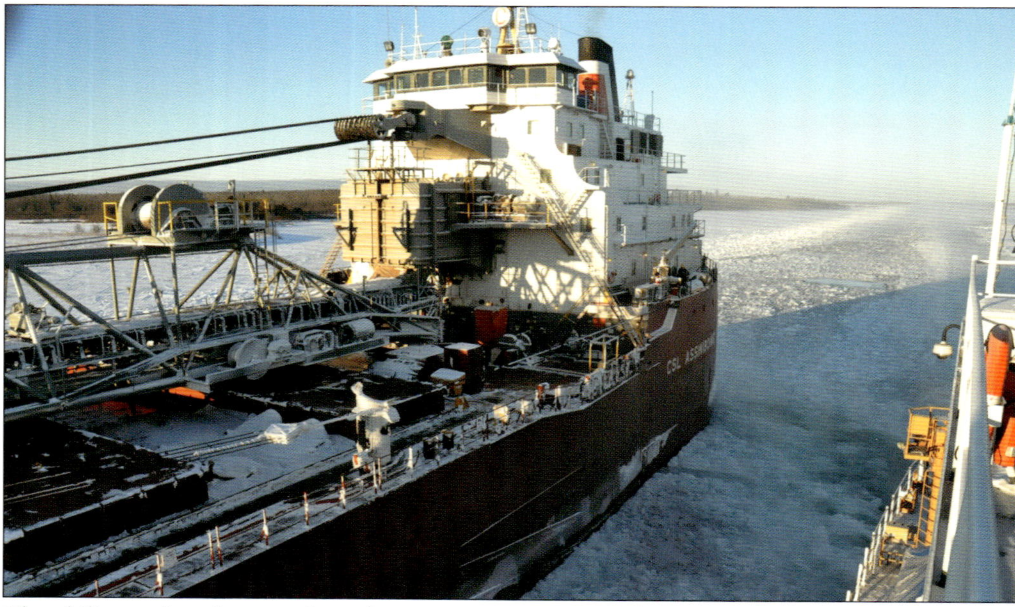

The ability to free ships stuck in the ice is a major part of the *Mackinaw's* legacy. The *Mac* can turn a tight circle around a distressed vessel and flush the remaining ice away in less than 15 minutes. The original *Mackinaw* required twice that time just to make those turns. Here, the new *Mac* assists the Canada Steamship Lines freighter *Assiniboine*. (Courtesy of U.S. Coast Guard.)

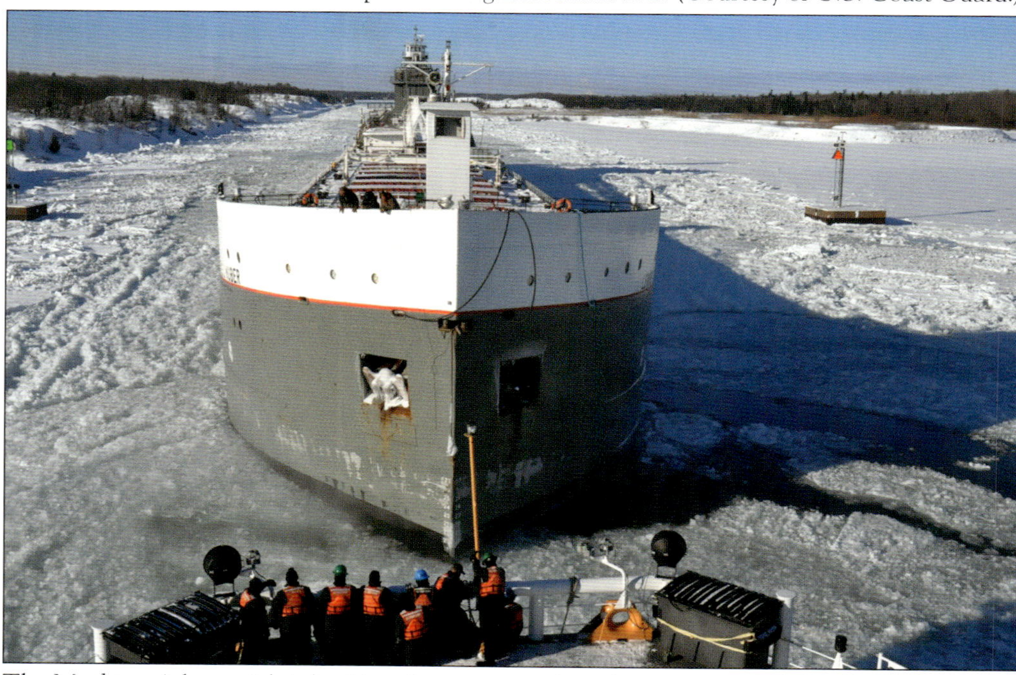

The *Mackinaw's* best trick is backing down on vessels and opening a track for them by using the prop wash from the Azipod engines. Here, the 616-foot *Lewis J. Kuber*, pushed by the tug *Olive L. Moore*, awaits assistance in the St. Marys River. Note the narrow configuration of the channel at this point. A stuck ship means nobody gets through. (Courtesy of U.S. Coast Guard.)

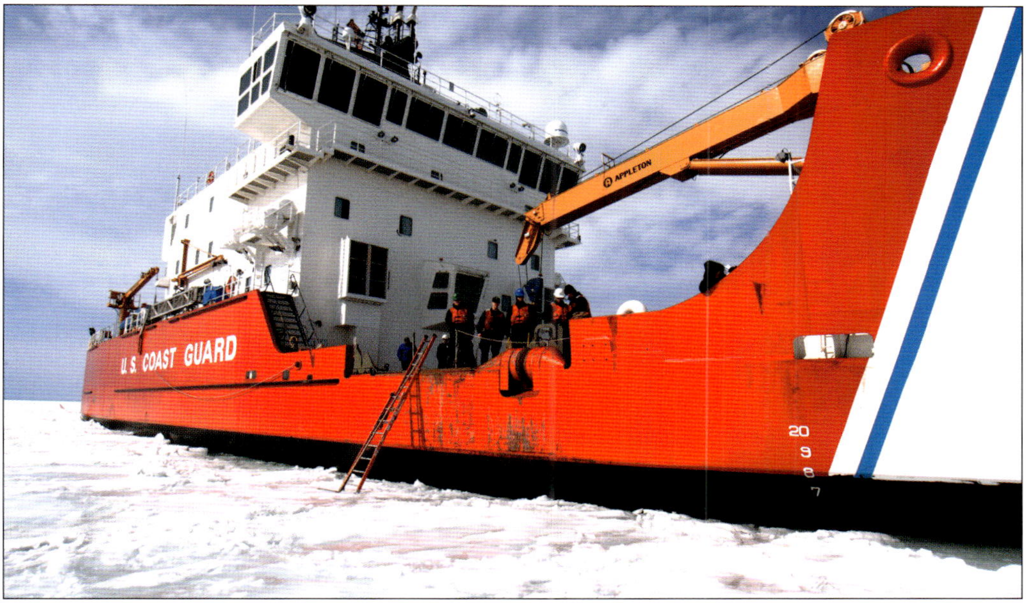

Ice measurements are a part of working the Great Lakes ice season. The ship's crew often measures ice thickness and records data involving locations and water depth. The information is shared with shipping companies and meteorologists for trip planning and weather forecasting. Crewmembers look forward to an opportunity to see their workplace from this angle. (Courtesy of U.S. Coast Guard.)

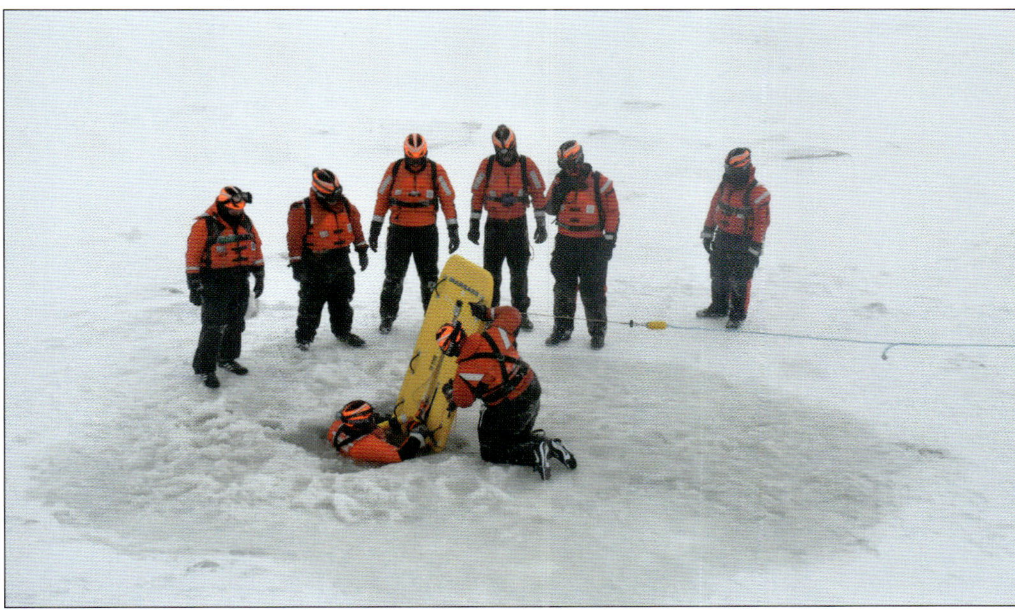

When the ship stops in stable ice, it is a great opportunity for training. *Mackinaw's* crew constantly drills on various facets of shipboard safety, and ice training is always popular. With backup for the backups, ice safety gear is donned and a "victim" gets in the water. With flotation and backboard at the ready, the crew practices retrieving the victim from the hole. (Courtesy of U.S. Coast Guard.)

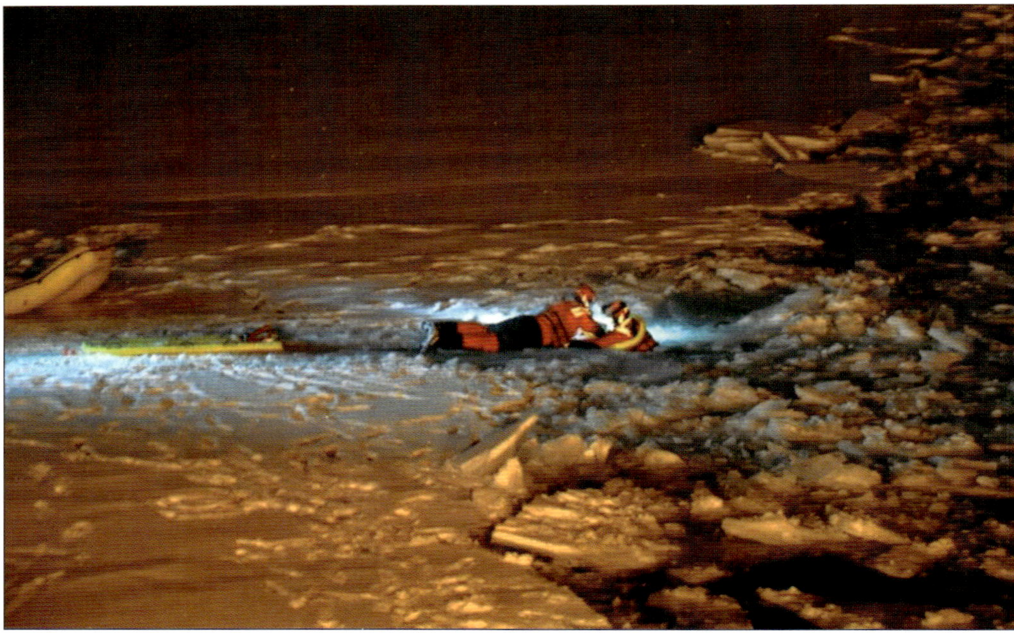

Any daytime emergency can become a nighttime emergency, so the crew adds darkness to the equation of the drill. The crew learns that sufficient lighting, when added to other standard safety gear, recreates the daytime atmosphere and discourages panic. Nonetheless, it is still different, and it is a great experience that builds confidence for a rescue team. (Courtesy of U.S. Coast Guard.)

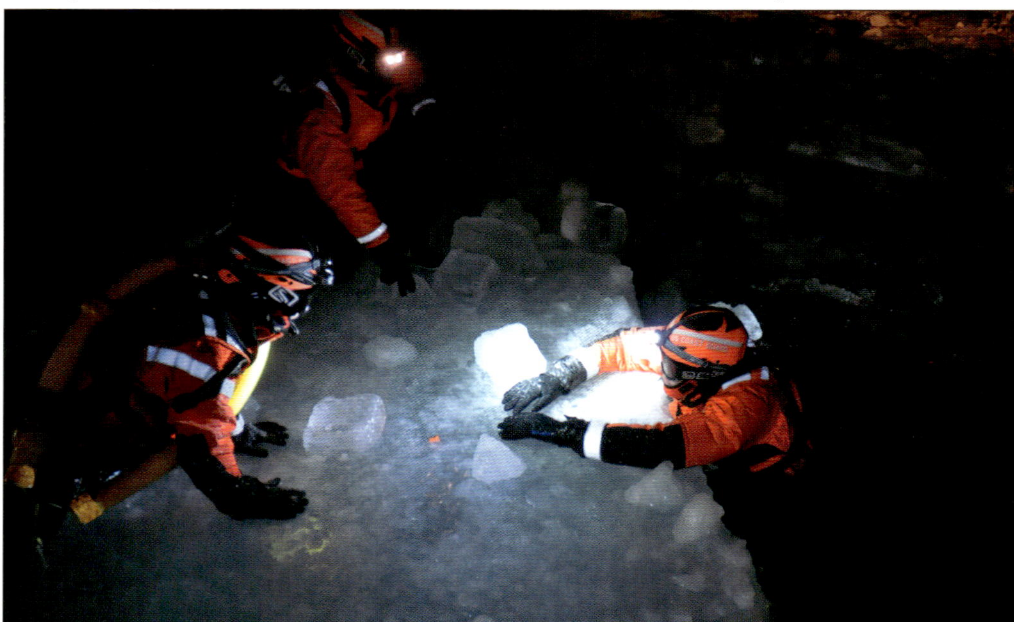

Familiarization with gear is a key component in rescue training. There can be no questions about how to operate any device while attempting to save someone's life. Otherwise, the life of the rescuer can soon be on the line, along with that of the original victim. Here, rescuers practice a night lifesaving drill in the ice. (Courtesy of U.S. Coast Guard.)

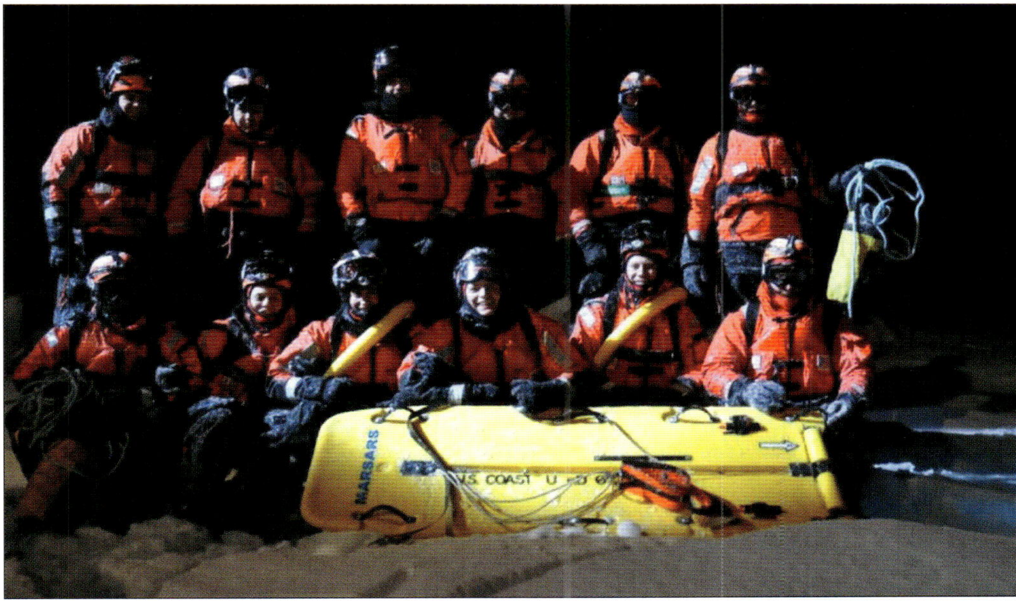

The crew's morale can be significantly elevated through successful drill training. The exhilaration of performing a task well, combining adventure with teamwork, and developing self-confidence goes a long way in raising spirits. This happy group posed in March 2014 after successful ice training exercises in Munuscong Lake in the St. Marys River. The drills were a welcome break from the tedium of constant icebreaking. (Courtesy of U.S. Coast Guard.)

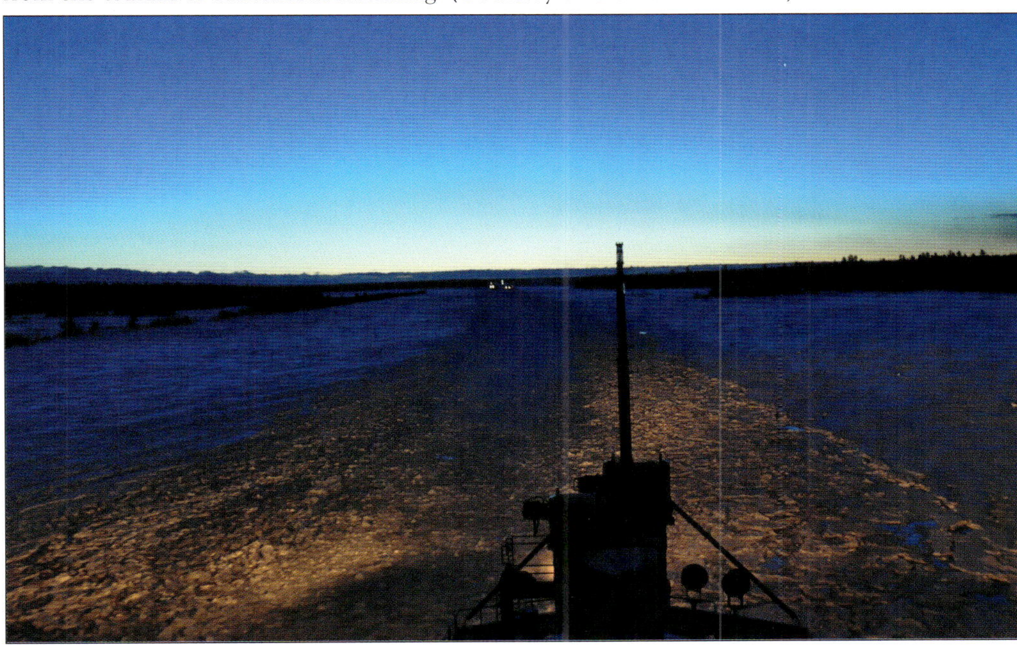

The colors and solitude of dawn and the expectation of a new day of moving ships on the St. Marys River can bring an inner peace. This view from the bridge would be accompanied by the aroma of hot coffee, a 24-hour staple. Each day, the officers assess the crew's readiness for the mission at hand, as well as their own. (Courtesy of U.S. Coast Guard.)

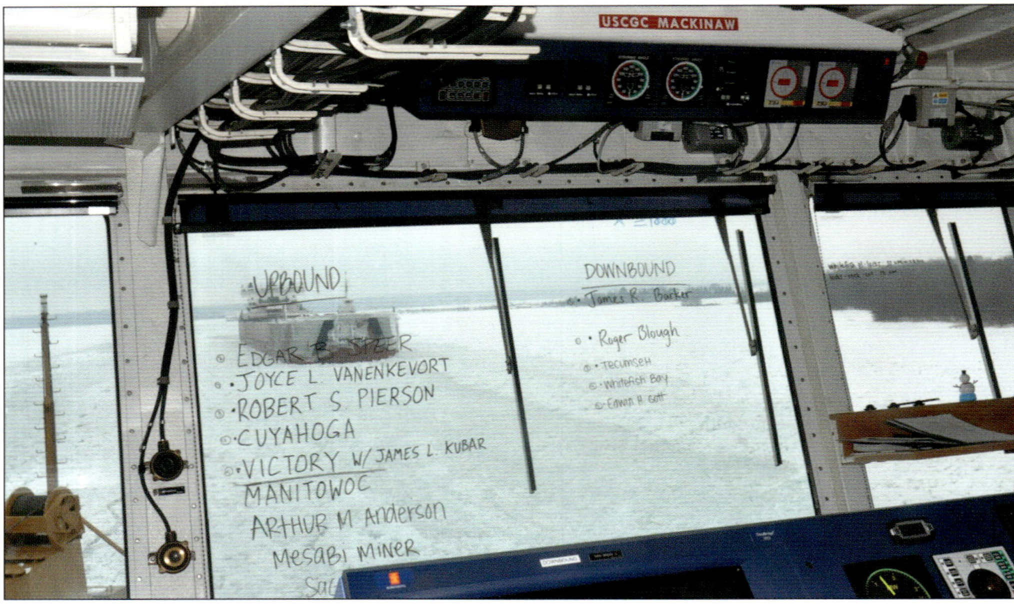

A day on the St. Marys River in March usually means lots of traffic. The *Mackinaw's* bridge crew keeps track of all traffic on the river and can see all vessels on an array of electronic equipment. In addition, ships active in the river are listed on the *Mac's* windshield, written with dry-erase markers. Each freighter, tug, and barge that moves past the *Mackinaw* is checked off the list throughout the day and night. (Courtesy of U.S. Coast Guard.)

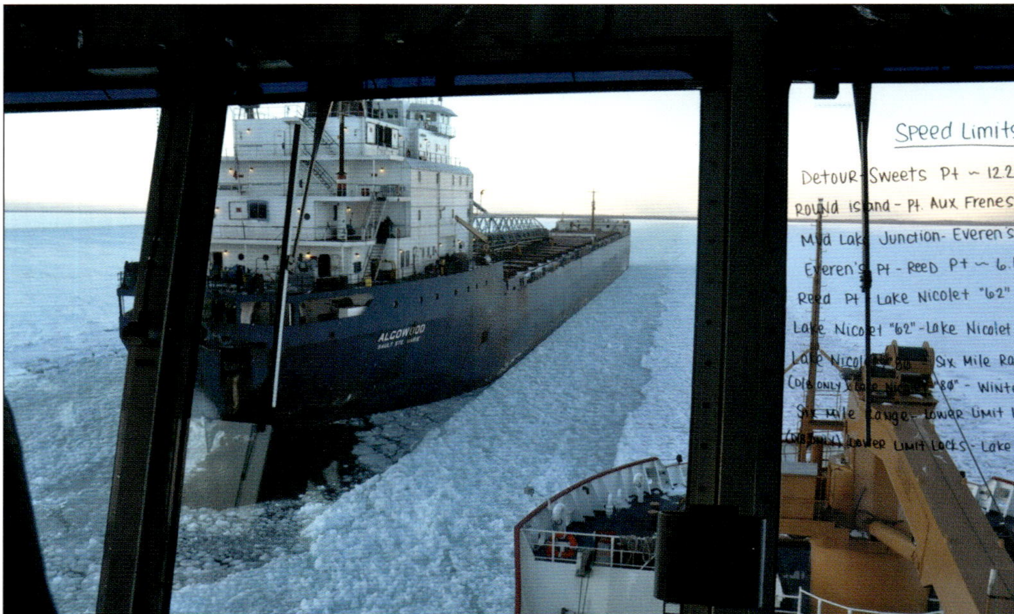

In addition to the ships, the *Mac* also tracks the river's speed limits. Vessels must observe speed zones to avoid damaging docks and eroding sensitive shorelines. The ships are visible to Soo Control on video monitors at selected points, and the ships must check in by radio, allowing for a timed estimation of their speed. (Courtesy of U.S. Coast Guard.)

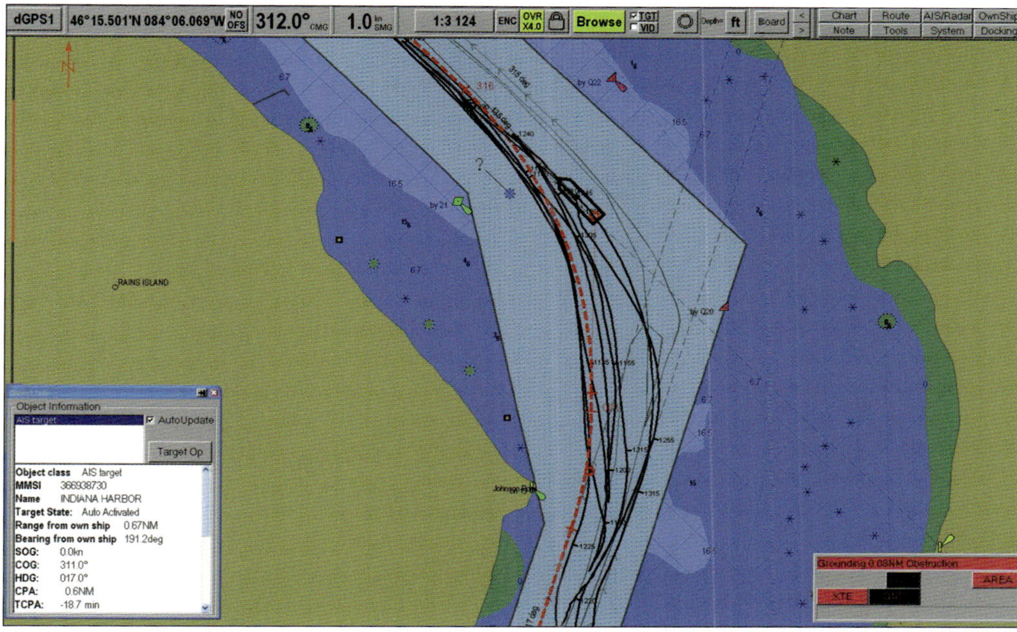

This computer display shows the channel depths and ship tracks of vessels on the St. Marys River. The equipment helps to prevent disorientation in the ice, which prevents visual estimations of reef locations and distance estimation. The crew utilizes electronic technology, visual observations, and standard paper charts to plot positions. (Courtesy of Kongsberg Maritime Inc.)

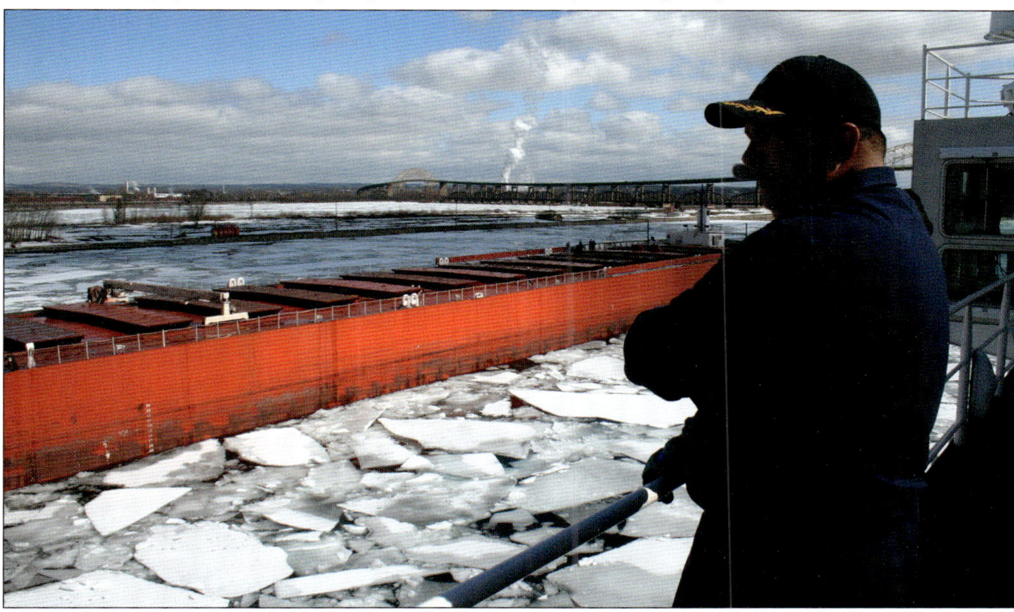

Cmdr. Scott Smith steps outside the bridge on a relatively balmy winter afternoon long enough to watch a freighter pass close by in the St. Marys River near Sault Ste. Marie, Michigan. The captain often receives a wave and a thumbs-up from those on other ships, recognizing the *Mackinaw's* service to lake carriers and international ships visiting the Great Lakes. Everybody on the water knows the *Mackinaw*. (Author's collection.)

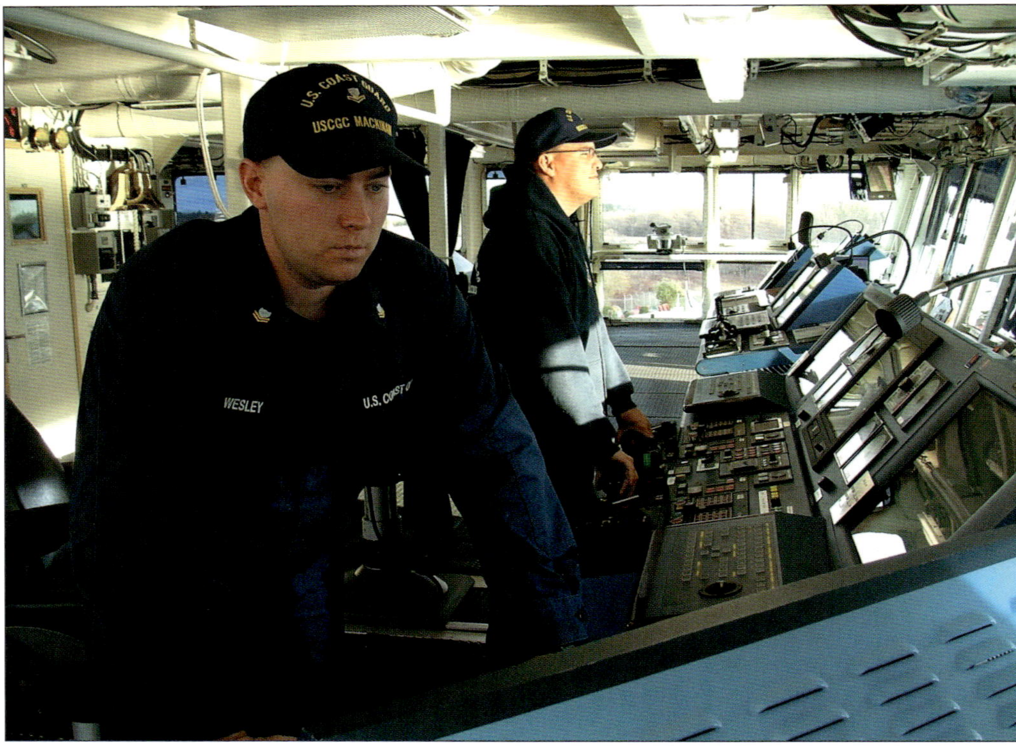

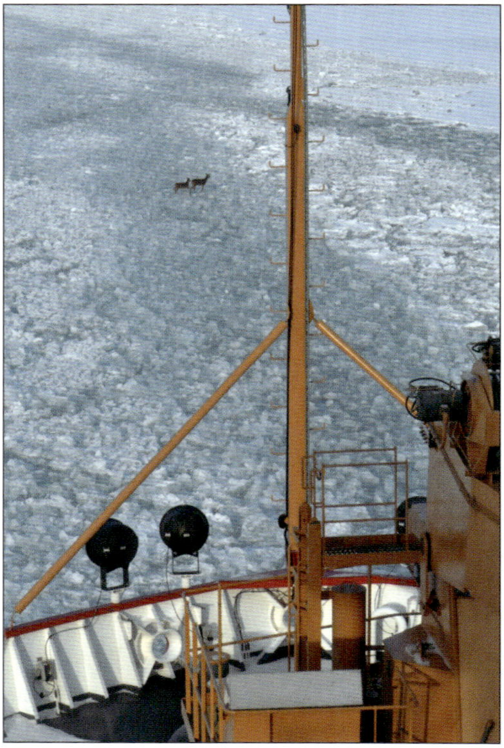

Lt. David Lieberman (right) is at the helm and Bosun's Mate 2nd Class Joe Wesley (left) updates weather forecasts following a day in the St. Marys River freeing the tug *Avenger IV*. After the crew of the *Mackinaw* freed the *Avenger IV*, it also freed the vessel the tug was escorting. Sometimes, ships get stuck in the fast-freezing ice while waiting for others to get clear. (Courtesy of U.S. Coast Guard.)

When the *Mackinaw's* lookouts thought they spotted a group of deer ahead in the refrozen track, crewmembers could not believe the whitetails showed no sign of fear that a 240-foot ship was bearing down on them. As the *Mac* got closer, the deer kept running ahead until they separated, leaving a pair off to the right of the track, still on the ship's heading. (Courtesy of U.S. Coast Guard.)

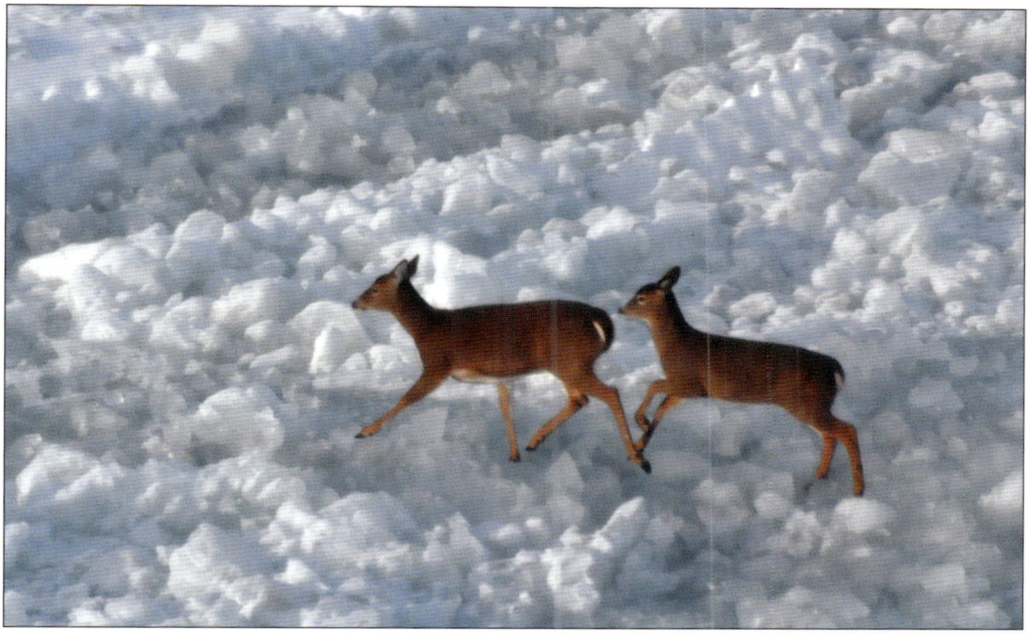

When the deer disappeared from sight under the *Mac's* bow, it was feared they would end up in broken ice and drown. The ship could not be stopped. Then, to the relief of the crew, the pair appeared safely on solid ice on the port side and rejoined the others. (Courtesy of U.S. Coast Guard.)

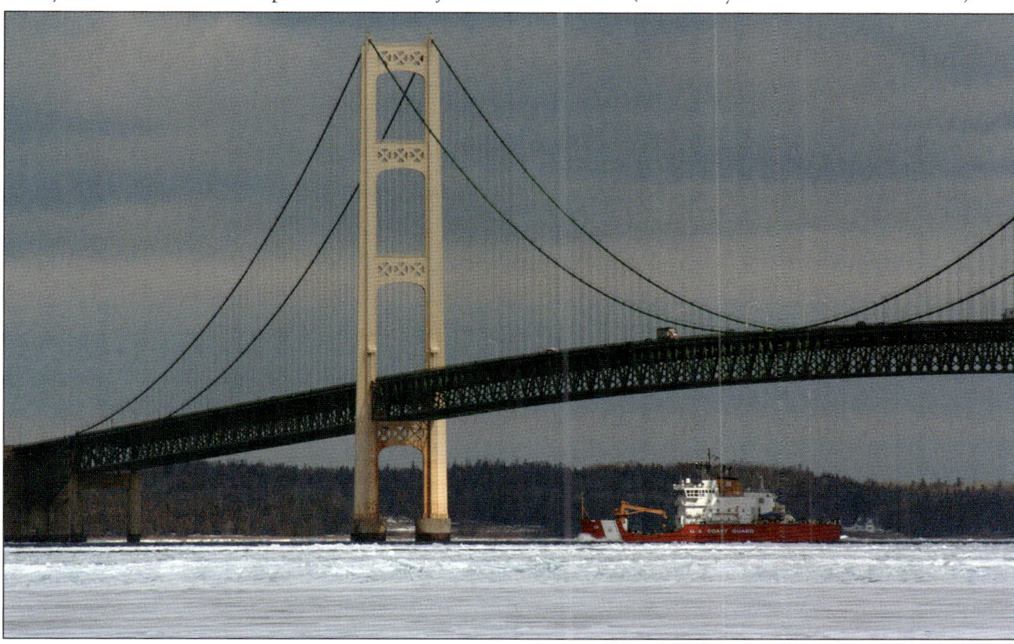

Grooming ship tracks in the Straits of Mackinac by day can lead to docking in Mackinaw City or St. Ignace at night—a short car ride home to family in Cheboygan. The Straits offer late-spring icebreaking work after Lake Superior and the St. Marys River are taken care of. Ice often remains in the Straits when none exists only a few miles away in Lake Huron or Lake Michigan. (Author's collection.)

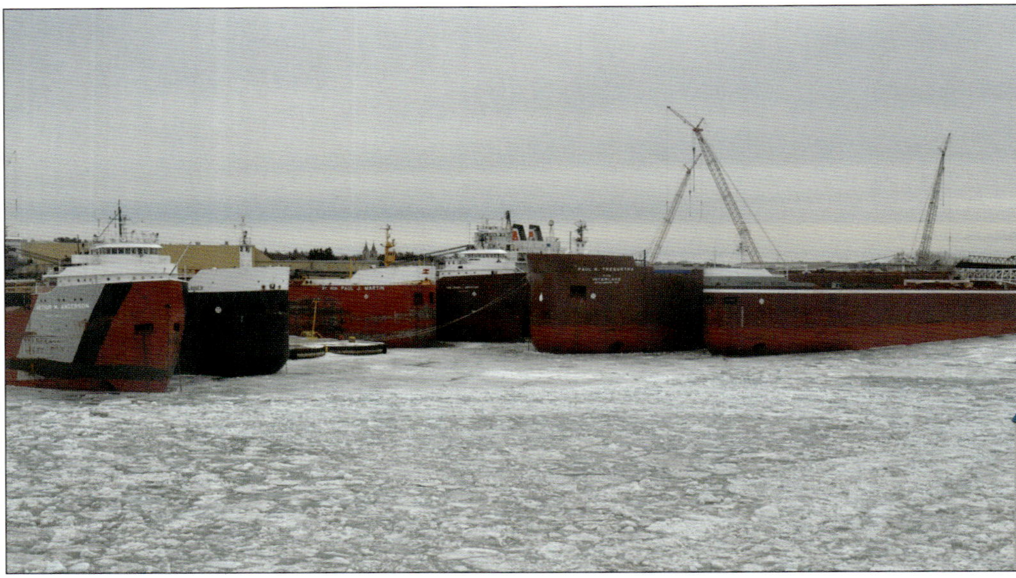

When Lake Michigan ports show up on the *Mackinaw's* duty list, it is a sure bet that Sturgeon Bay will be a destination. The freighters who slept here for winter layup are ready to awaken, and need the harbor cleared of ice to get under way. They are all glad to see the big red icebreaker arrive. Being in heavy ice can take a toll on a ship's hull. Below, crewmen from the *Mackinaw* use a small boat to inspect the hull of the *Roger Blough*, scraped by large windrows of ice. The crewmen make a thorough inspection for the *Blough's* captain, who will report the findings to his company. Upon a closer look, the damage to the *Blough* is obvious. The inspection allows the shipping company to make plans for repairs and minimize time spent away from the shipping season. (Both, courtesy of U.S. Coast Guard.)

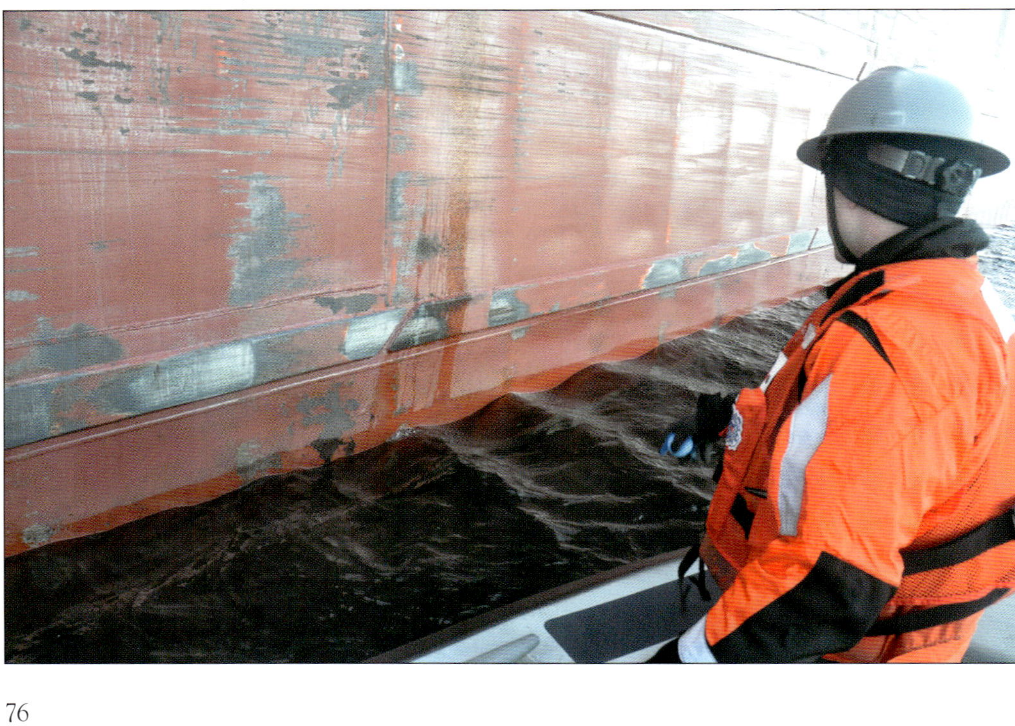

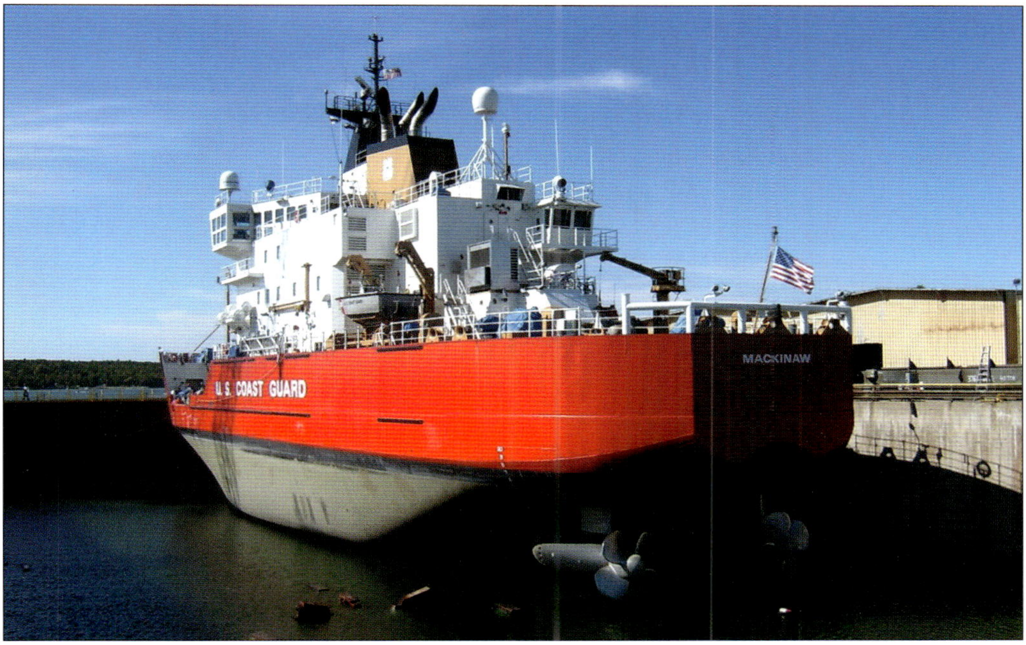

After a season of icebreaking, the *Mackinaw* goes into a "Charlie" maintenance period to repair the nicks, scrapes, and mechanical and electrical glitches that come with being at sea for six weeks or more. The maintenance work may or may not include dry-dock. If repairs to the hull or the Azipods are necessary, the ship will sail into the dry-dock well, and all the water will be drained, leaving it high and dry (above). The resulting look is always impressive and reminds those who saw the ship's launch of that April day in 2005. Below, the presence of yard workers gives a perspective on the *Mac's* size. (Both, courtesy of U.S. Coast Guard.)

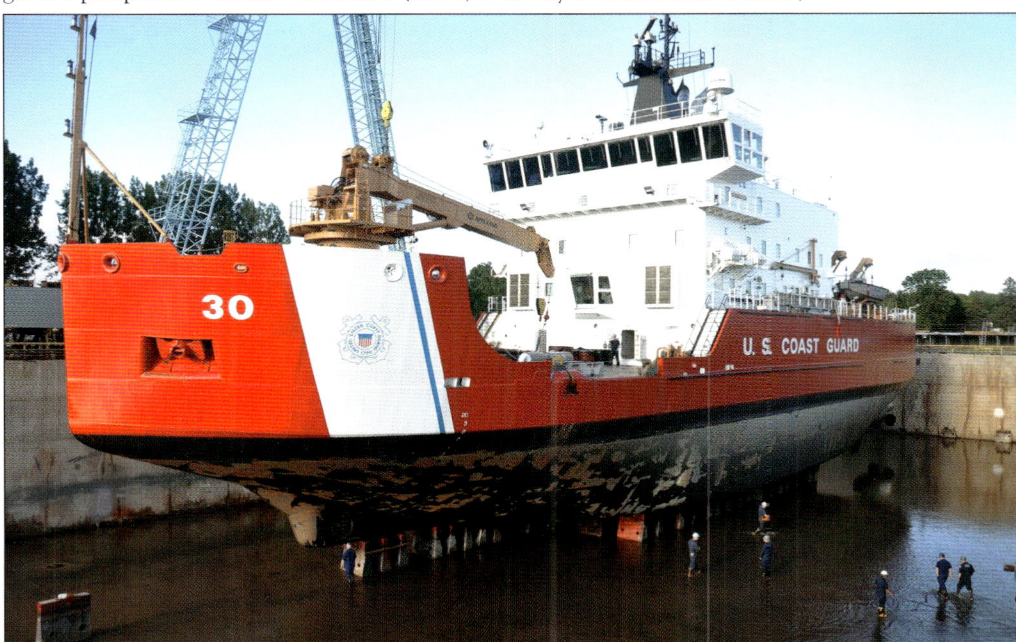

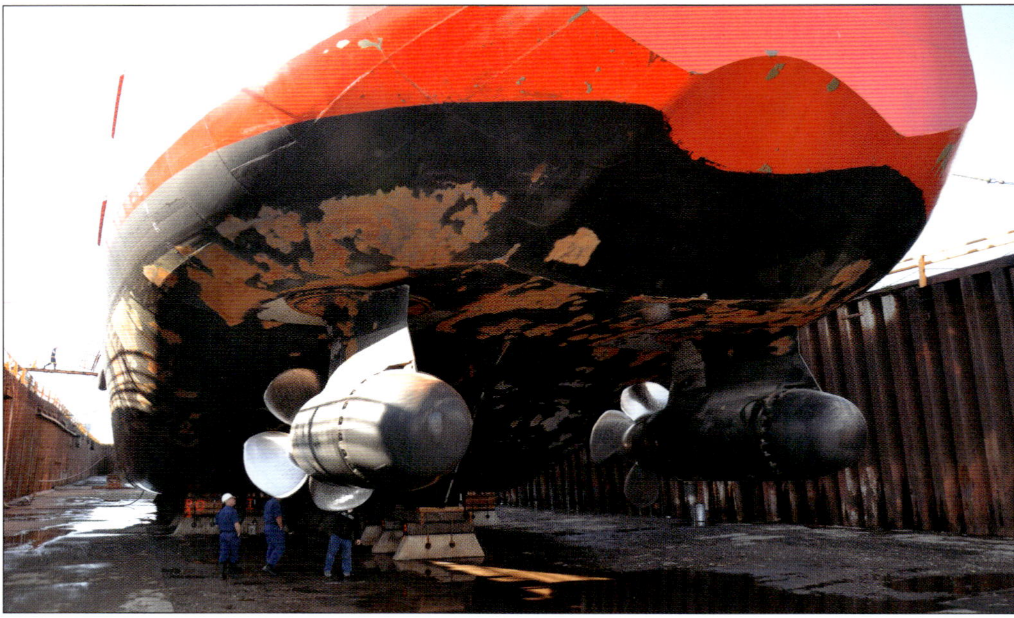

This stern perspective of the dry-docked *Mackinaw* gives an underside look at the ship's giant Azipod propellers. The oil seals on the pods have leaked on occasion, causing the ship to miss some scheduled missions. Maintenance workers have explored several means of keeping the pod assembly watertight. (Courtesy of U.S. Coast Guard.)

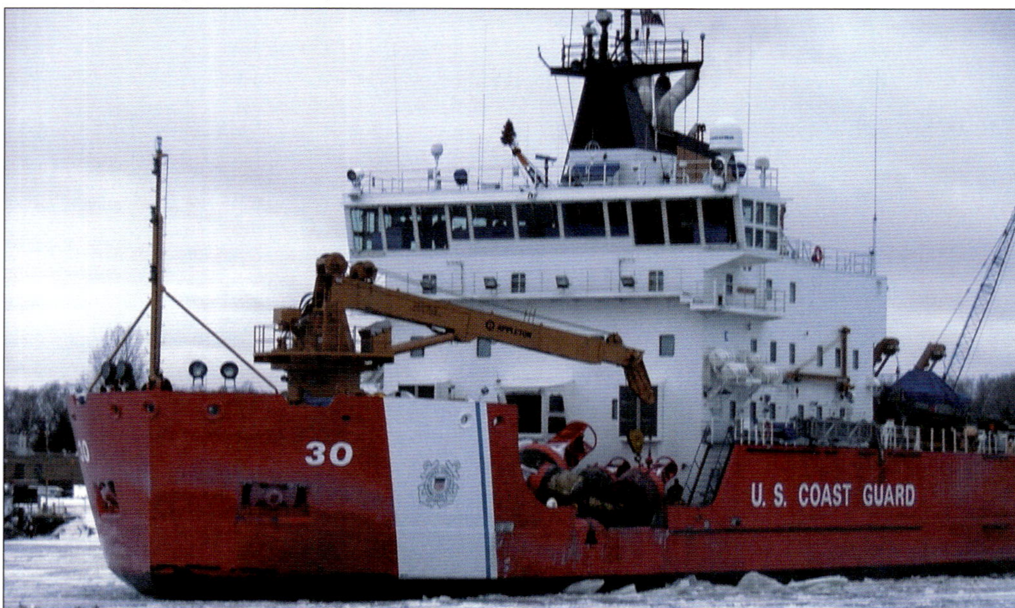

Ship-watchers often gather to observe the cutter return home. When the *Mac* is in town, Coast Guard family life returns to normal. Crewmembers are visible again in local stores, churches, and at athletic events. Local contractors arrive to service the vessel in various ways, from cleaning and septic service, to welding and painting. The word gets out pretty fast—"The *Mac* is back!" (Author's collection.)

Seven

MISSIONS OF A GREAT LAKES QUEEN

Another role that was passed from the original *Mackinaw* to the new *Mackinaw* involved the public relations legacy of the Coast Guard in the Great Lakes. Few who witnessed the old *Mac* shepherding yachts from Chicago to Mackinac or ferrying a load of Christmas trees to Chicago will forget the sight.

Cmdr. John Little embraced these traditions early on in his command and saw to it that the new cutter was immediately accepted as the original ship's full-fledged successor. Little encouraged Cheboygan children to board the new *Mac* as a "ghost ship" at Halloween, asked families and friends to come aboard for an annual dependents' cruise, and routinely opened the vessel for tours in his home port and while the cutter visited other communities. Nearly all subsequent commanding officers have followed that plan.

The *Mackinaw* customarily serves as the backdrop for the National Memorial Service at the Coast Guard Festival in Grand Haven, Michigan. The service is held to honor the memory of the USS *Escanaba*, lost during World War II, as well as all Coast Guard men and women who have given their lives in service to the nation.

When escorting yachts in the races from Port Huron to Mackinac or from Chicago to Mackinac, the ship is the command center for information, safety, and medical backup. In years when storms have brought tragedy to the race, yacht crews have found comfort in seeing *Mackinaw's* profile on the horizon.

As the Christmas Tree Ship, *Mackinaw* has reprised the tradition of the *Rouse Simmons*, Capt. Herman Schuenemann's three-masted schooner that sank on November 23, 1912, off the coast of Wisconsin with 16 crewmen and more than 5,000 Christmas trees bound for underprivileged children in Chicago.

Most years, *Mackinaw* loads approximately 1,200 trees cut in the Cheboygan area and carries them to Chicago, where the trees are unloaded to community organizations designated by the Chicago Christmas Ship Committee and distributed to deserving families. The ship routinely stops en route over the *Rouse Simmons* gravesite and holds a memorial service.

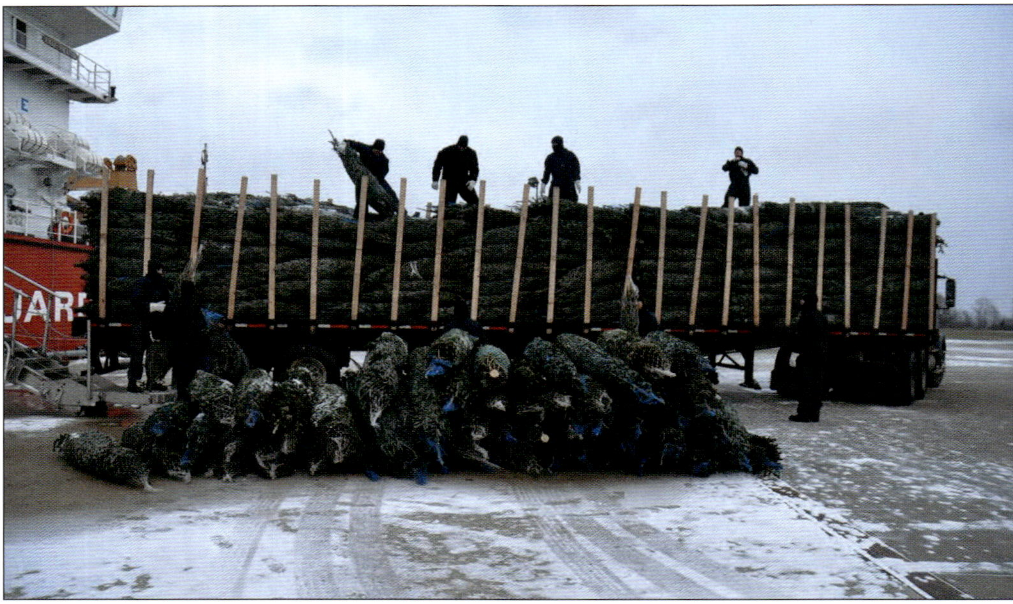

Crewmembers load more than 1,200 Christmas trees onto the ship in Cheboygan in 2013. The trees are grown on local Christmas tree farms and brought to the dock. Space is cleared on the ship's fantail deck for transport. The *Mackinaw*, serving as the Christmas Tree Ship, arrived in Chicago one week later and unloaded the trees for distribution to deserving families. (Courtesy of U.S. Coast Guard.)

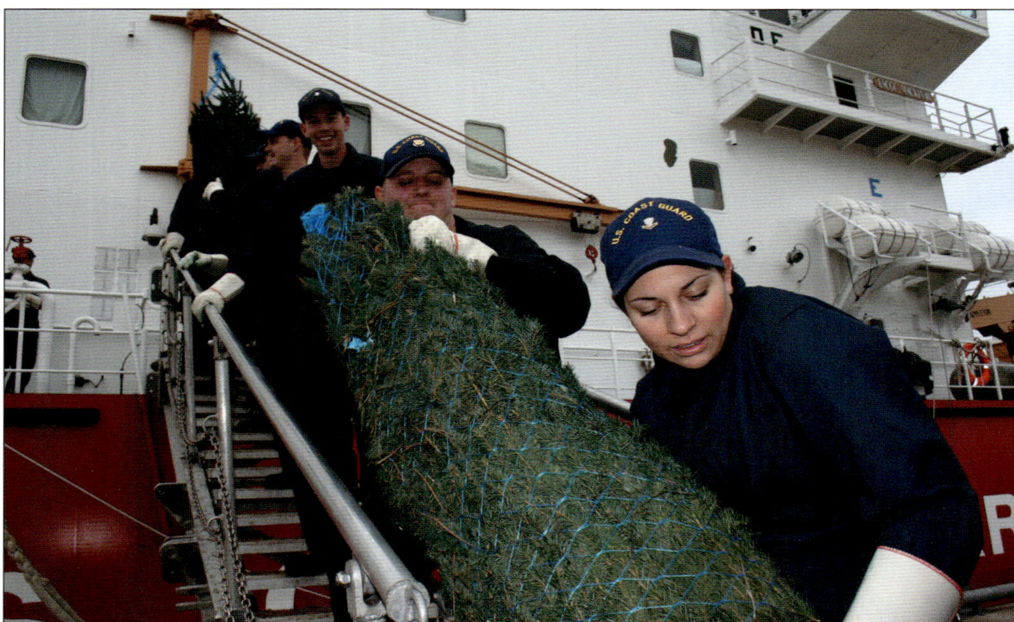

When handling a constant relay of Christmas trees, *Mackinaw* crewmembers learned to wear heavy gloves and long sleeves. Everyone pitches in on this job; having the full crew involved makes the task an enjoyable one. Over the years, crews have used conveyor systems, cranes, and old-fashioned bucket brigades to load the ship. (Author's collection.)

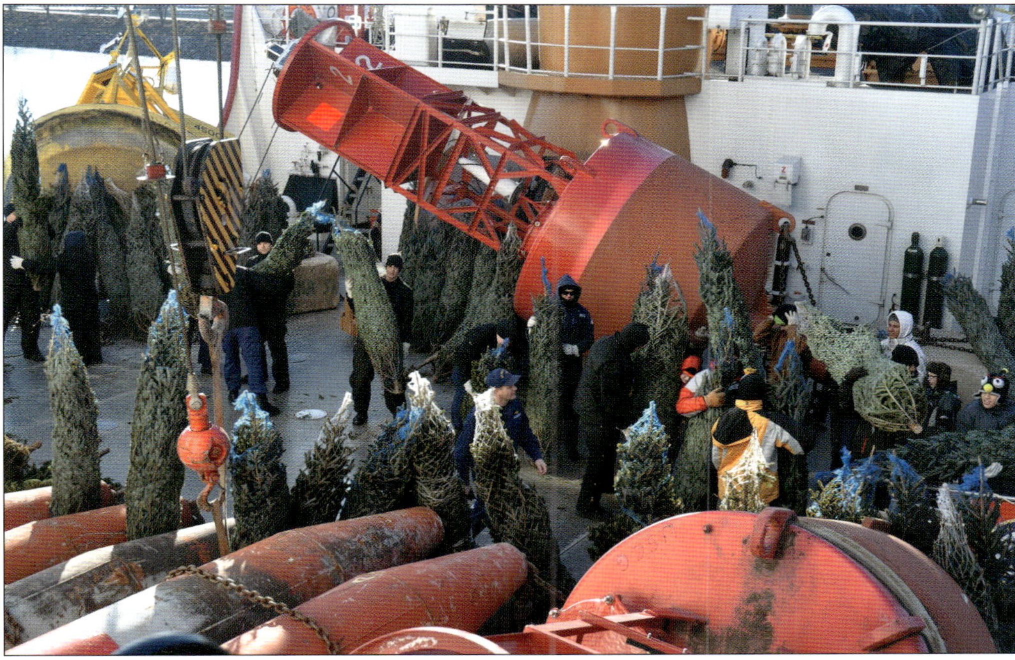

The *Mac* usually works Lake Michigan buoys on the way to Chicago, so the relay brings the Christmas trees right onto the buoy deck on the way to the fantail at the stern. The trees are bundled, secured to the deck, and covered with a tarpaulin for the trip. (Courtesy of U.S. Coast Guard.)

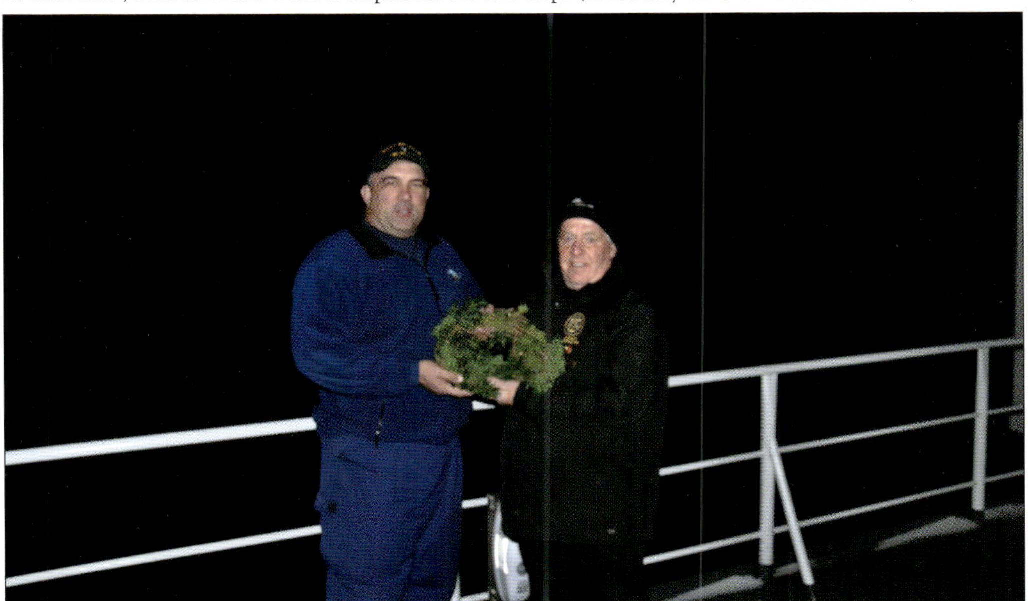

Cmdr. Scott Smith (left) and Lloyd Karzen of the Chicago Christmas Ship Committee pose before tossing a wreath overboard to commemorate the sinking of the *Rouse Simmons*. The *Mackinaw* traditionally stops at the wreck site, off the coast of Two Rivers, Wisconsin, to honor and reflect on the conditions that Capt. Herman Schuenemann must have faced on November 23, 1912, when he was lost with his crew and entire cargo. (Courtesy of U.S. Coast Guard.)

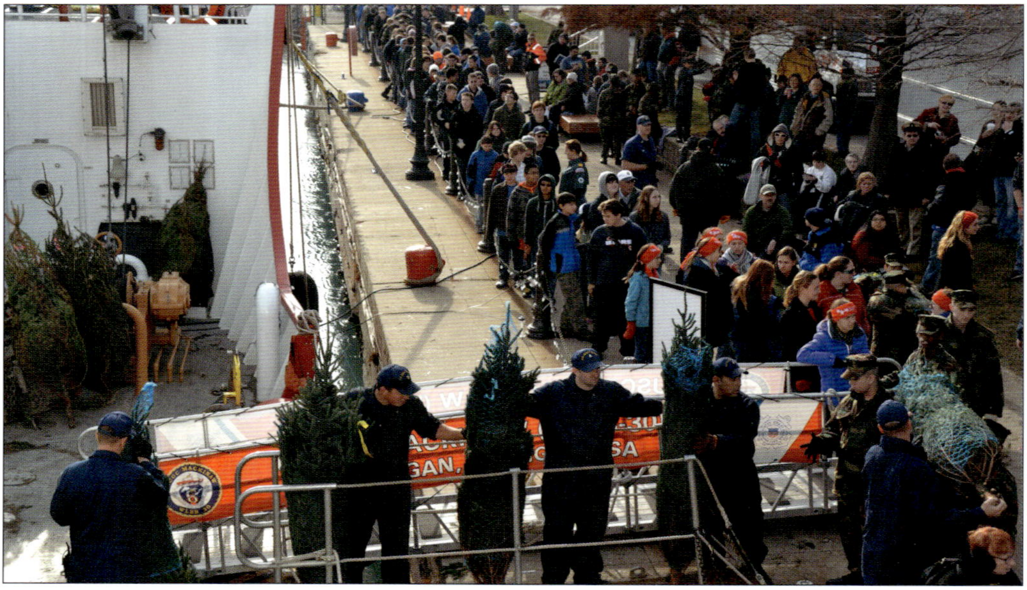

Volunteers from youth organizations including the Sea Cadets, Sea Scouts, and Young Marines help unload the trees in Chicago. Various charitable organizations assist in distributing the trees to needy families, replicating the mission of the original Christmas Tree Ship. Crewmembers usually host tours for several thousand people. Often, the crew is able to take in a sporting event while enjoying shore liberty in town. (Courtesy of U.S. Coast Guard.)

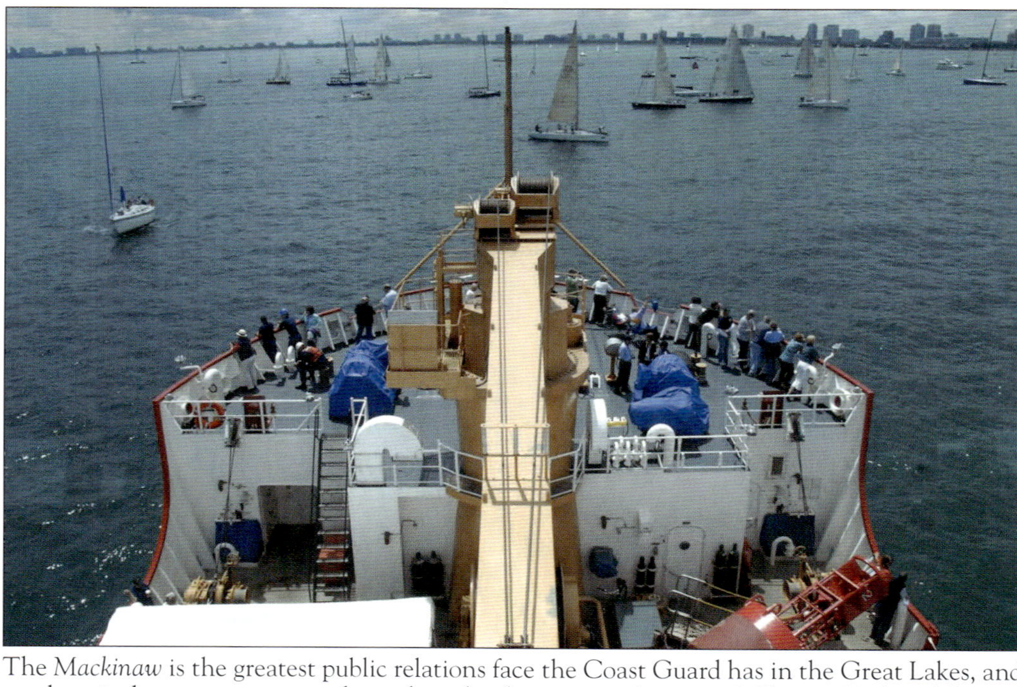

The *Mackinaw* is the greatest public relations face the Coast Guard has in the Great Lakes, and nowhere is that more apparent than when the ship escorts the annual Chicago Yacht Club Race to Mackinac. The *Mac* provides a platform for spectators at the starting line, then heads up the lake to catch the racers and provide support when needed. (Courtesy of U.S. Coast Guard.)

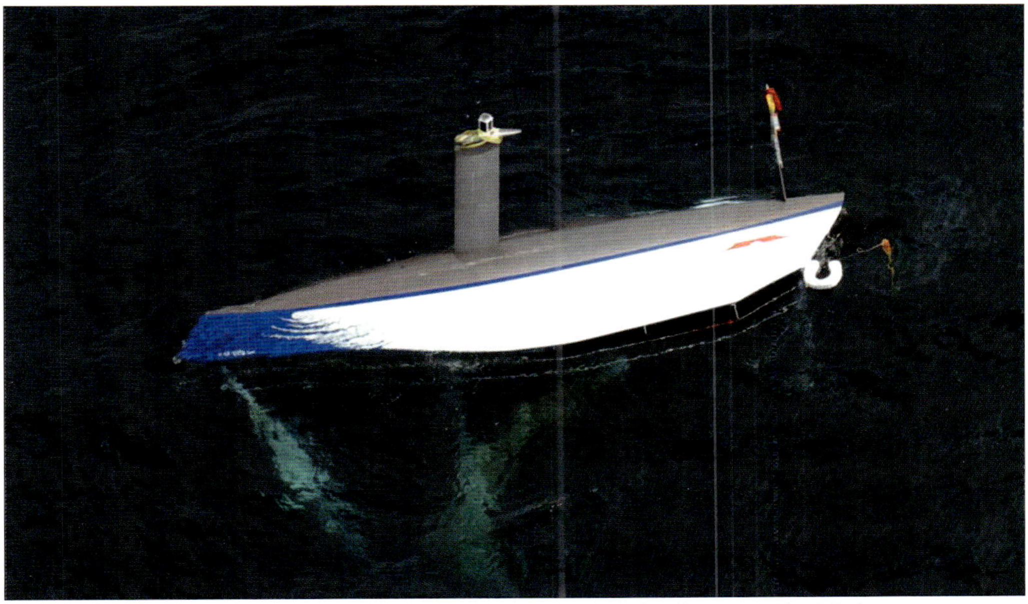

During the 2011 race, an overnight severe thunderstorm hit the fleet on Lake Michigan, capsizing the yacht *Wing Nuts* and throwing eight sailors into the water, two of whom drowned. The *Mackinaw* arrived during the night on location, approximately 13 nautical miles northwest of Charlevoix and 10 miles east of South Fox Island, to assume the role of on-scene commander and to coordinate ongoing search efforts. (Courtesy of The Associated Press.)

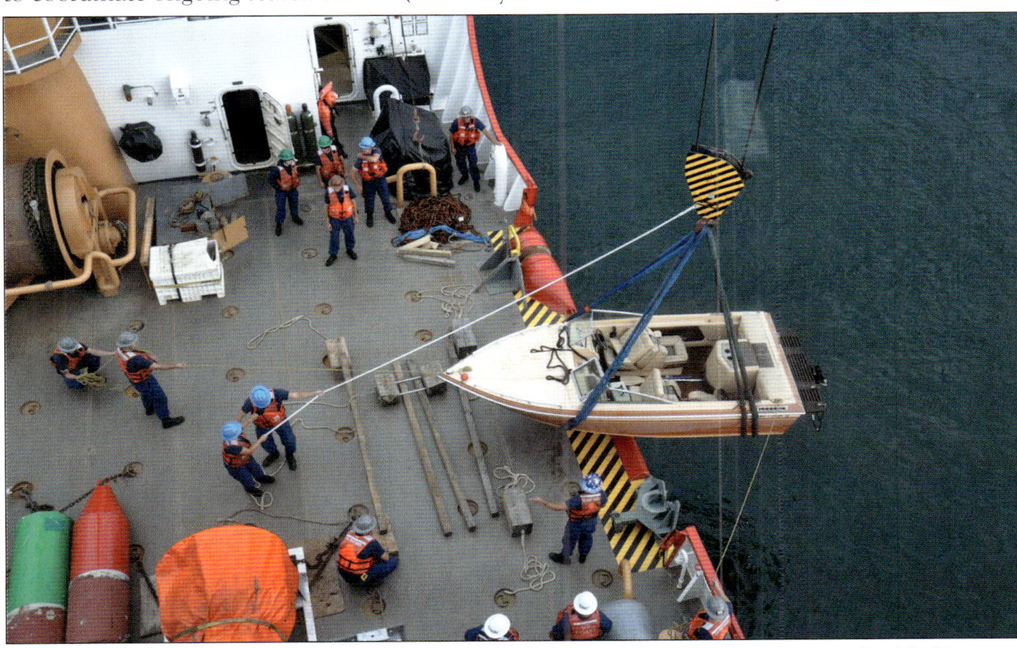

A 2012 search-and-rescue mission involved the rescue of three people from a disabled boat in the vicinity of the Soo Locks. Crewmembers from the *Mackinaw* brought the boaters aboard, then used the cutter's crane to lift the boat out of the water to salvage it, due to incoming severe weather. (Courtesy of U.S. Coast Guard.)

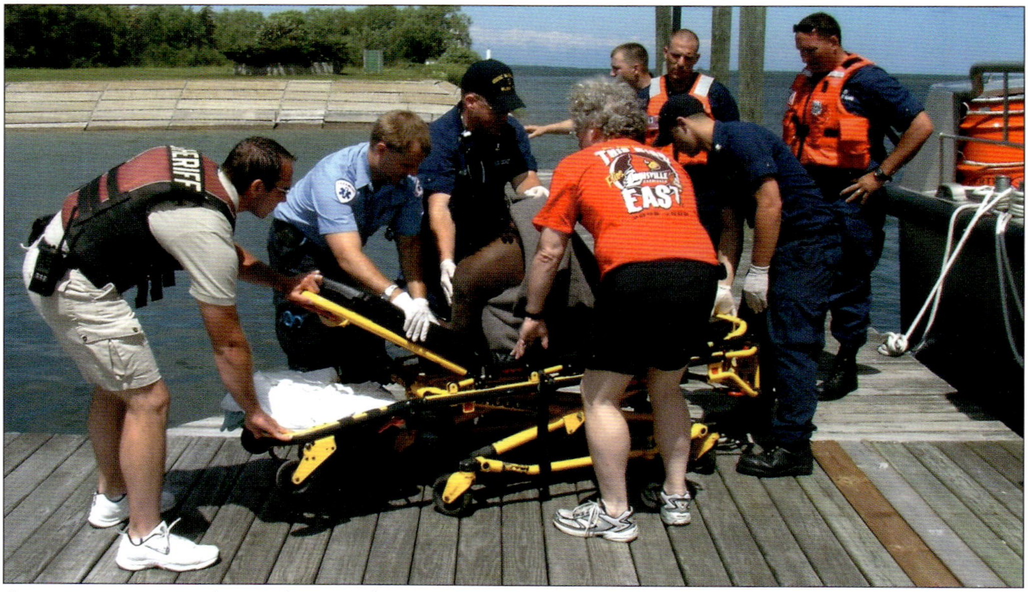

A summer canoe ride nearly turned into tragedy for two Kentucky visitors who lived to tell about it because they were wearing life jackets. Will Stout, 21, of Louisville, Kentucky, and his sister Erika Conner, 22, of Fort Knox, Kentucky, went for a canoe ride from a beach in Beaugrand Township and encountered conditions far beyond what a canoe could handle. It capsized, throwing brother and sister into the waves. The *Mackinaw* sent out a 23-foot rescue boat, and crewmen pulled the canoeists aboard. They had been in the 59-degree water for nearly an hour and suffered hypothermia. When the family wanted to thank the *Mac's* crew, Cmdr. John Little had them all aboard as guests, conducted a ceremony, and saw to it that even the family's youngest siblings received T-shirts and caps from the *Mackinaw*. (Both, author's collection.)

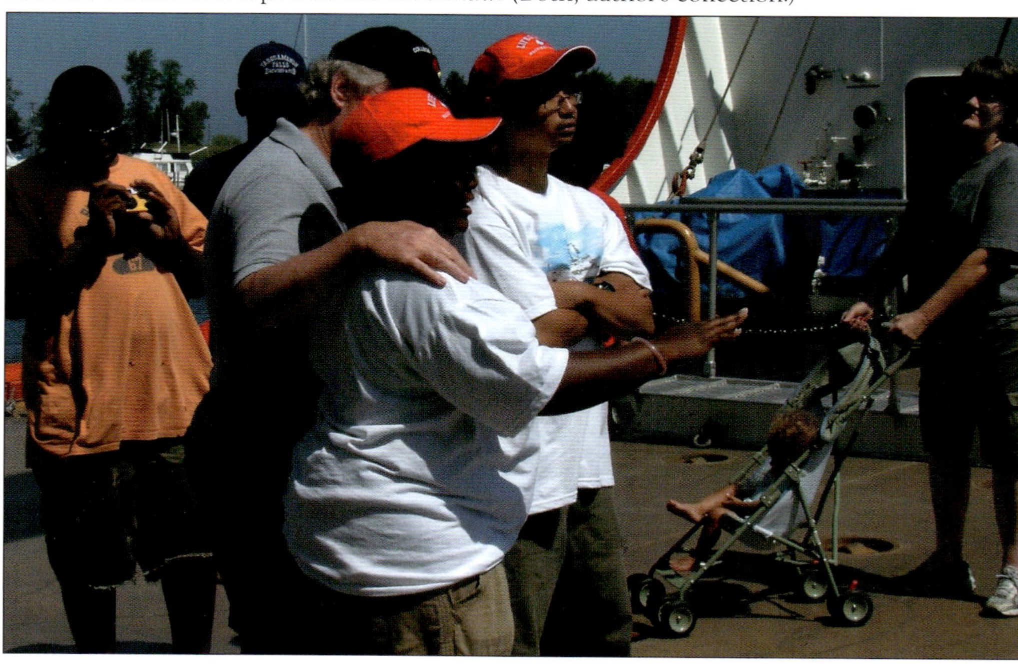

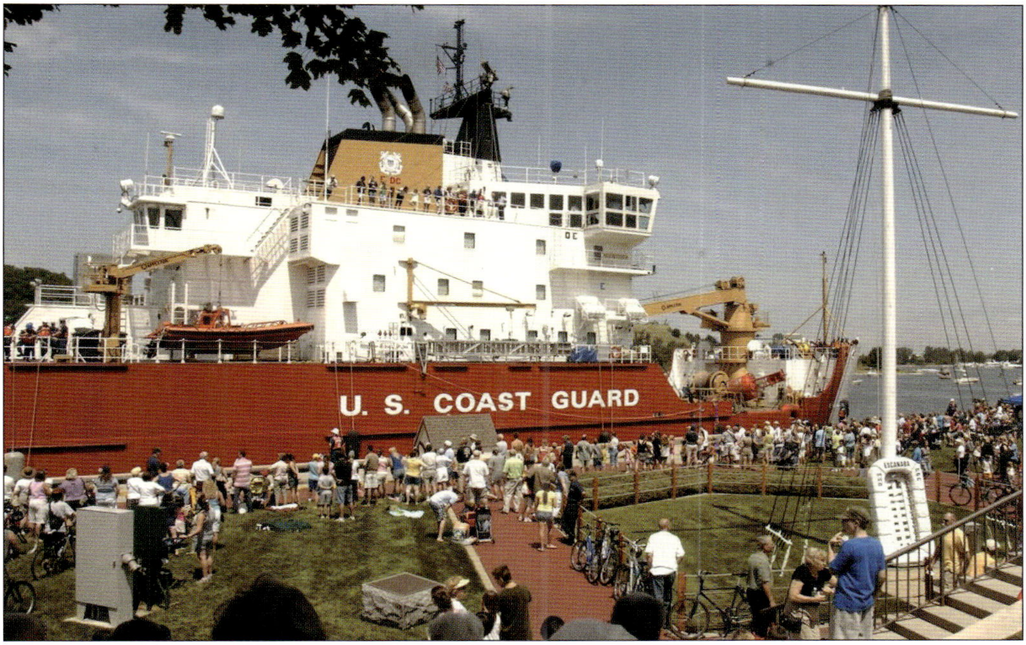

The *Mackinaw* is the star of the show everywhere it goes in the Great Lakes, especially when it visits the Coast Guard Festival in Grand Haven, Michigan. Often surrounded by other cutters, the *Mac* serves as the backdrop for the National Memorial Service, held to honor the memory of the USS *Escanaba*. That vessel was lost during World War II, and the ceremony honors the *Escanaba* crew as well as all Coast Guard men and women who have given their lives in service to the nation. The *Mackinaw* is also center stage for a huge fireworks celebration and hosts thousands of visitors on tours during its week at the festival. (Both, courtesy of U.S. Coast Guard.)

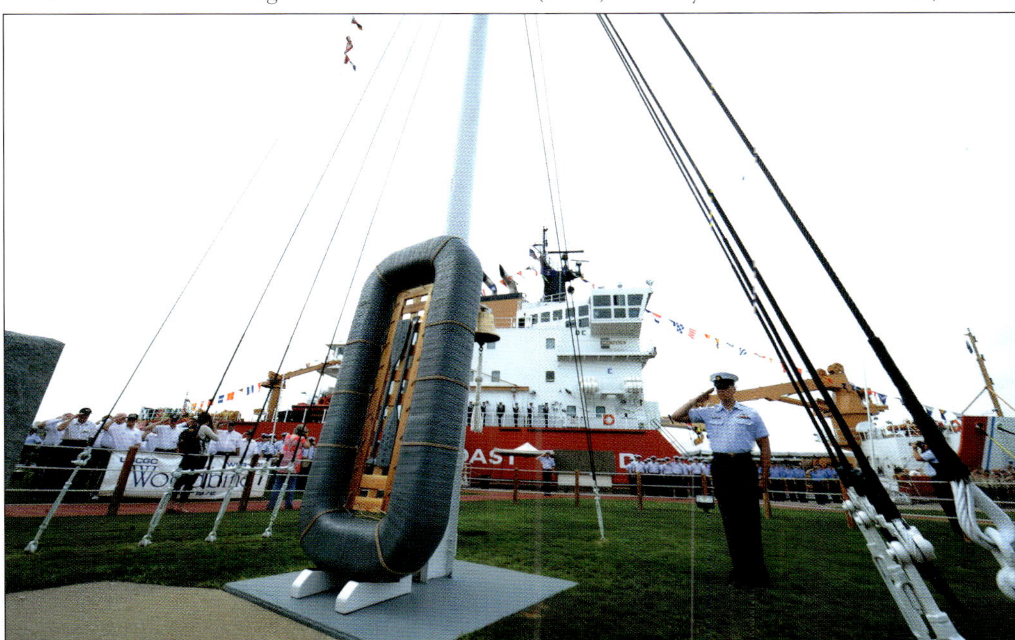

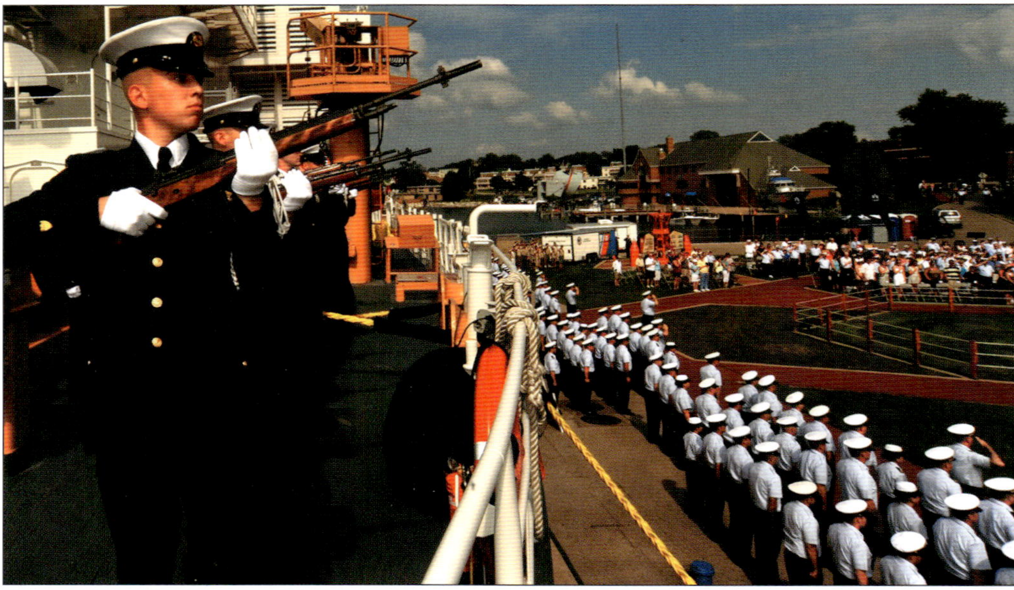

The *Mackinaw* is capable of putting on quite a public display. When crewmembers don their dress blues and the ship is in its usual spit-polished condition, visitors line up to see it inside and out. Well-positioned signage directs visitors throughout the ship to see most operating systems and decks, and crewmembers have a flair for showing off the "Queen of the Great Lakes." Families by the dozen happily wait in line for their chance to see the great ship. There is never a charge for a tour. The crew immediately begins the cleanup after 4,000 people have trekked through the ship, only to do it all again the next day. (Both, courtesy of U.S. Coast Guard.)

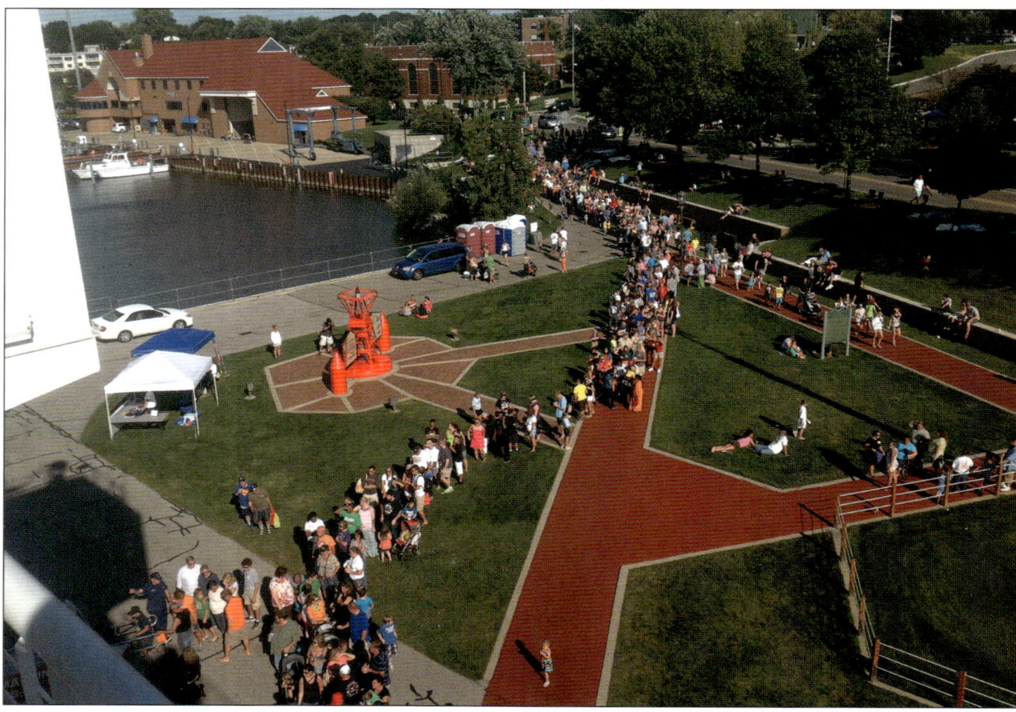

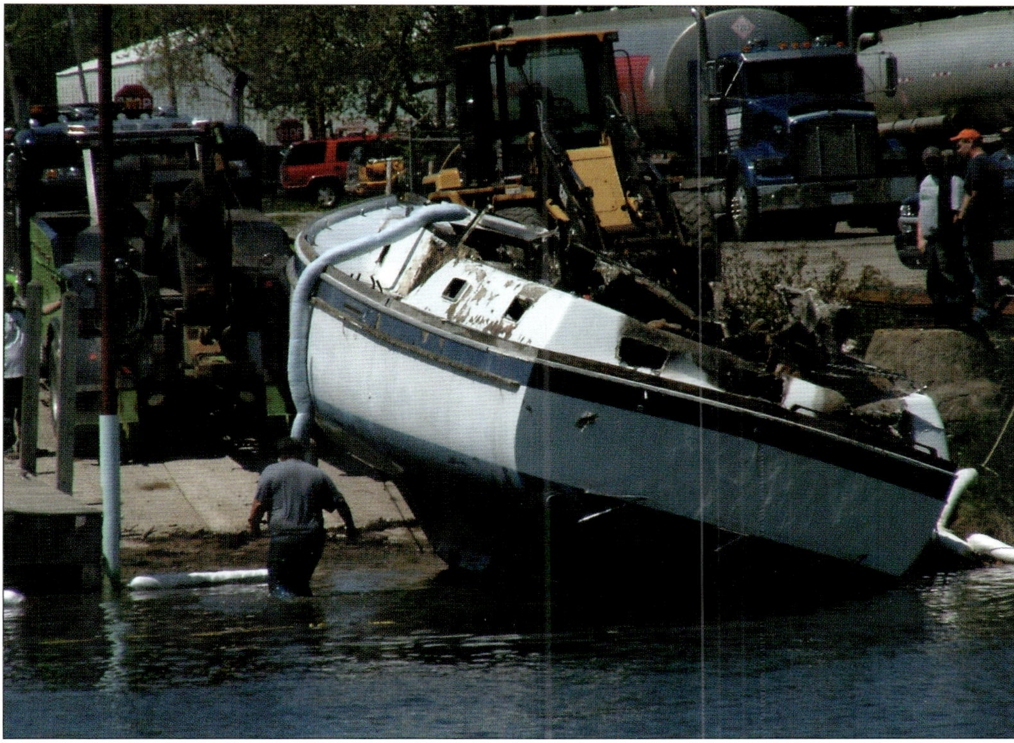

The *Mac's* role in law enforcement played out locally when a man upset with his insurance company decided to sink his burned-out cabin cruiser. Wayne Duffiney of Cheboygan was spotted by the *Mackinaw's* watch crew towing his damaged 44-foot Gulfstar from the Cheboygan River into Lake Huron. A Coast Guard helicopter found the vessel submerged in the South Channel with only the tip of the bow visible and ordered it removed. (Author's collection.)

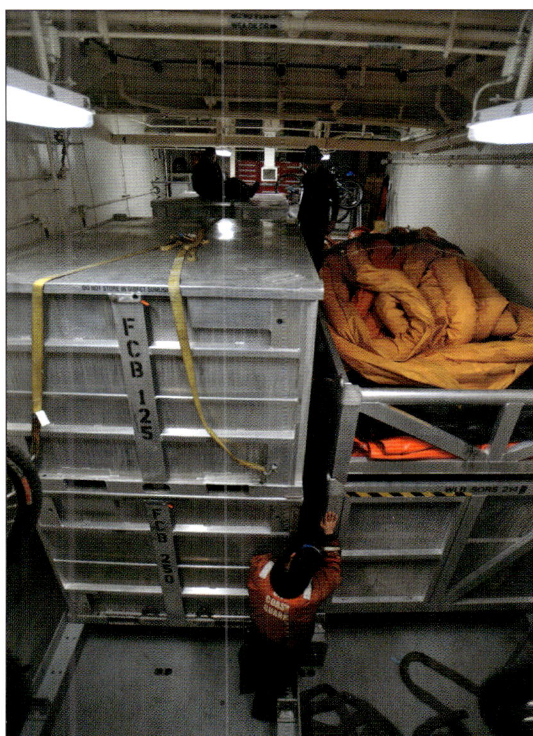

These cases contain oil skimmers, vacuum pumps, and hoses that are capable of handling an oil spill emergency in the Great Lakes. A van can deliver the materials to any waiting ship that is capable of deploying the unit. The *Mackinaw* is equipped to accept and utilize the gear, and it can also serve as a command center for such an operation. (Courtesy of U.S. Coast Guard.)

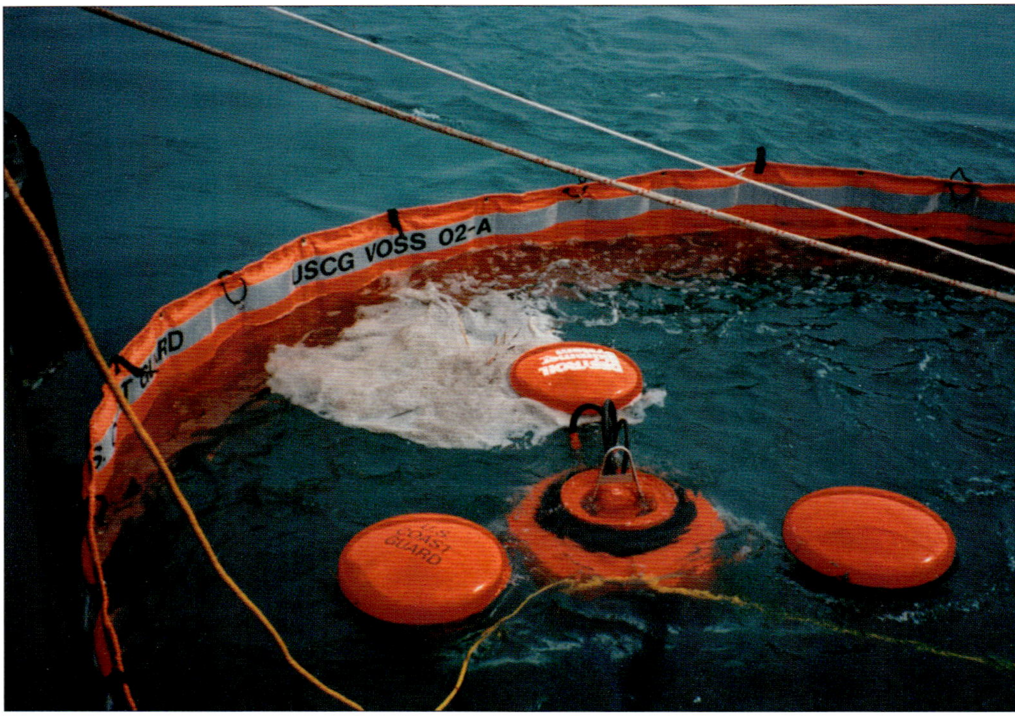

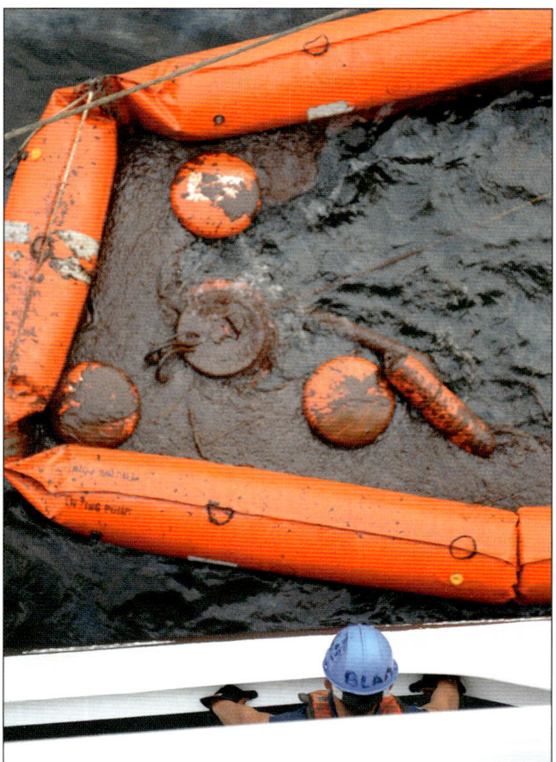

Oil spill response involves evolving technology, and the *Mackinaw* is equipped to utilize tools including the Vessel of Opportunity Skimming System. The VOSS is a highly portable skimmer unit that can be delivered to the *Mac* and deployed to recover floating oil. It can also be adapted for use as a submersible pump for removing oil from a ship or barge. The skimmer uses a weir-type device to shave the oil from the water's surface into a containment box, where it is vacuumed out with a hose. It can also be adapted for lighter oils. The skimmer is supported in the water by three corner floats. It can also handle debris up to an inch in diameter. There are 22 units ready for deployment in the United States, nine of them in the Great Lakes as of 2014. (Both, courtesy of U.S. Coast Guard.)

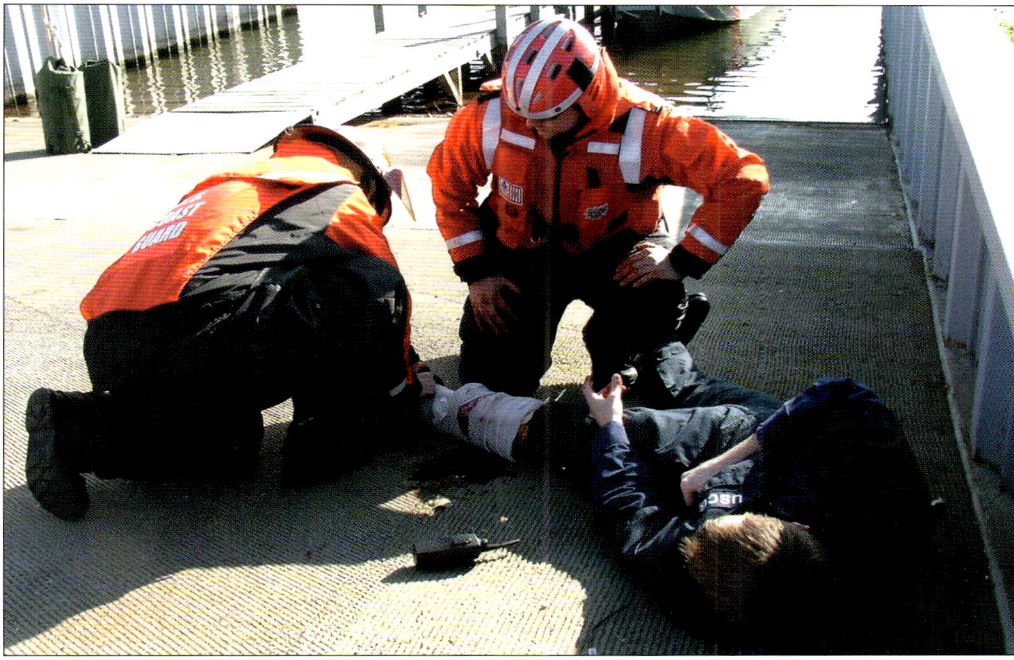

Mackinaw's crewmembers routinely train to enhance medical knowledge and to ensure readiness. This drill took place across the Cheboygan River from the ship's berth, at the launch ramp of the Cheboygan County Marina. The "wounded" sailor was taken ashore from a kayak to have a leg wound treated and bandaged. (Author's collection.)

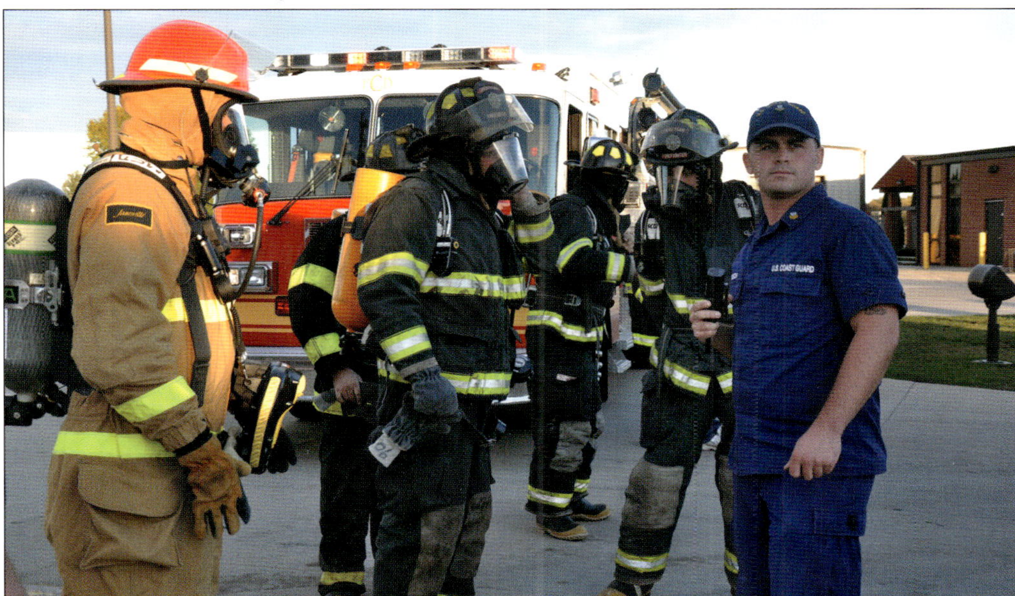

Storekeeper 1st Class Blake Rausch (right) worked with local firefighters as part of a coordinated fire drill with *Mackinaw's* crewmembers. The drill allowed Cheboygan Fire Department personnel to familiarize themselves with the ship's layout and logistics in the event of a fire emergency requiring shore-side assistance. (Courtesy of U.S. Coast Guard.)

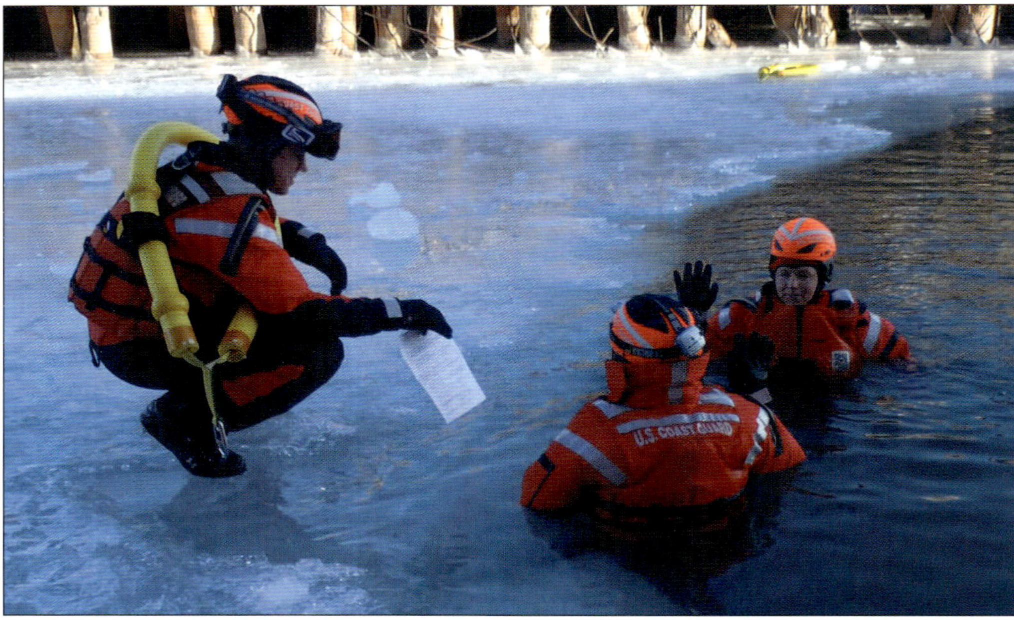

Petty Officer 1st Class Erin Hunter (right) recited the oath of enlistment and reenlisted for four years of duty in the Coast Guard during a break from ice-rescue training near Detour Village, Michigan, on January 10, 2013. Ensign Katie Braynard (center) administered the oath to Hunter while Bosun's Mate 3rd Class Zach Emery was on the ice at left with safety gear. (Courtesy of U.S. Coast Guard.)

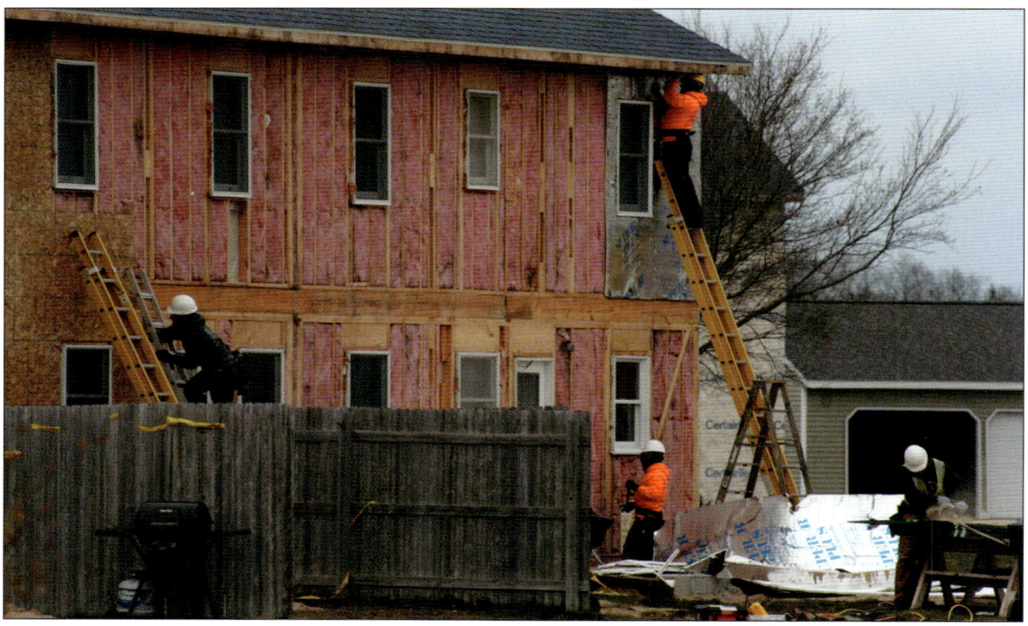

Many *Mackinaw* families live in the Coast Guard Housing Complex, one of the nicest neighborhoods in Cheboygan. This 2013 maintenance job involved the installation of new siding on all housing units and added upgraded insulation. Many single crewmembers rent from landlords, who prefer Coast Guard tenants. Newcomers usually live aboard briefly when first reporting for duty. (Author's collection.)

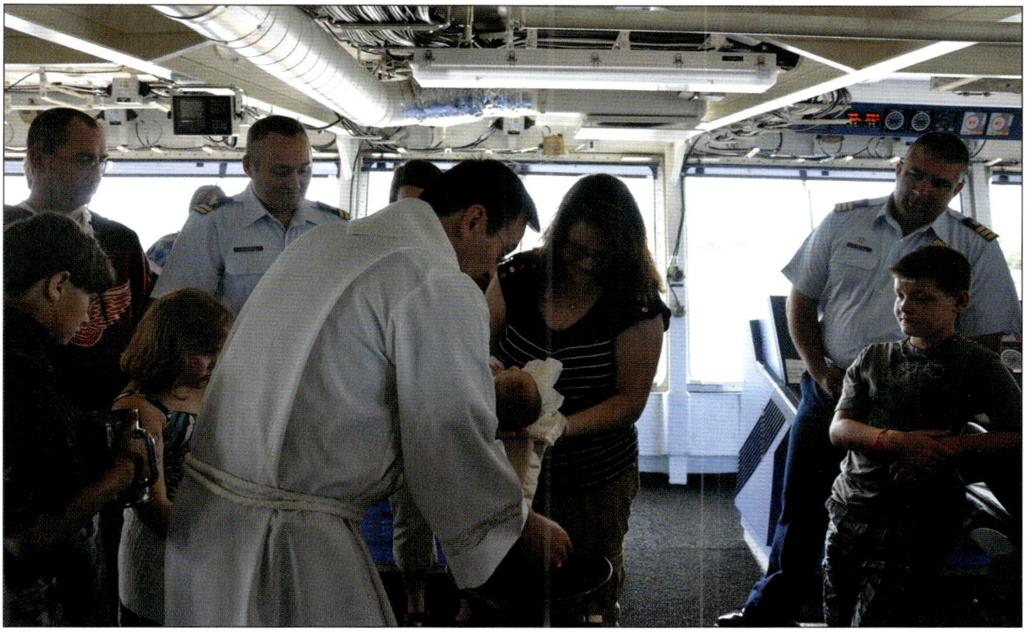

A *Mackinaw* tradition was continued when Carter Cichoracki was baptized in the ship's bell. Carter is the second Cichoracki child to be christened on the bridge of the *Mackinaw*. His sister, Isabella Lynne, was baptized in August 2010, and her name is engraved inside the ship's bell, right next to her brother's. The parents are Cory and Margaret Cichoracki. (Author's collection.)

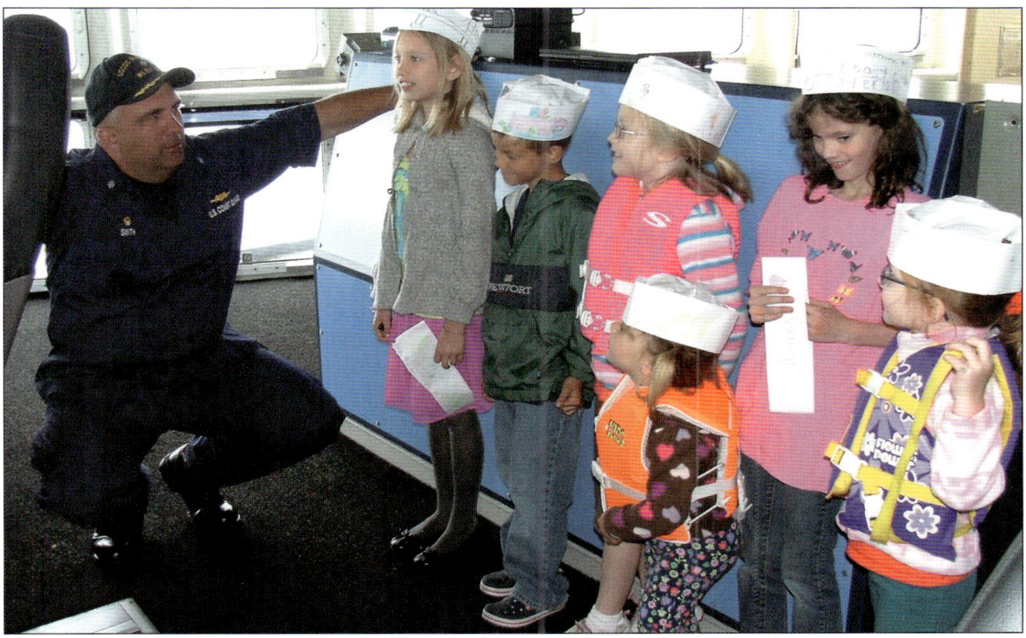

Cmdr. Scott Smith encouraged activities that involved *Mackinaw* families. The annual Dependents Cruise gives family members a chance to ride aboard the ship for a day and see what life at sea is like. Smith knew how to win over the youngsters, as he demonstrated with these six children of *Mackinaw* sailors. (Author's collection.)

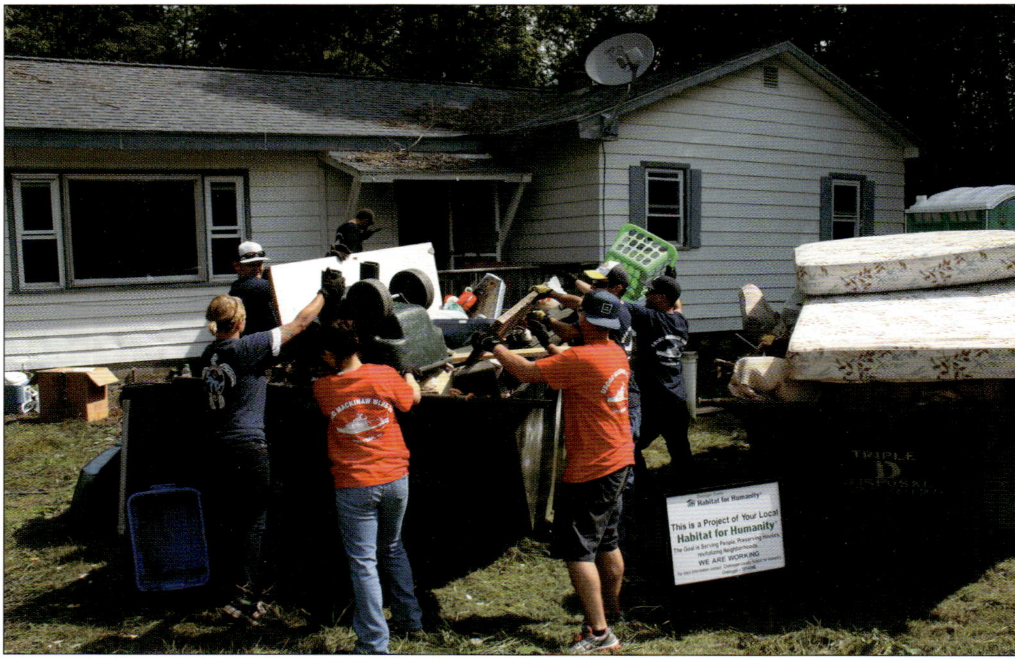

The *Mac* crew pitched in to help clear a vacant house and yard of stored junk in 2013 to prepare it for refurbishment by Habitat for Humanity. The crew's enthusiasm to get involved in community projects goes a long way toward endearing the ship's company to the locals. (Author's collection.)

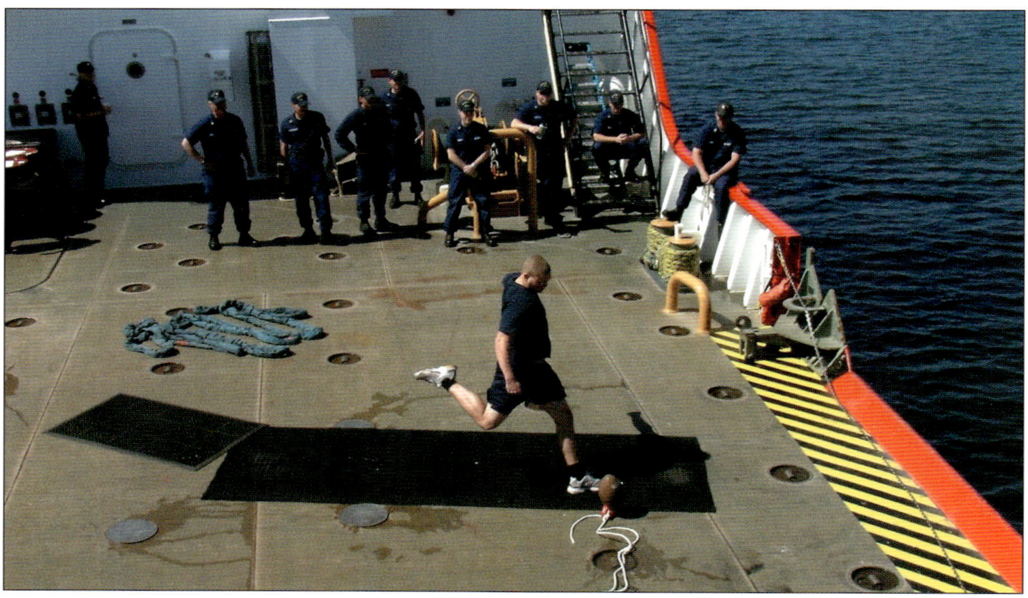

Ensign David Lieberman, who holds several football kicking records at the Coast Guard Academy, accepted a challenge in 2010 to kick a ball across the Cheboygan River. His longest kick from the deck of the ship was measured by a rangefinder at 69 yards. Since the river was more than 100 yards wide there, Lieberman tried again from the Water Street Marina. He was successful at 72 yards. (Author's collection.)

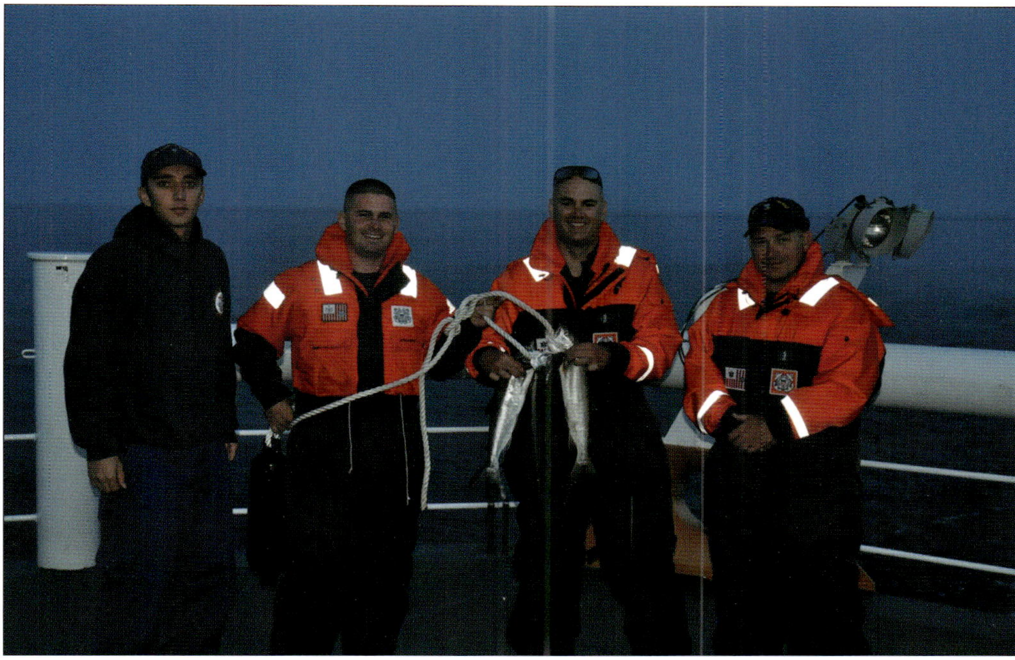

Excellent opportunities abound for the sportsmen stationed aboard the *Mackinaw*. Fishing, hunting, skiing, snowmobiling, scuba diving, and recreational boating are some of the pastimes pursued while off duty. Occasionally, fishing from the ship produces a tasty meal for the crew, as these anglers proved by dropping a line over the side. (Courtesy of U.S. Coast Guard.)

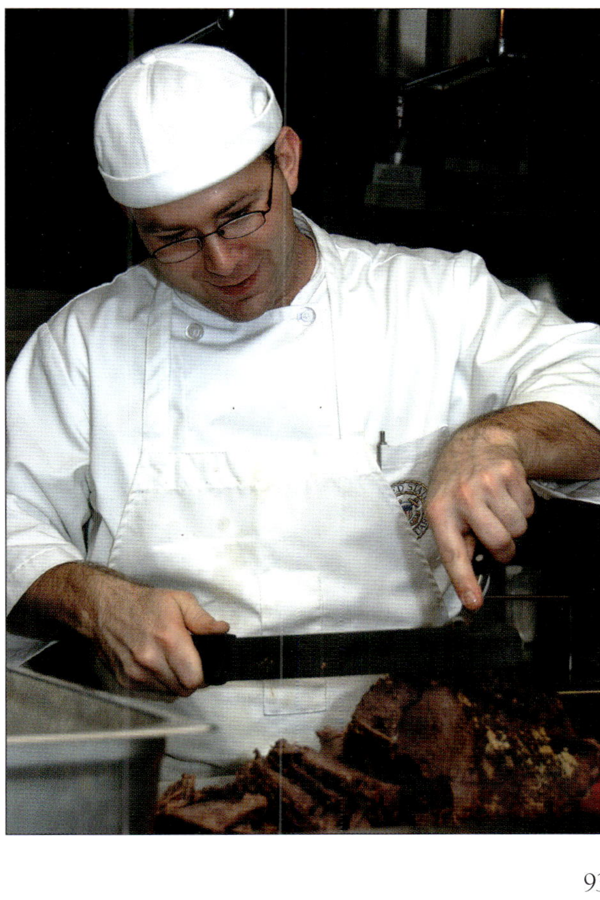

Mackinaw's food service is considered to be the best in the Coast Guard. Petty Officer 2nd Class Eddie Fuchs, a food service specialist, is an award-winning chef who competed as part of a U.S. Army team at the World Culinary Olympics in Germany. Fuchs is part of a tradition of great cooks aboard the ship. (Courtesy of U.S. Coast Guard.)

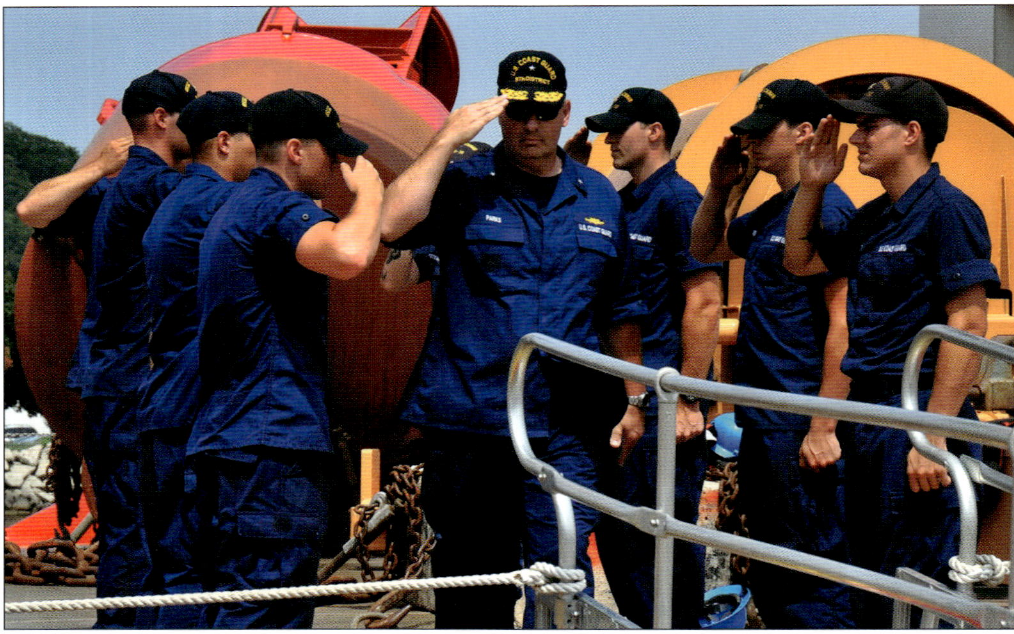

Rear Adm. Michael Parks visited the ship near the end of a buoy-tending run before he retired after 35 years of Coast Guard service. Parks assumed command of the 9th District in April 2010. The district spans the five Great Lakes, the St. Lawrence Seaway, and parts of the surrounding states. (Courtesy of U.S. Coast Guard.)

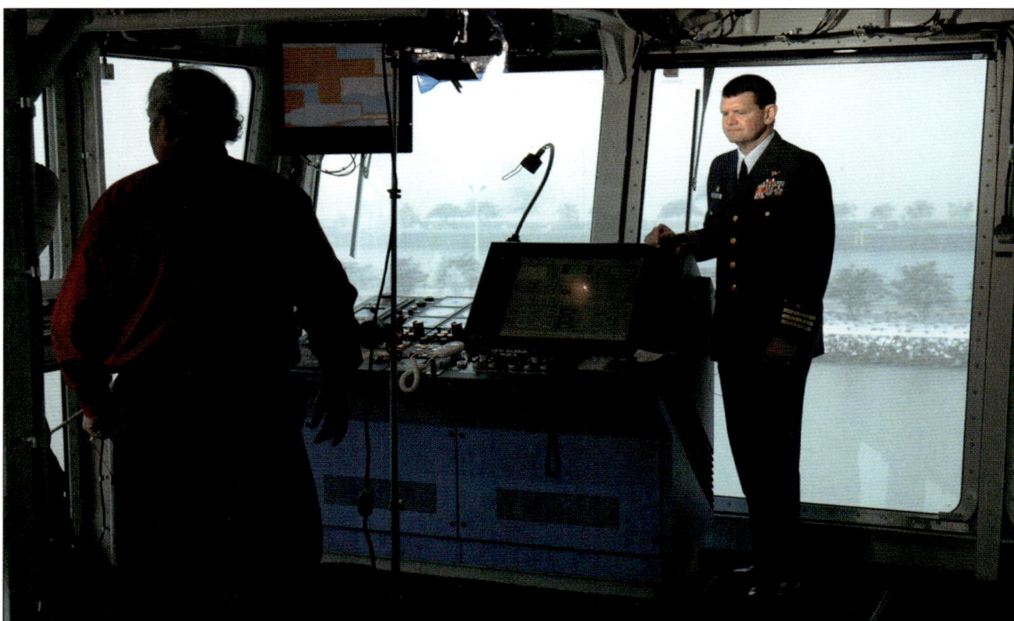

Cmdr. John Little immersed himself in the community. Although he lived onboard the ship, he was very visible walking about town, riding a bicycle for exercise, and attending civic events. Little handled media opportunities with ease and expertly dealt with the public. He perfectly prepared the ship and crew to assume the legacy of its predecessor. (Courtesy of U.S. Coast Guard.)

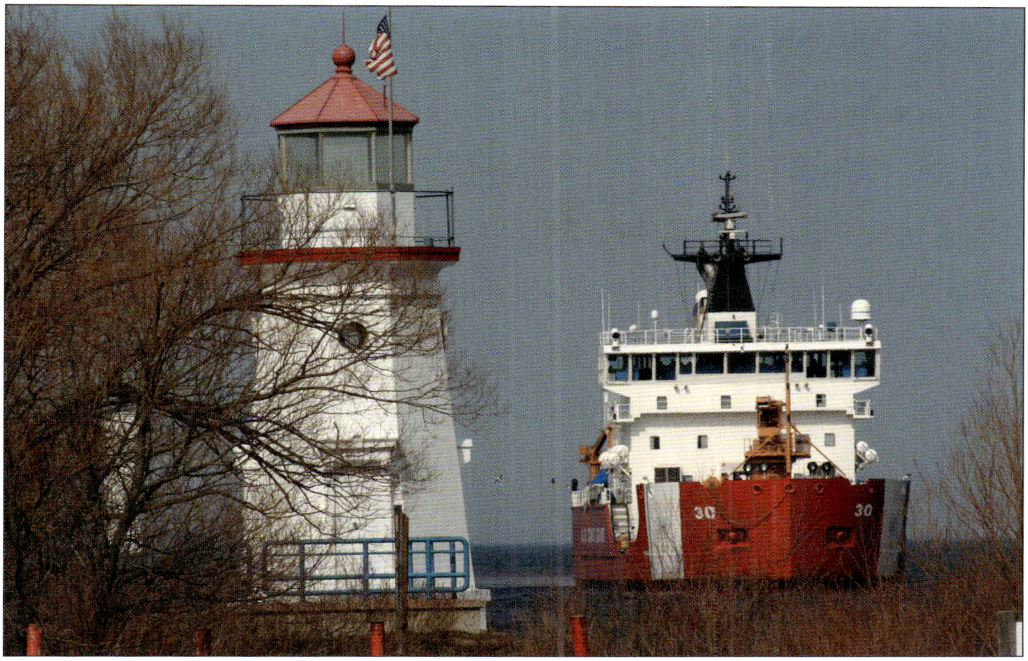

Mackinaw's familiar profile passes another Cheboygan icon, the Cheboygan Crib Light, while entering the Cheboygan River following another successful mission on the Great Lakes. The entrance to the river is tricky for the ship, since its large superstructure tends to catch prevailing northwesterly winds. (Author's collection.)

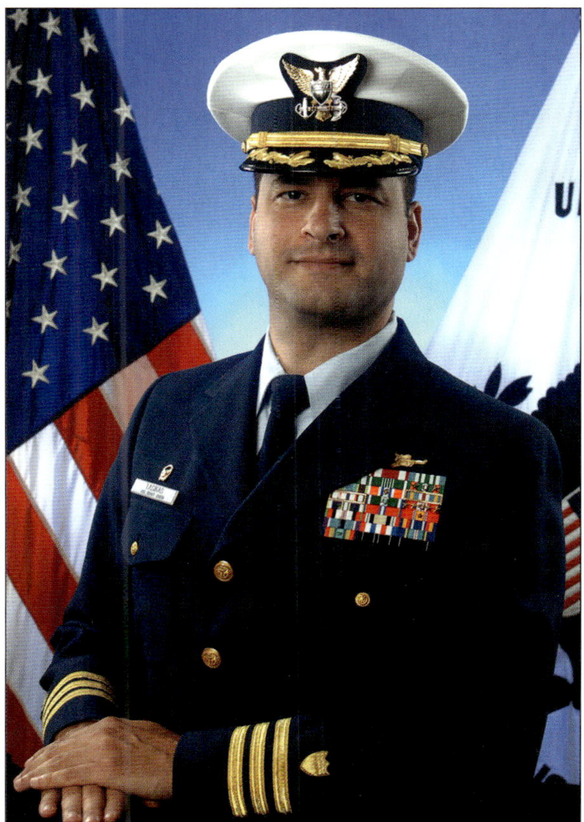

Cmdr. Vasilios Tasikas became the new skipper of the *Mackinaw* on June 18, 2014. In his previous assignment, he captained the cutter *Mobile Bay*. Experienced in legal and military-justice matters in addition to his ship-handling capabilities, Tasikas is also a veteran of deployments to Iraq and Afghanistan. (Courtesy of U.S. Coast Guard.)

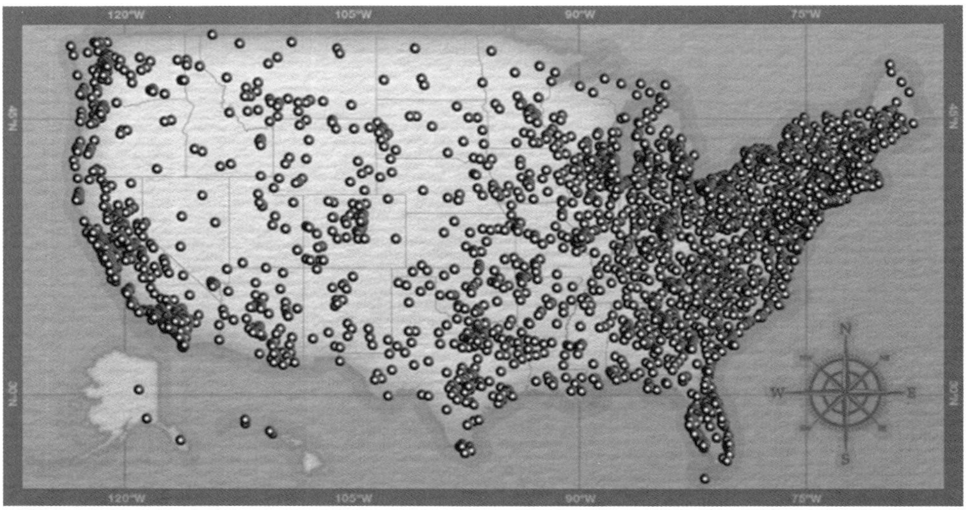